D1163566

DATE DUE

ULTIMATE
ARMOR WARS

ARMOR WARS

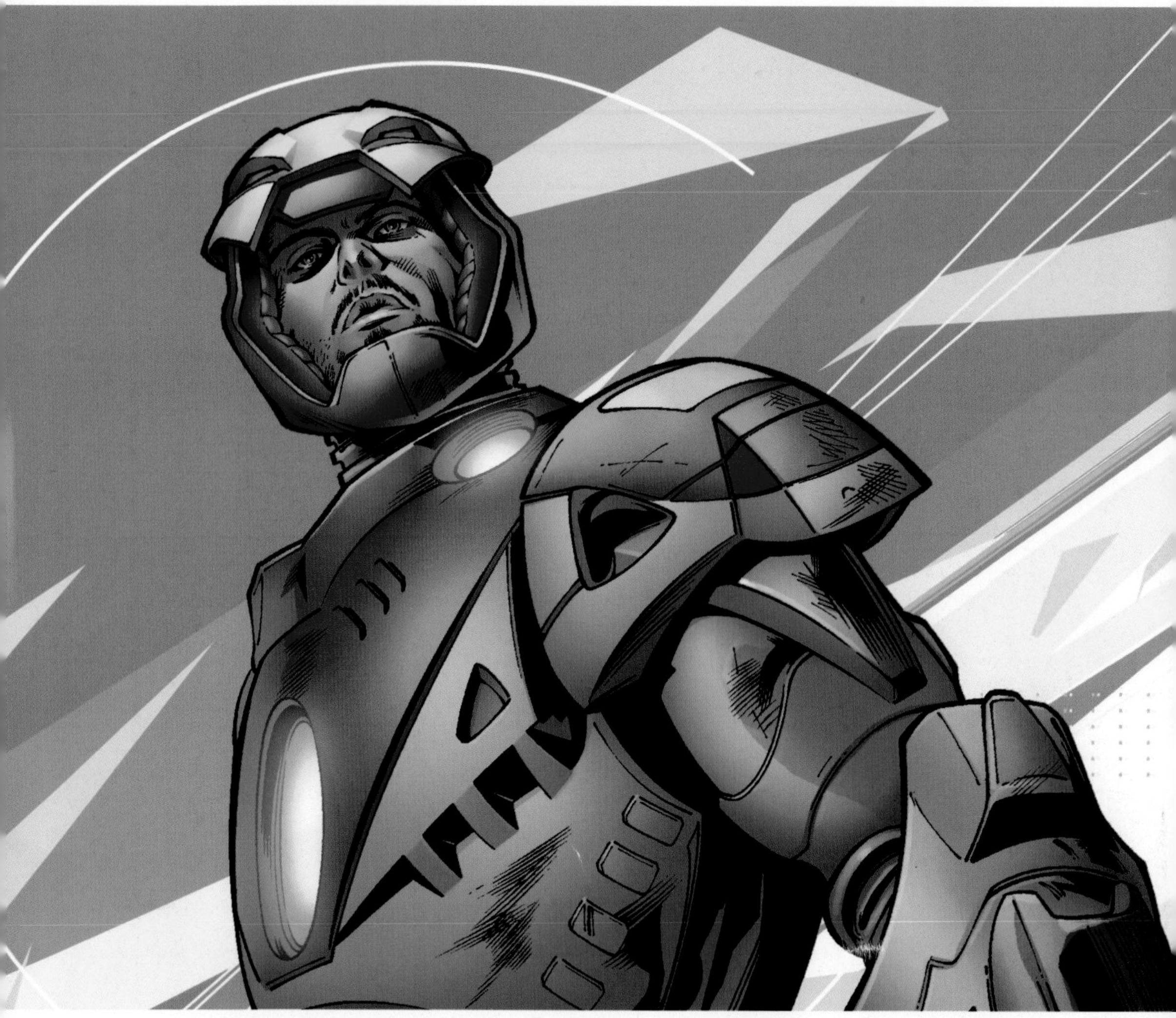

WRITER:
WARREN ELLIS
PENCILER:
STEVE KURTH
INKERS: **JEFF HUET** WITH **ALLEN MARTINEZ** & **SCOTT HANNA**
COLORIST: **GURU EFX** LETTERER: **VC'S JOE SABINO**
COVER ARTIST: **BRANDON PETERSON**
ASSISTANT EDITOR: **SANA AMANAT**
ASSOCIATE EDITOR: **LAUREN SANKOVITCH**
SENIOR EDITOR: **MARK PANICCIA**

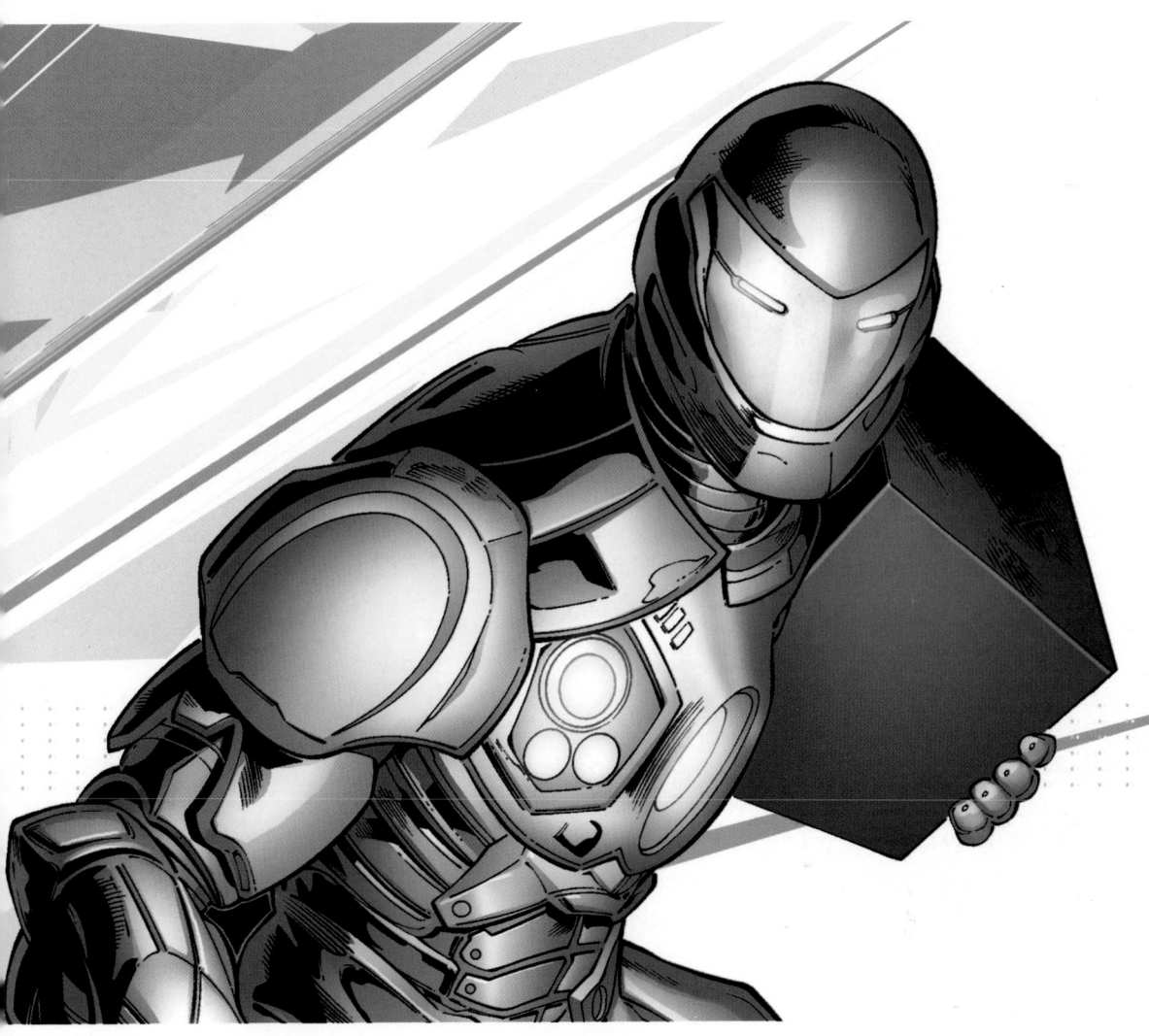

COLLECTION EDITOR: **JENNIFER GRÜNWALD**
ASSISTANT EDITOR: **ALEX STARBUCK**   ASSOCIATE EDITOR: **JOHN DENNING**
EDITOR, SPECIAL PROJECTS: **MARK D. BEAZLEY**
SENIOR EDITOR, SPECIAL PROJECTS: **JEFF YOUNGQUIST**
SENIOR VICE PRESIDENT OF SALES: **DAVID GABRIEL**
BOOK DESIGNER: **RODOLFO MURAGUCHI**

EDITOR IN CHIEF: **JOE QUESADA**   PUBLISHER: **DAN BUCKLEY**
EXECUTIVE PRODUCER: **ALAN FINE**

ULTIMATE COMICS IRON MAN: ARMOR WARS. Contains material originally published in magazine form as ULTIMATE COMICS ARMOR WARS #1-4. First printing 2010. ISBN# 978-0-7851-4250-8. Published by MARVEL WORLDWIDE, INC., a subsidiary of MARVEL ENTERTAINMENT, LLC. OFFICE OF PUBLICATION: 417 5th Avenue, New York, NY 10016. Copyright © 2009 and 2010 Marvel Characters, Inc. All rights reserved. $19.99 per copy in the U.S. (GST #R127032852); Canadian Agreement #40668537. All characters featured in this issue and the distinctive names and likenesses thereof, and all related indicia are trademarks of Marvel Characters, Inc. No similarity between any of the names, characters, persons, and/or institutions in this magazine with those of any living or dead person or institution is intended, and any such similarity which may exist is purely coincidental. **Printed in the U.S.A.** ALAN FINE, EVP - Office of the President, Marvel Worldwide, Inc. and EVP & CMO Marvel Characters B.V.; DAN BUCKLEY, Chief Executive Officer and Publisher - Print, Animation & Digital Media; JIM SOKOLOWSKI, Chief Operating Officer; DAVID GABRIEL, SVP of Publishing Sales & Circulation; DAVID BOGART, SVP of Business Affairs & Talent Management; MICHAEL PASCIULLO, VP Merchandising & Communications; JIM O'KEEFE, VP of Operations & Logistics; DAN CARR, Executive Director of Publishing Technology; JUSTIN F. GABRIE, Director of Publishing & Editorial Operations; SUSAN CRESPI, Editorial Operations Manager; ALEX MORALES, Publishing Operations Manager; STAN LEE, Chairman Emeritus. For information regarding advertising in Marvel Comics or on Marvel.com, please contact Ron Stern, VP of Business Development, at rstern@marvel.com. For Marvel subscription inquiries, please call 800-217-9158. **Manufactured between 2/1/10 and 3/3/10 by R.R. DONNELLEY, INC., SALEM, VA, USA.**

10 9 8 7 6 5 4 3 2 1

PREVIOUSLY

Tony Stark lives two lives: one as a billionaire industrial playboy, the other as Iron Man, high-tech hero of the government-sponsored superhuman defense initiative known as the Ultimates. Iron Man and the Ultimates helped protect the country from foreign threats until the Ultimatum struck—a doomsday event launched by Magneto as vengeance against humankind.

Heroes fought the ultimate battle, and paid the ultimate price. In a tragic clash of mind over metal, Magneto overrode Tony's hardware, forcing Tony's hand to kill Wolverine. Though scarred by this horrific event, our heroes still managed to persevere, defeating Magneto and his mutant army.

The world reeks with destruction and evil still lurks within its rubble. But Tony is ready to take it all on, with a drink in one hand and an iron fist in the other.

1

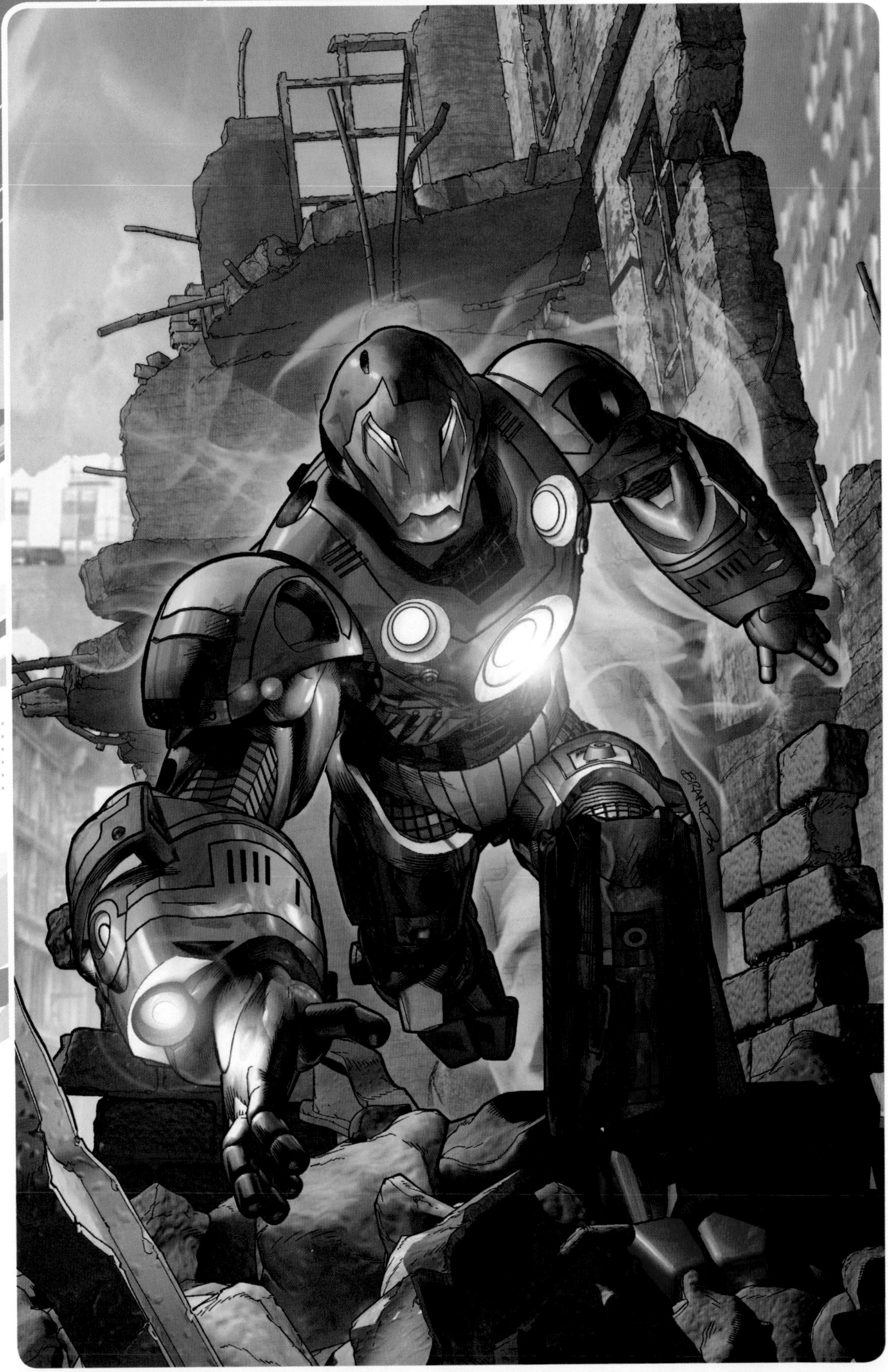

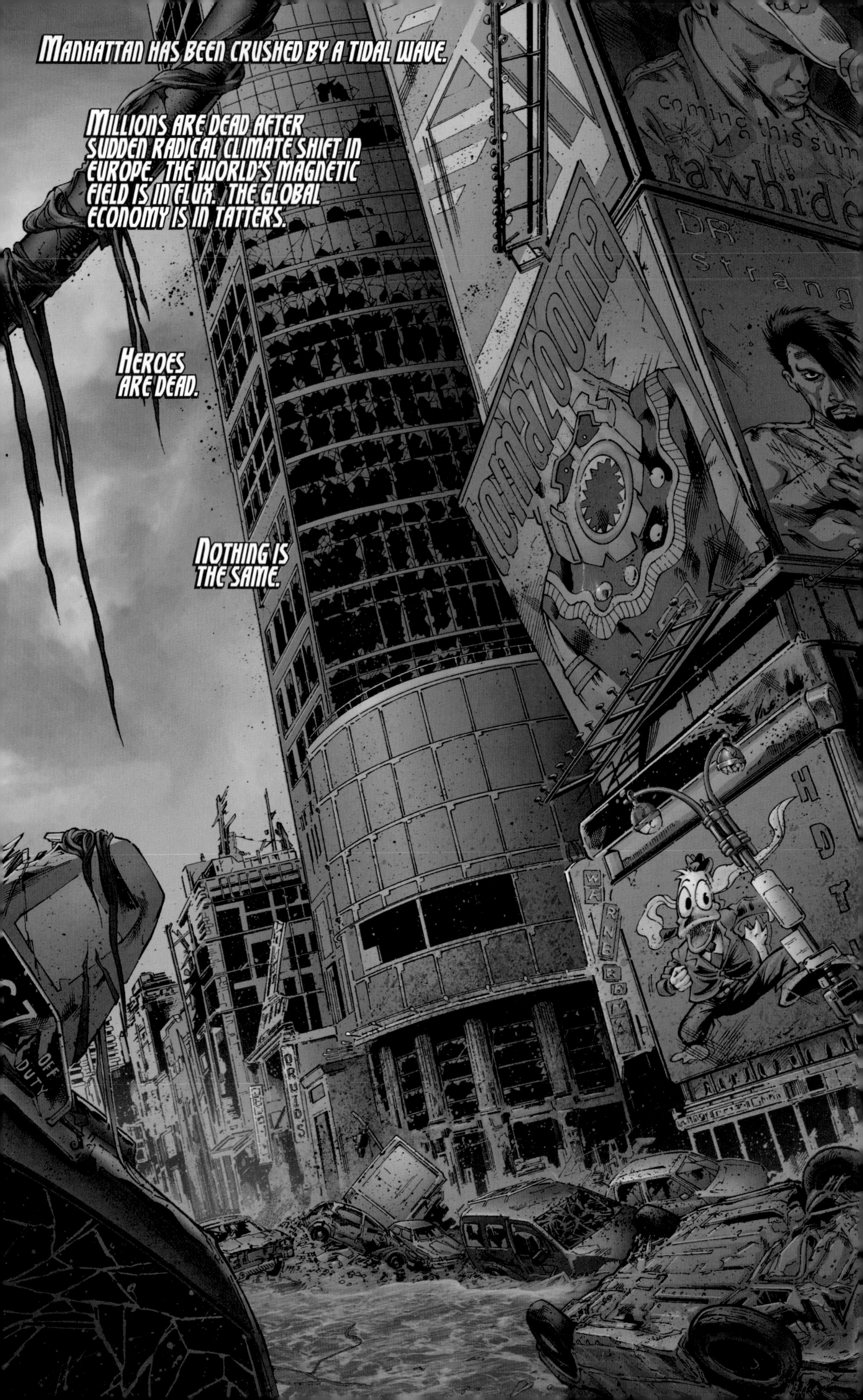

Manhattan has been crushed by a tidal wave.
Millions are dead after sudden radical climate shift in Europe. The world's magnetic field is in flux. The global economy is in tatters.
Heroes are dead.
Nothing is the same.
rawhide
DRUIDS
OFF DUTY

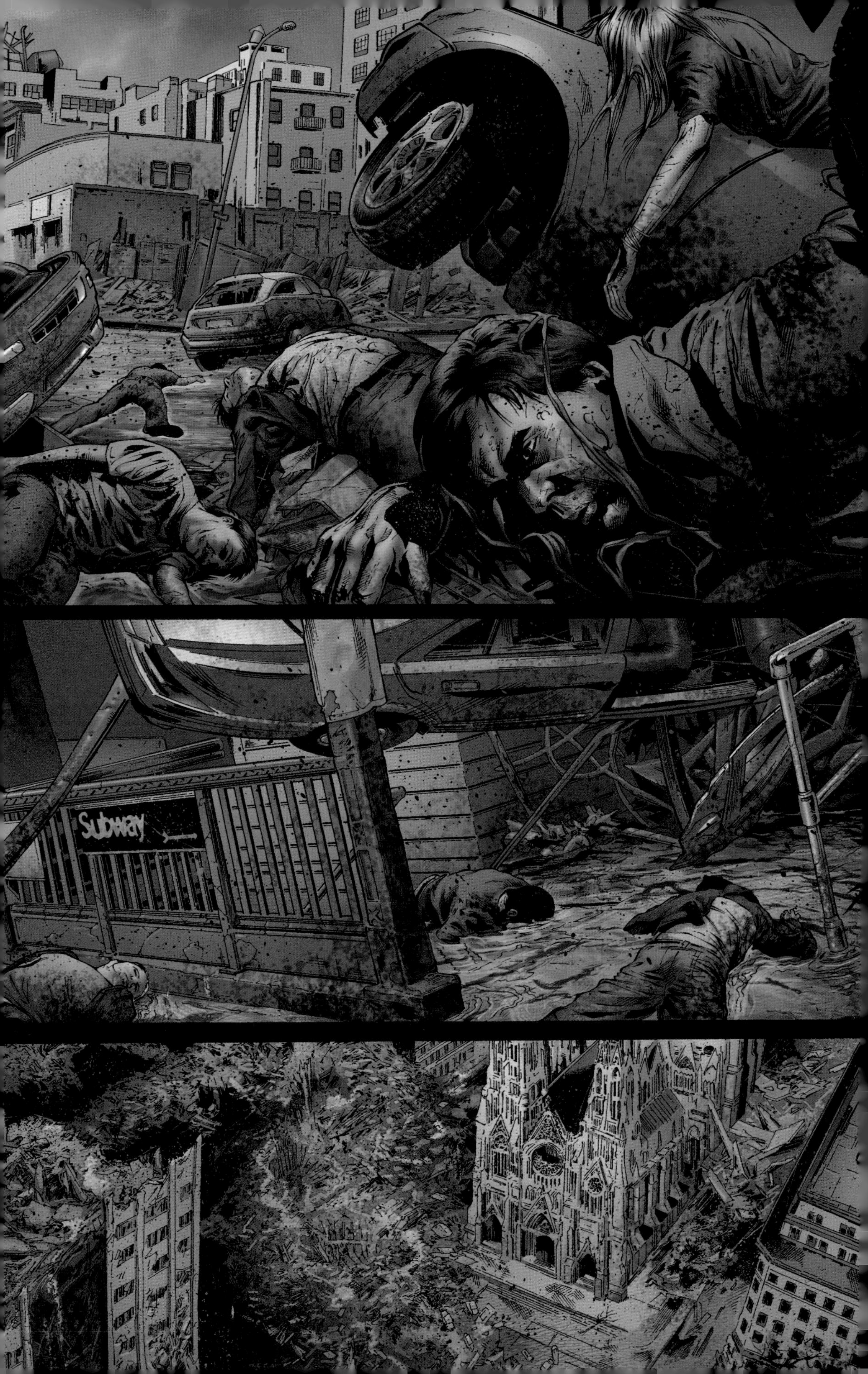
Subway

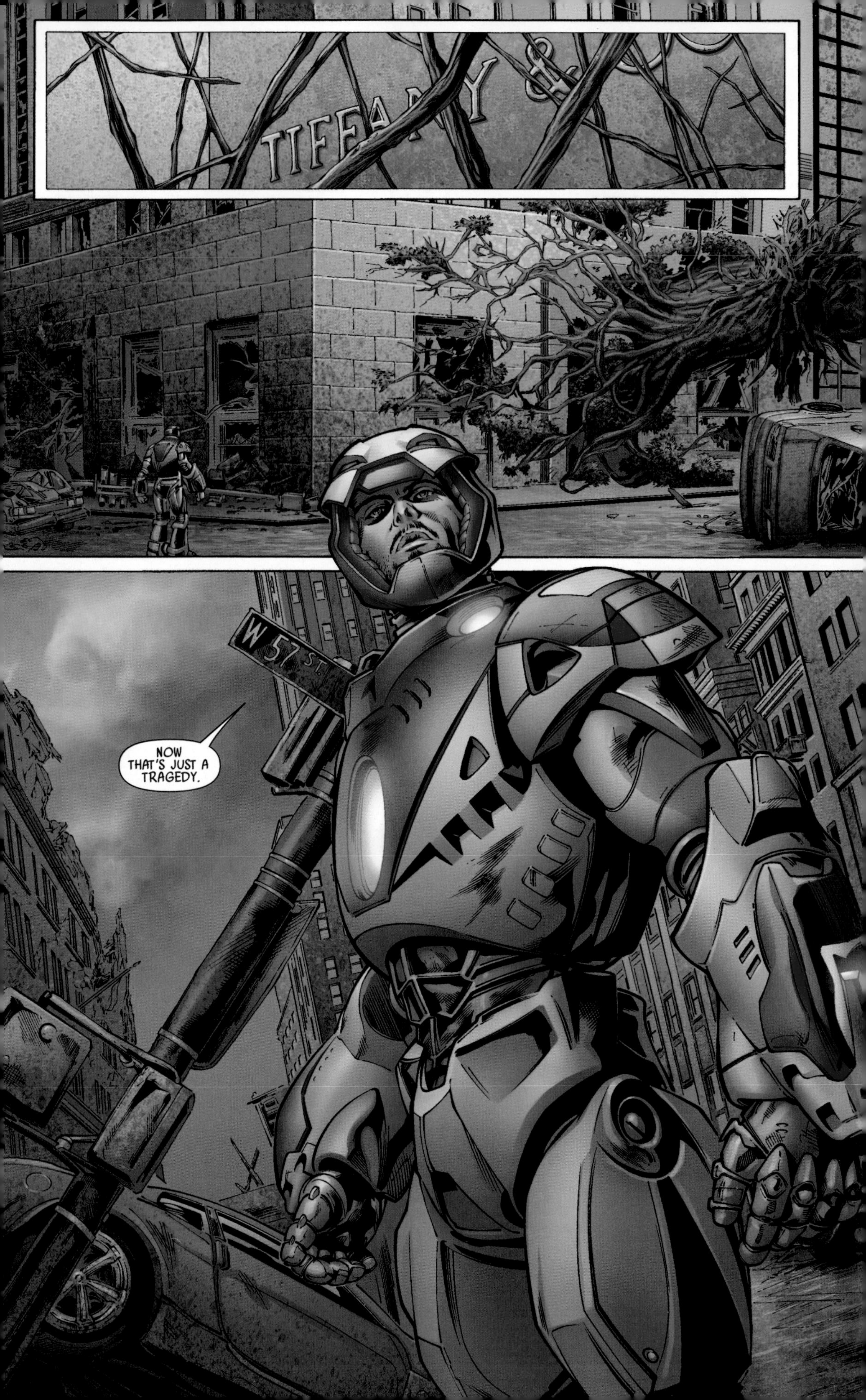
TIFFANY &
W 57 ST.
NOW THAT'S JUST A TRAGEDY.

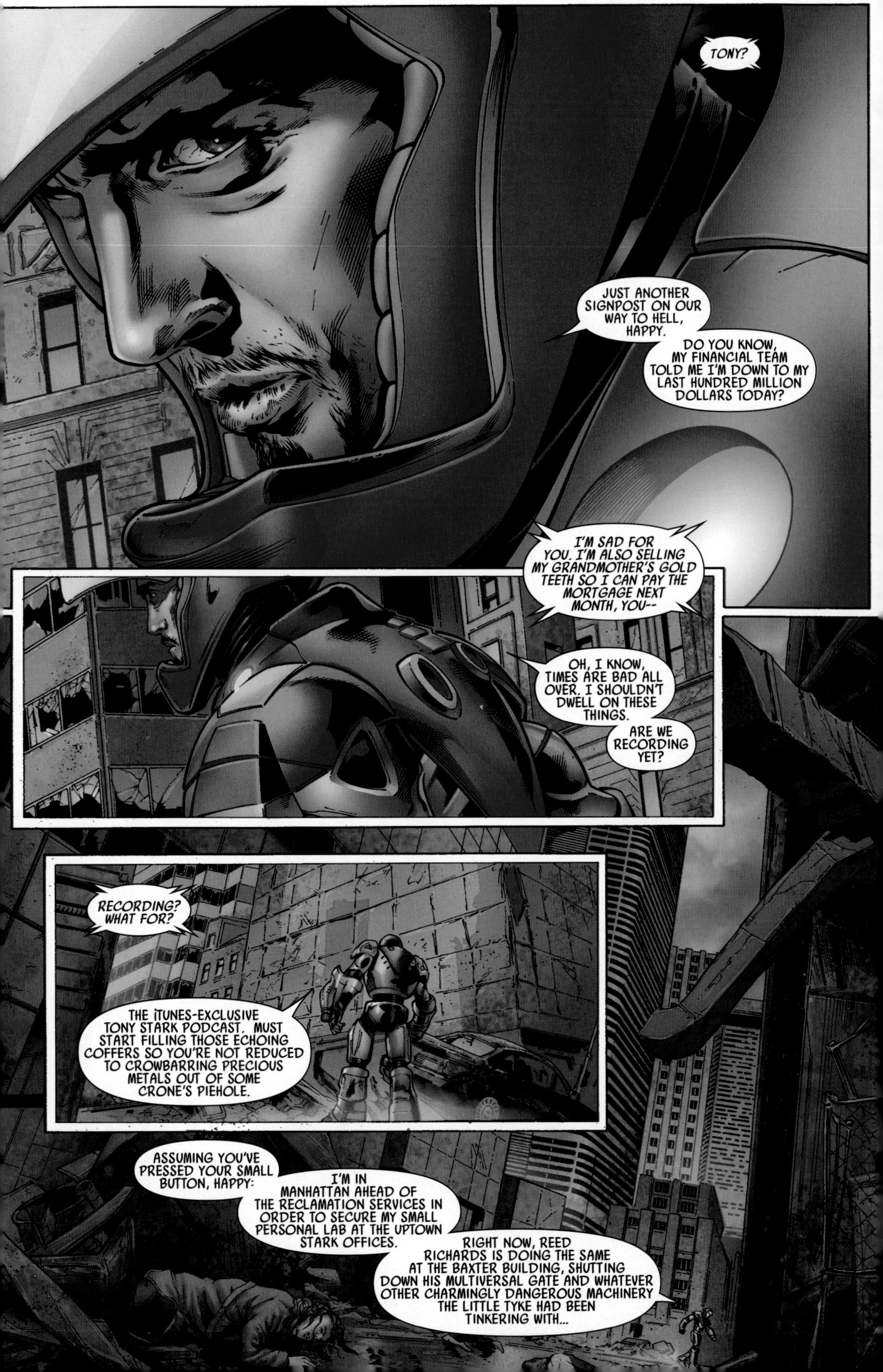
TONY?
JUST ANOTHER SIGNPOST ON OUR WAY TO HELL, HAPPY.
DO YOU KNOW, MY FINANCIAL TEAM TOLD ME I'M DOWN TO MY LAST HUNDRED MILLION DOLLARS TODAY?
I'M SAD FOR YOU. I'M ALSO SELLING MY GRANDMOTHER'S GOLD TEETH SO I CAN PAY THE MORTGAGE NEXT MONTH, YOU--
OH, I KNOW, TIMES ARE BAD ALL OVER. I SHOULDN'T DWELL ON THESE THINGS.
ARE WE RECORDING YET?
RECORDING? WHAT FOR?
THE iTUNES-EXCLUSIVE TONY STARK PODCAST. MUST START FILLING THOSE ECHOING COFFERS SO YOU'RE NOT REDUCED TO CROWBARRING PRECIOUS METALS OUT OF SOME CRONE'S PIEHOLE.
ASSUMING YOU'VE PRESSED YOUR SMALL BUTTON, HAPPY:
I'M IN MANHATTAN AHEAD OF THE RECLAMATION SERVICES IN ORDER TO SECURE MY SMALL PERSONAL LAB AT THE UPTOWN STARK OFFICES.
RIGHT NOW, REED RICHARDS IS DOING THE SAME AT THE BAXTER BUILDING, SHUTTING DOWN HIS MULTIVERSAL GATE AND WHATEVER OTHER CHARMINGLY DANGEROUS MACHINERY THE LITTLE TYKE HAD BEEN TINKERING WITH...

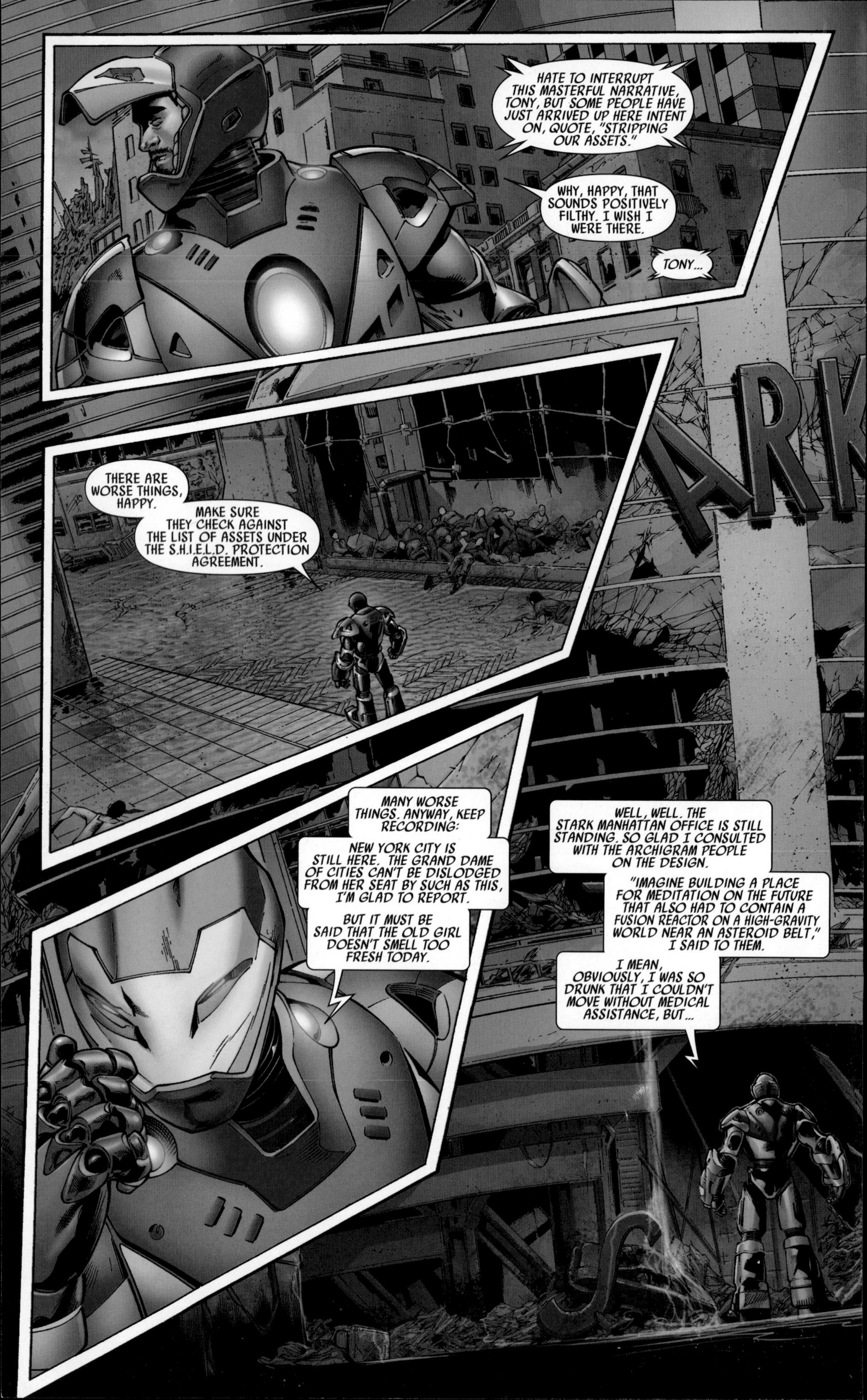
HATE TO INTERRUPT THIS MASTERFUL NARRATIVE, TONY, BUT SOME PEOPLE HAVE JUST ARRIVED UP HERE INTENT ON, QUOTE, "STRIPPING OUR ASSETS."
WHY, HAPPY, THAT SOUNDS POSITIVELY FILTHY. I WISH I WERE THERE.
TONY...
ARK
THERE ARE WORSE THINGS, HAPPY.
MAKE SURE THEY CHECK AGAINST THE LIST OF ASSETS UNDER THE S.H.I.E.L.D. PROTECTION AGREEMENT.
MANY WORSE THINGS. ANYWAY, KEEP RECORDING:
NEW YORK CITY IS STILL HERE. THE GRAND DAME OF CITIES CAN'T BE DISLODGED FROM HER SEAT BY SUCH AS THIS, I'M GLAD TO REPORT.
BUT IT MUST BE SAID THAT THE OLD GIRL DOESN'T SMELL TOO FRESH TODAY.
WELL, WELL. THE STARK MANHATTAN OFFICE IS STILL STANDING. SO GLAD I CONSULTED WITH THE ARCHIGRAM PEOPLE ON THE DESIGN.
"IMAGINE BUILDING A PLACE FOR MEDITATION ON THE FUTURE THAT ALSO HAD TO CONTAIN A FUSION REACTOR ON A HIGH-GRAVITY WORLD NEAR AN ASTEROID BELT," I SAID TO THEM.
I MEAN, OBVIOUSLY, I WAS SO DRUNK THAT I COULDN'T MOVE WITHOUT MEDICAL ASSISTANCE, BUT...

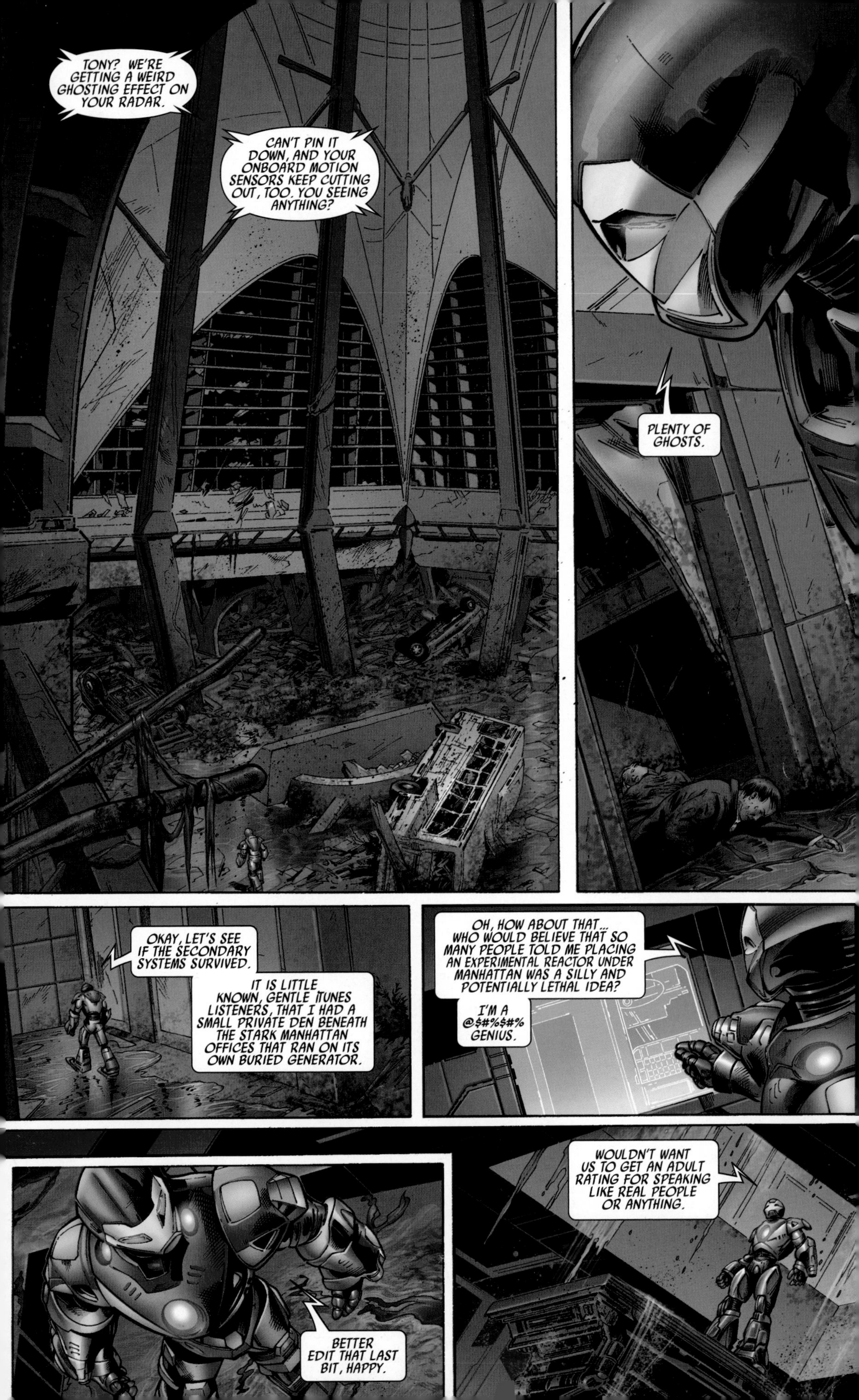
TONY? WE'RE GETTING A WEIRD GHOSTING EFFECT ON YOUR RADAR.
CAN'T PIN IT DOWN, AND YOUR ONBOARD MOTION SENSORS KEEP CUTTING OUT, TOO. YOU SEEING ANYTHING?
PLENTY OF GHOSTS.
OKAY, LET'S SEE IF THE SECONDARY SYSTEMS SURVIVED.
IT IS LITTLE KNOWN, GENTLE ITUNES LISTENERS, THAT I HAD A SMALL PRIVATE DEN BENEATH THE STARK MANHATTAN OFFICES THAT RAN ON ITS OWN BURIED GENERATOR.
OH, HOW ABOUT THAT... WHO WOULD BELIEVE THAT SO MANY PEOPLE TOLD ME PLACING AN EXPERIMENTAL REACTOR UNDER MANHATTAN WAS A SILLY AND POTENTIALLY LETHAL IDEA?
I'M A @$#%$#% GENIUS.
BETTER EDIT THAT LAST BIT, HAPPY.
WOULDN'T WANT US TO GET AN ADULT RATING FOR SPEAKING LIKE REAL PEOPLE OR ANYTHING.

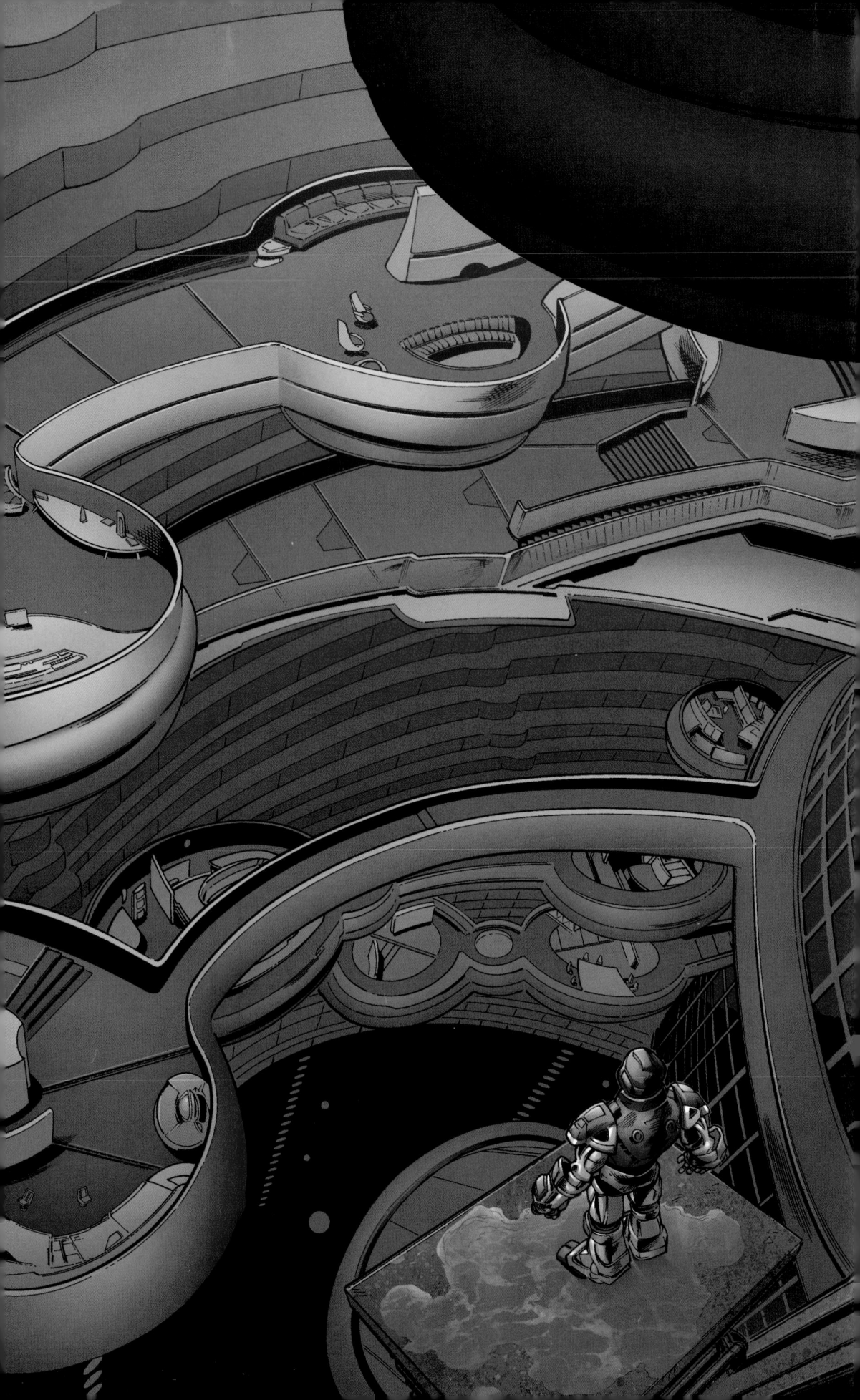

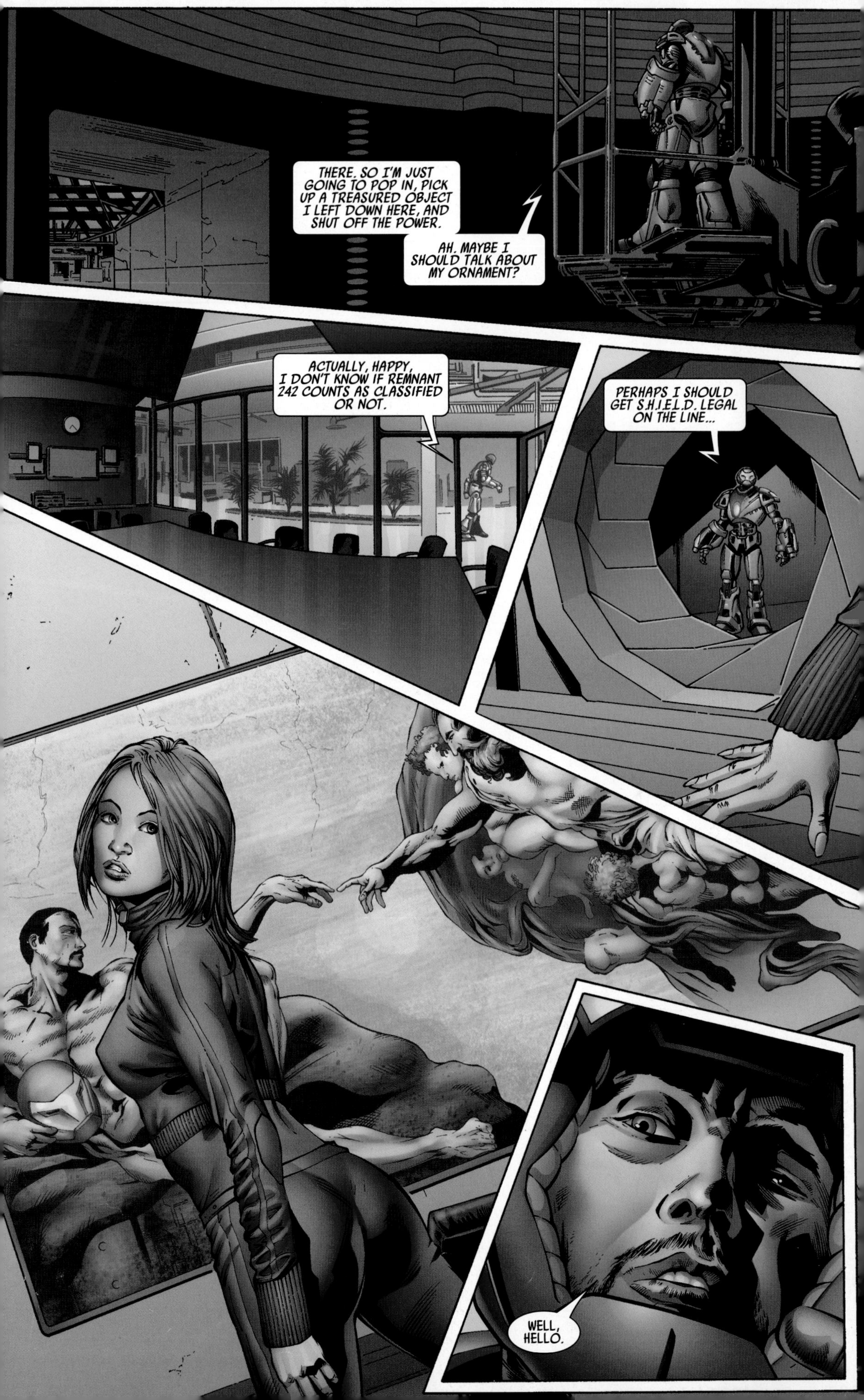
THERE. SO I'M JUST GOING TO POP IN, PICK UP A TREASURED OBJECT I LEFT DOWN HERE, AND SHUT OFF THE POWER.
AH. MAYBE I SHOULD TALK ABOUT MY ORNAMENT?
ACTUALLY, HAPPY, I DON'T KNOW IF REMNANT 242 COUNTS AS CLASSIFIED OR NOT.
PERHAPS I SHOULD GET S.H.I.E.L.D. LEGAL ON THE LINE...
WELL, HELLO.

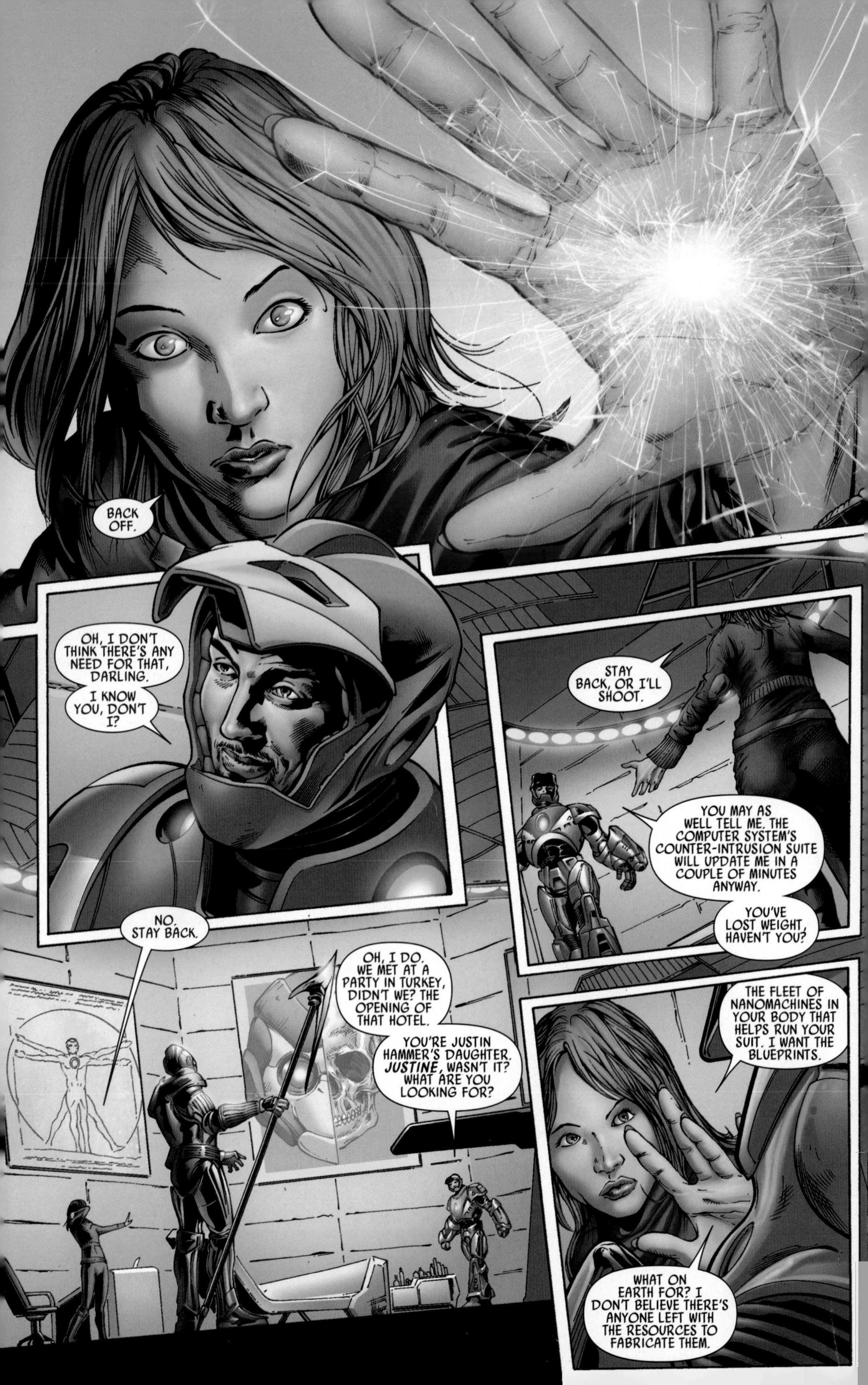
BACK OFF.
OH, I DON'T THINK THERE'S ANY NEED FOR THAT, DARLING.
I KNOW YOU, DON'T I?
STAY BACK, OR I'LL SHOOT.
YOU MAY AS WELL TELL ME. THE COMPUTER SYSTEM'S COUNTER-INTRUSION SUITE WILL UPDATE ME IN A COUPLE OF MINUTES ANYWAY.
YOU'VE LOST WEIGHT, HAVEN'T YOU?
NO. STAY BACK.
OH, I DO. WE MET AT A PARTY IN TURKEY, DIDN'T WE? THE OPENING OF THAT HOTEL.
YOU'RE JUSTIN HAMMER'S DAUGHTER. JUSTINE, WASN'T IT? WHAT ARE YOU LOOKING FOR?
THE FLEET OF NANOMACHINES IN YOUR BODY THAT HELPS RUN YOUR SUIT. I WANT THE BLUEPRINTS.
WHAT ON EARTH FOR? I DON'T BELIEVE THERE'S ANYONE LEFT WITH THE RESOURCES TO FABRICATE THEM.

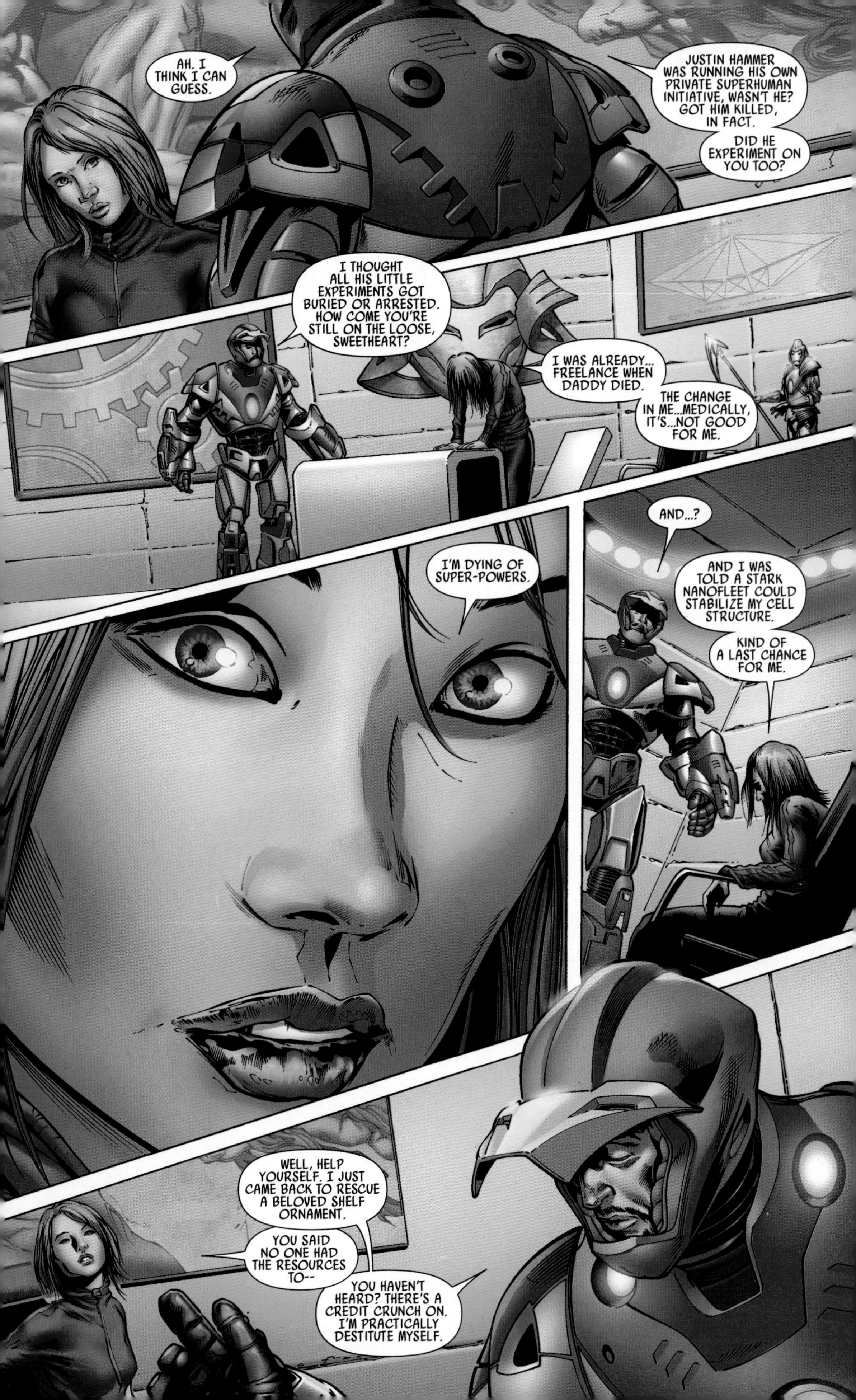
AH. I THINK I CAN GUESS.
JUSTIN HAMMER WAS RUNNING HIS OWN PRIVATE SUPERHUMAN INITIATIVE, WASN'T HE? GOT HIM KILLED, IN FACT.
DID HE EXPERIMENT ON YOU TOO?
I THOUGHT ALL HIS LITTLE EXPERIMENTS GOT BURIED OR ARRESTED. HOW COME YOU'RE STILL ON THE LOOSE, SWEETHEART?
I WAS ALREADY... FREELANCE WHEN DADDY DIED.
THE CHANGE IN ME...MEDICALLY, IT'S...NOT GOOD FOR ME.
I'M DYING OF SUPER-POWERS.
AND...?
AND I WAS TOLD A STARK NANOFLEET COULD STABILIZE MY CELL STRUCTURE.
KIND OF A LAST CHANCE FOR ME.
WELL, HELP YOURSELF. I JUST CAME BACK TO RESCUE A BELOVED SHELF ORNAMENT.
YOU SAID NO ONE HAD THE RESOURCES TO--
YOU HAVEN'T HEARD? THERE'S A CREDIT CRUNCH ON. I'M PRACTICALLY DESTITUTE MYSELF.

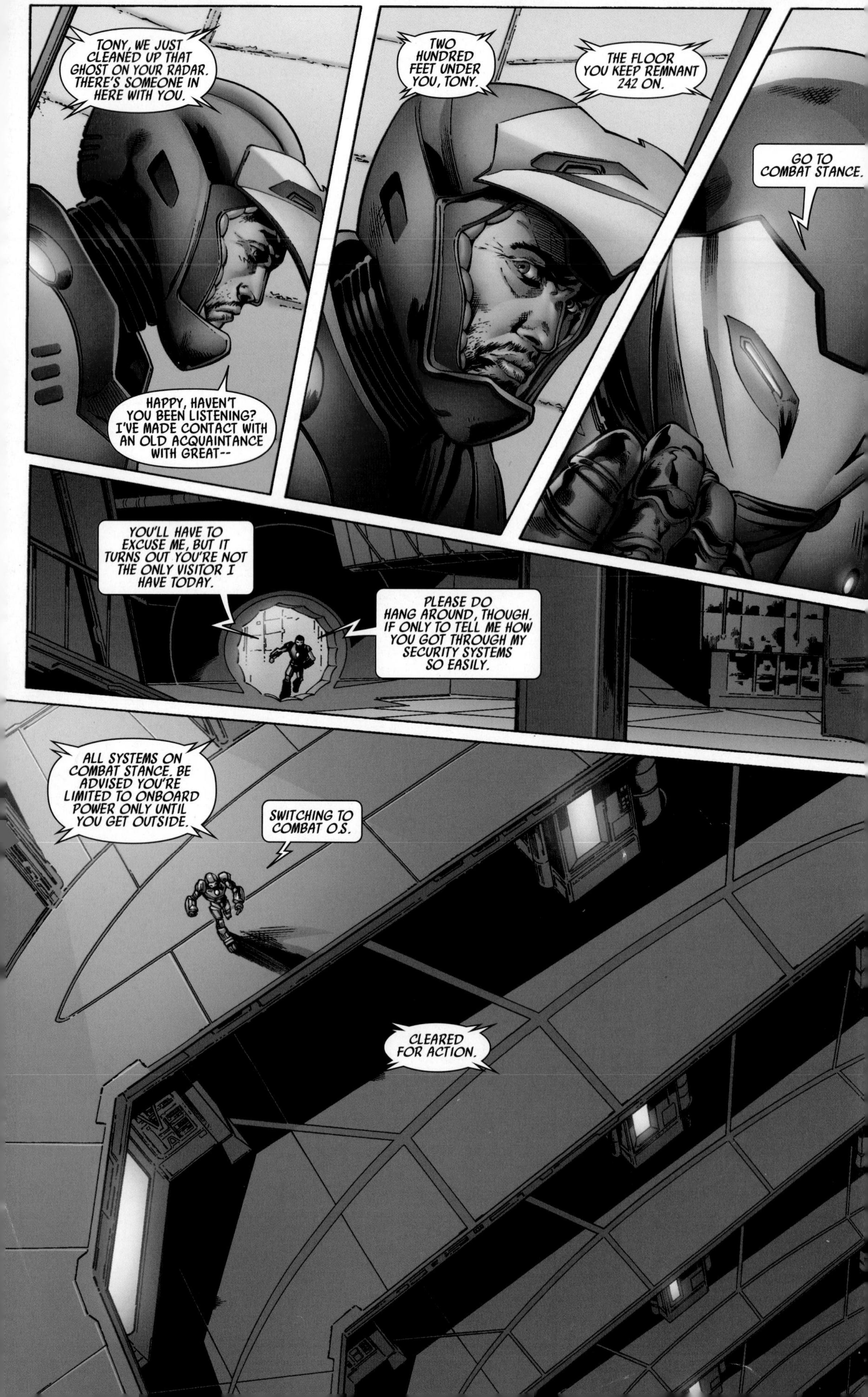

TONY, WE JUST CLEANED UP THAT GHOST ON YOUR RADAR. THERE'S SOMEONE IN HERE WITH YOU.
HAPPY, HAVEN'T YOU BEEN LISTENING? I'VE MADE CONTACT WITH AN OLD ACQUAINTANCE WITH GREAT--
TWO HUNDRED FEET UNDER YOU, TONY.
THE FLOOR YOU KEEP REMNANT 242 ON.
GO TO COMBAT STANCE.
YOU'LL HAVE TO EXCUSE ME, BUT IT TURNS OUT YOU'RE NOT THE ONLY VISITOR I HAVE TODAY.
PLEASE DO HANG AROUND, THOUGH. IF ONLY TO TELL ME HOW YOU GOT THROUGH MY SECURITY SYSTEMS SO EASILY.
ALL SYSTEMS ON COMBAT STANCE. BE ADVISED YOU'RE LIMITED TO ONBOARD POWER ONLY UNTIL YOU GET OUTSIDE.
SWITCHING TO COMBAT O.S.
CLEARED FOR ACTION.

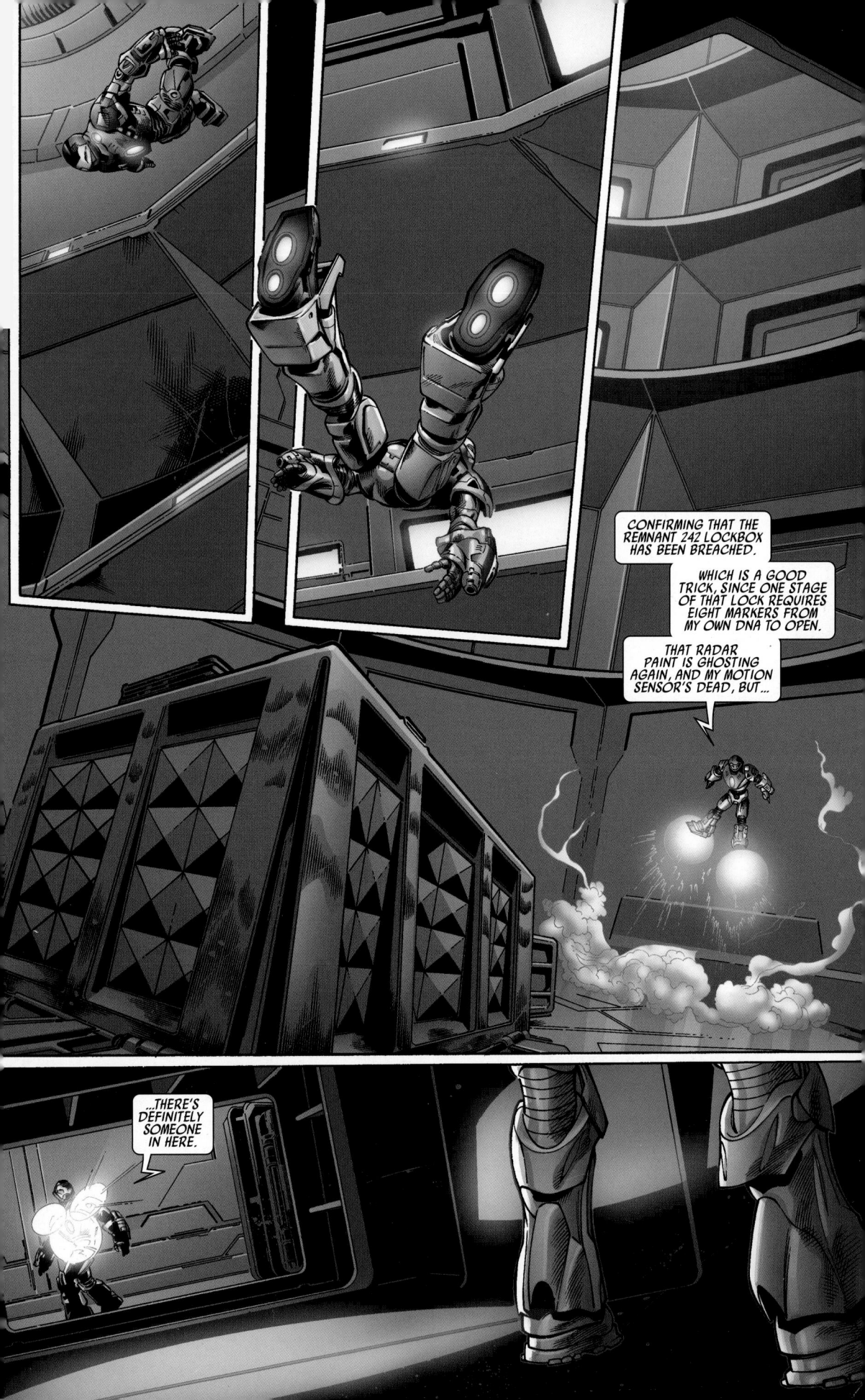

CONFIRMING THAT THE REMNANT 242 LOCKBOX HAS BEEN BREACHED.

WHICH IS A GOOD TRICK, SINCE ONE STAGE OF THAT LOCK REQUIRES EIGHT MARKERS FROM MY OWN DNA TO OPEN.

THAT RADAR PAINT IS GHOSTING AGAIN, AND MY MOTION SENSOR'S DEAD, BUT...

...THERE'S DEFINITELY SOMEONE IN HERE.

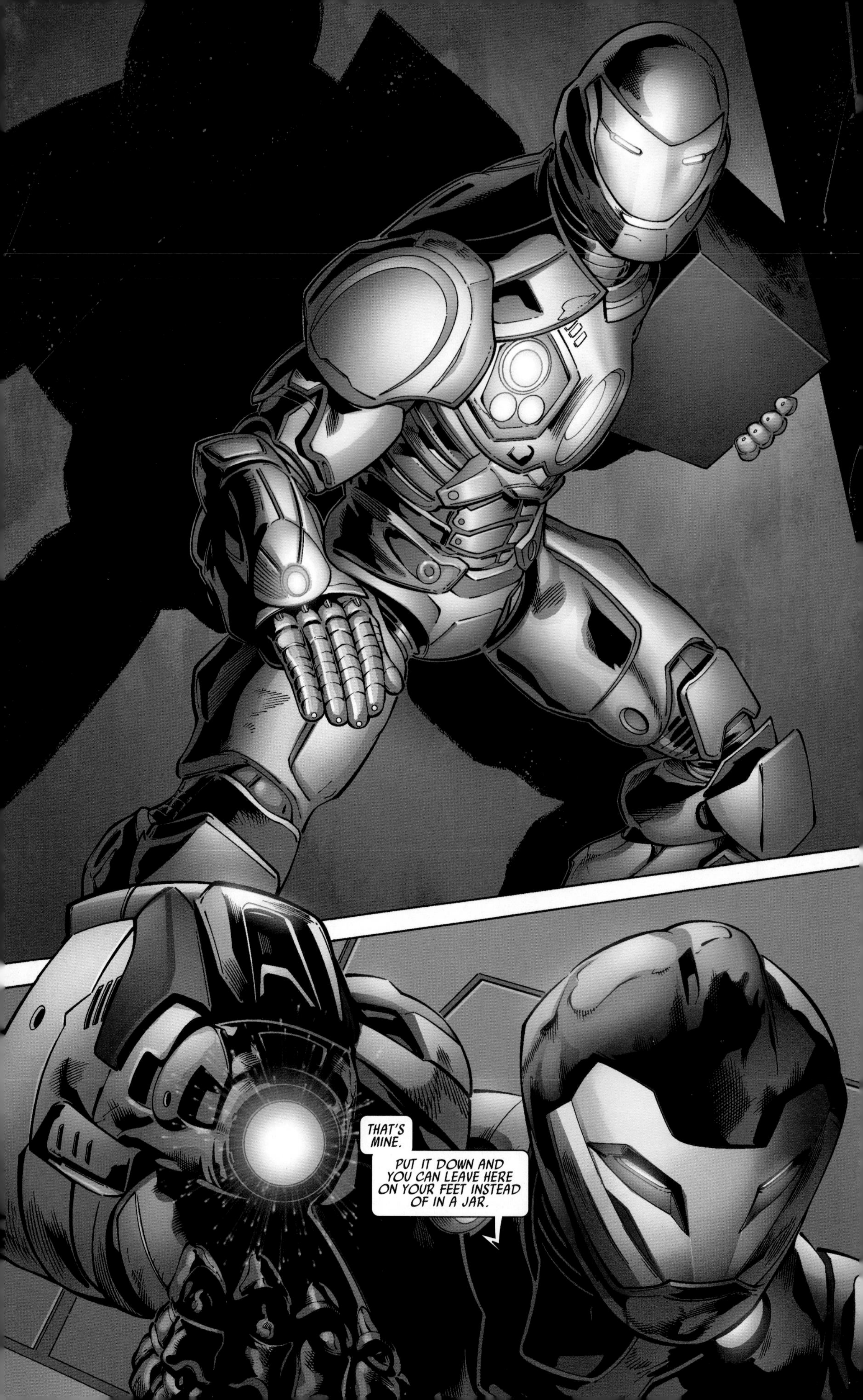
THAT'S MINE.
PUT IT DOWN AND YOU CAN LEAVE HERE ON YOUR FEET INSTEAD OF IN A JAR.

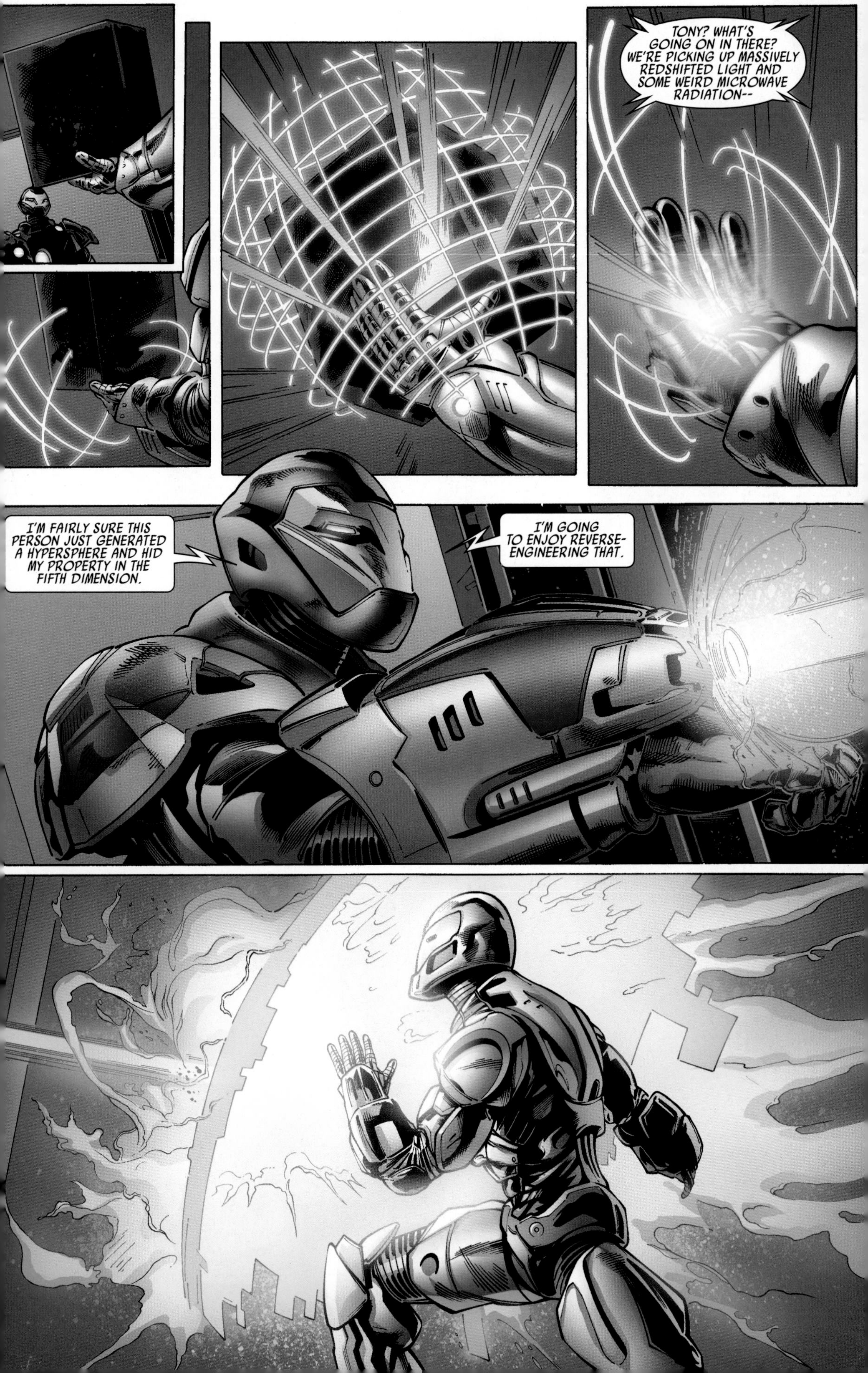
TONY? WHAT'S GOING ON IN THERE? WE'RE PICKING UP MASSIVELY REDSHIFTED LIGHT AND SOME WEIRD MICROWAVE RADIATION--
I'M FAIRLY SURE THIS PERSON JUST GENERATED A HYPERSPHERE AND HID MY PROPERTY IN THE FIFTH DIMENSION.
I'M GOING TO ENJOY REVERSE-ENGINEERING THAT.

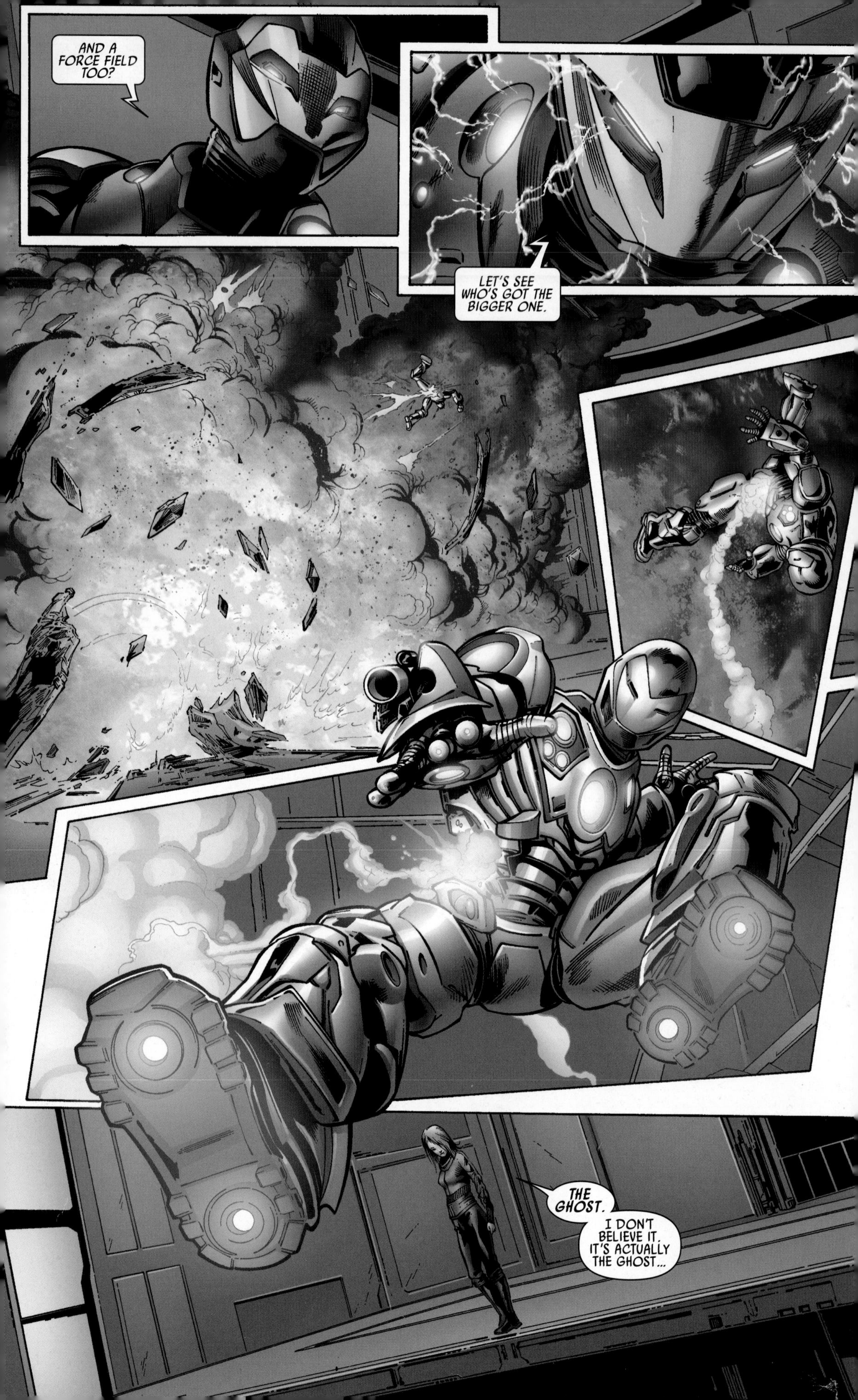
AND A FORCE FIELD TOO?
LET'S SEE WHO'S GOT THE BIGGER ONE.
THE GHOST.
I DON'T BELIEVE IT. IT'S ACTUALLY THE GHOST...

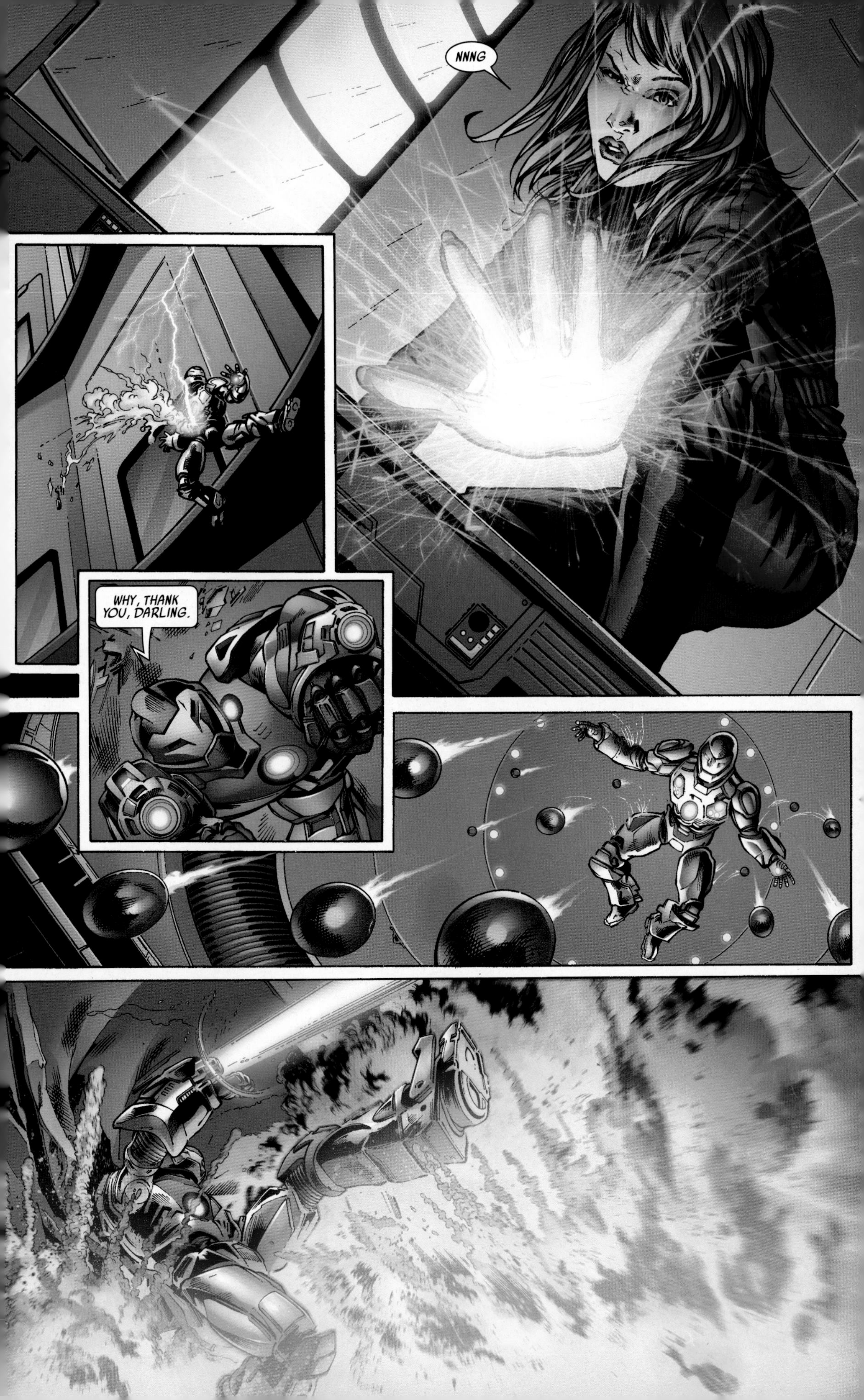
NNNG
WHY, THANK YOU, DARLING.

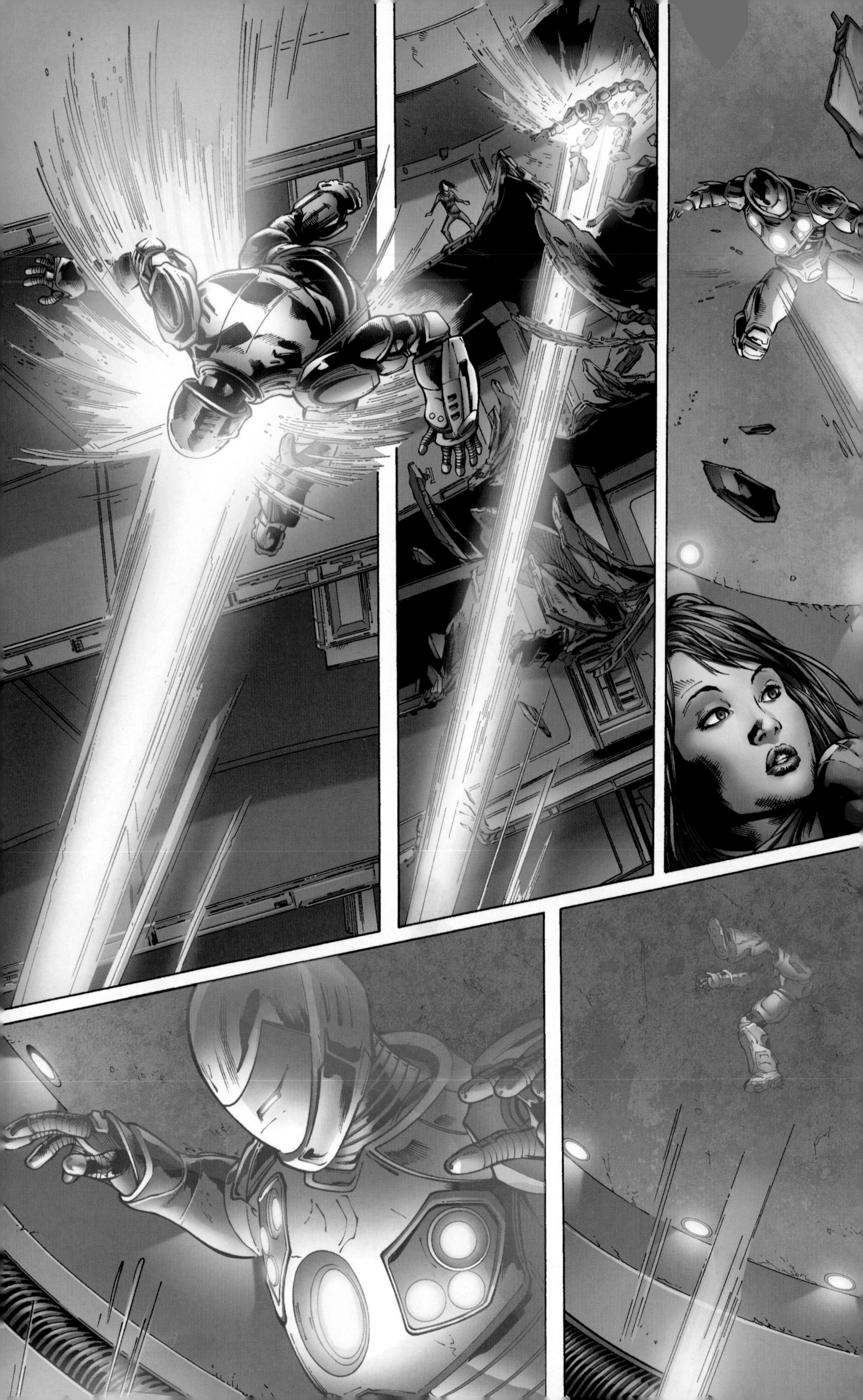

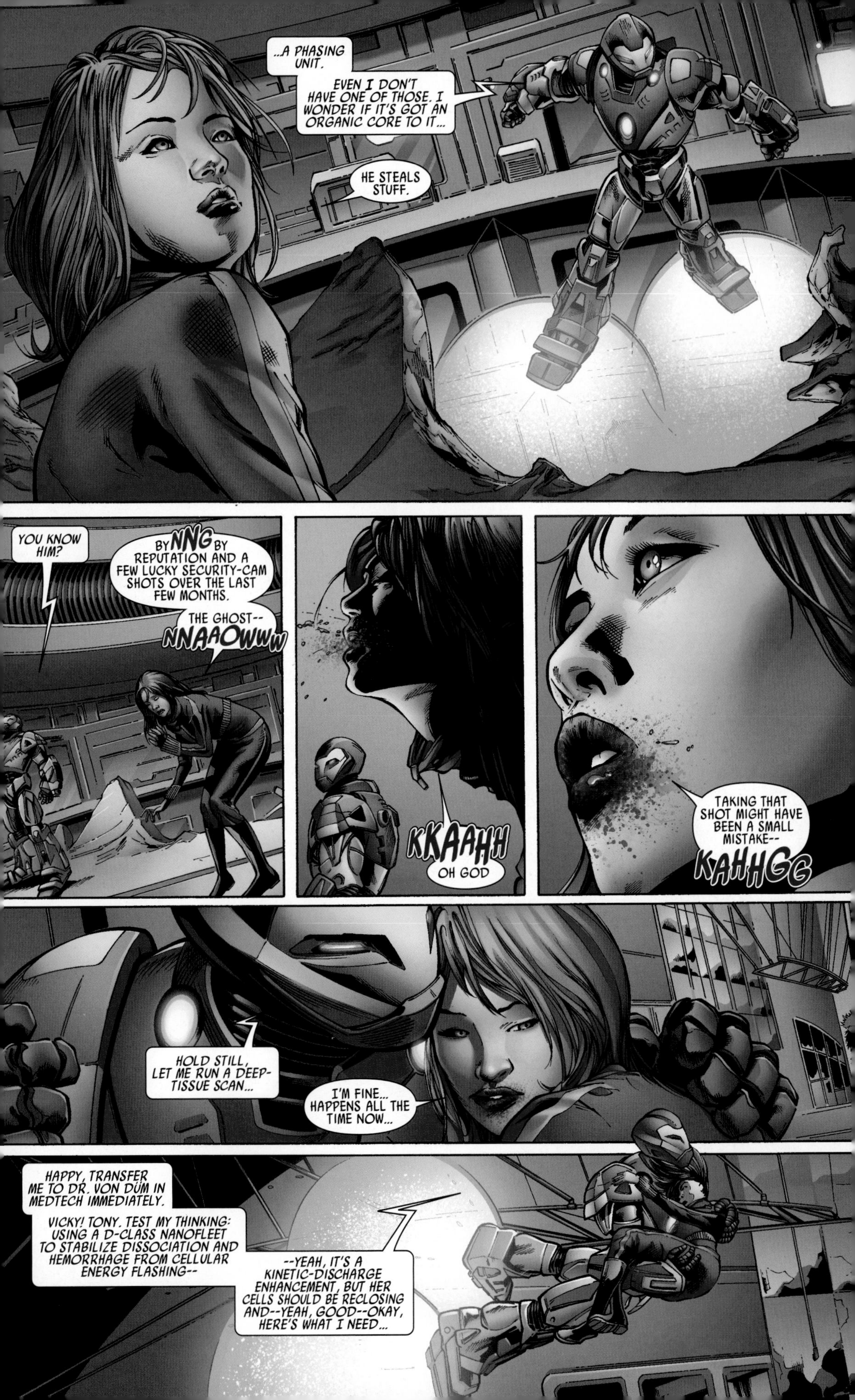
...A PHASING UNIT.
EVEN I DON'T HAVE ONE OF THOSE. I WONDER IF IT'S GOT AN ORGANIC CORE TO IT...
HE STEALS STUFF.
YOU KNOW HIM?
BY NNG BY REPUTATION AND A FEW LUCKY SECURITY-CAM SHOTS OVER THE LAST FEW MONTHS.
THE GHOST--
NNAAOWWW
KKAAHH
OH GOD
TAKING THAT SHOT MIGHT HAVE BEEN A SMALL MISTAKE--
KAHHGG
HOLD STILL, LET ME RUN A DEEP-TISSUE SCAN...
I'M FINE... HAPPENS ALL THE TIME NOW...
HAPPY, TRANSFER ME TO DR. VON DÜM IN MEDTECH IMMEDIATELY.
VICKY! TONY. TEST MY THINKING: USING A D-CLASS NANOFLEET TO STABILIZE DISSOCIATION AND HEMORRHAGE FROM CELLULAR ENERGY FLASHING--
--YEAH, IT'S A KINETIC-DISCHARGE ENHANCEMENT, BUT HER CELLS SHOULD BE RECLOSING AND--YEAH, GOOD--OKAY, HERE'S WHAT I NEED...

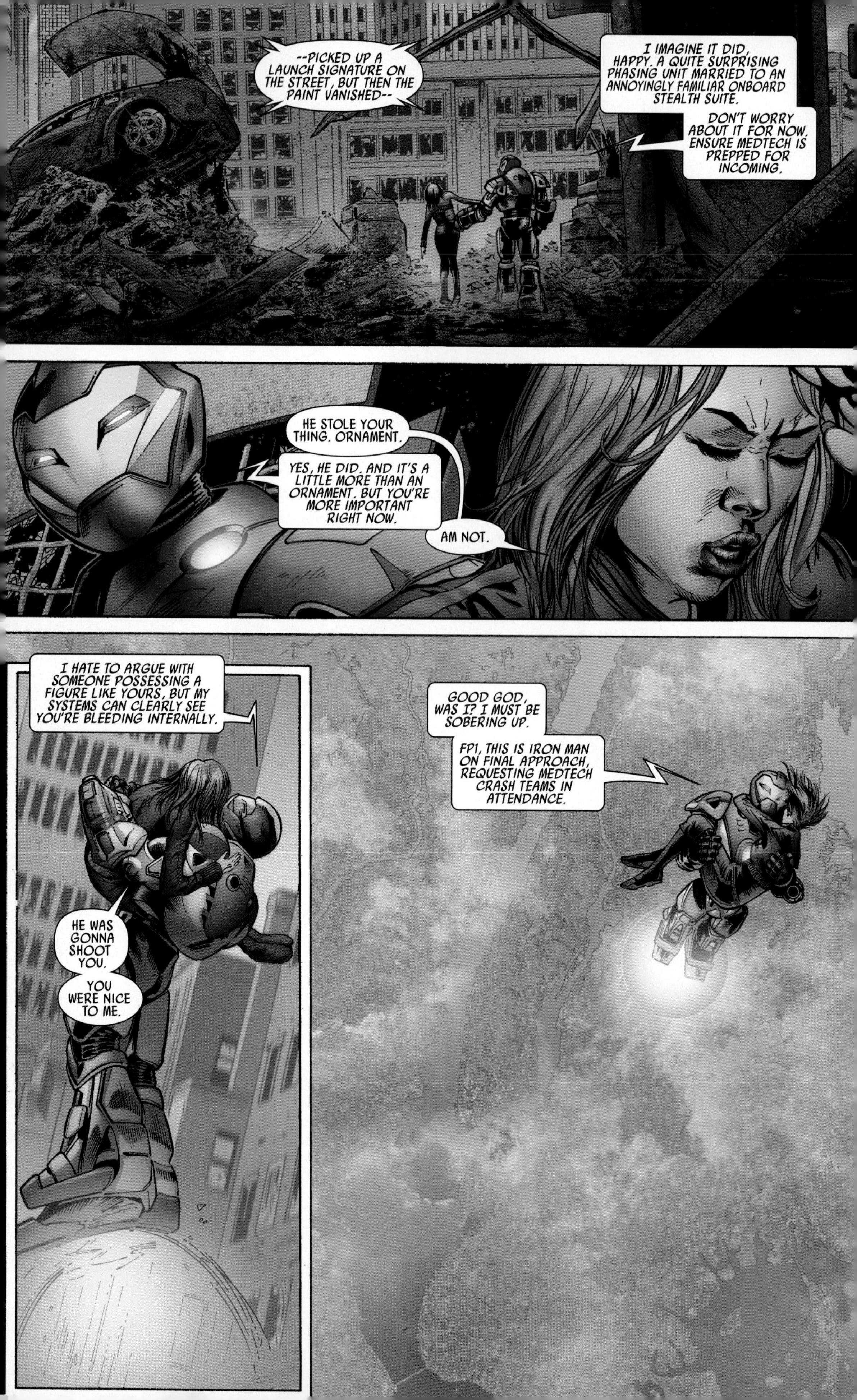
--PICKED UP A LAUNCH SIGNATURE ON THE STREET, BUT THEN THE PAINT VANISHED--
I IMAGINE IT DID, HAPPY. A QUITE SURPRISING PHASING UNIT MARRIED TO AN ANNOYINGLY FAMILIAR ONBOARD STEALTH SUITE.
DON'T WORRY ABOUT IT FOR NOW. ENSURE MEDTECH IS PREPPED FOR INCOMING.
HE STOLE YOUR THING. ORNAMENT.
YES, HE DID. AND IT'S A LITTLE MORE THAN AN ORNAMENT. BUT YOU'RE MORE IMPORTANT RIGHT NOW.
AM NOT.
I HATE TO ARGUE WITH SOMEONE POSSESSING A FIGURE LIKE YOURS, BUT MY SYSTEMS CAN CLEARLY SEE YOU'RE BLEEDING INTERNALLY.
HE WAS GONNA SHOOT YOU.
YOU WERE NICE TO ME.
GOOD GOD, WAS I? I MUST BE SOBERING UP.
FP1, THIS IS IRON MAN ON FINAL APPROACH, REQUESTING MEDTECH CRASH TEAMS IN ATTENDANCE.

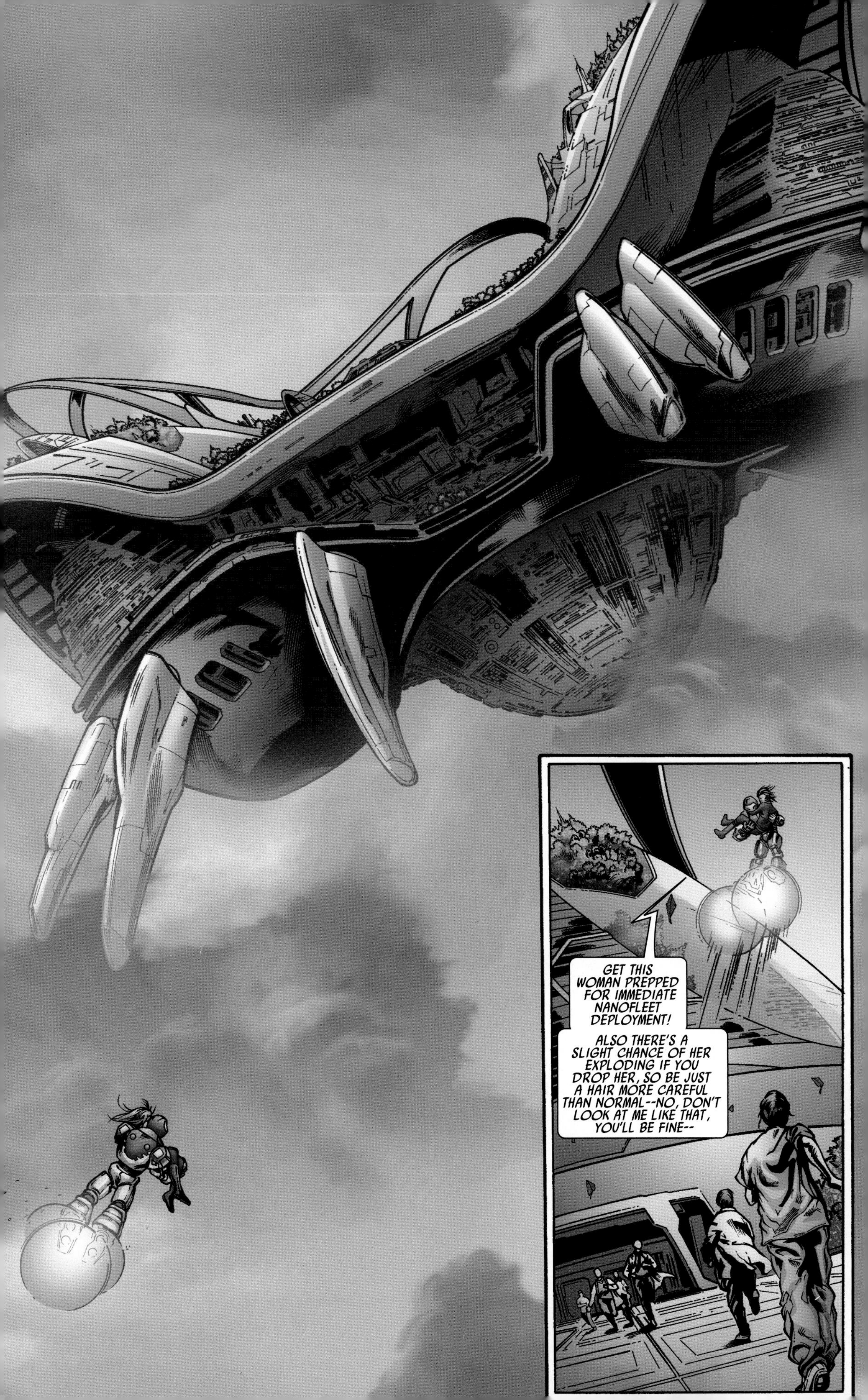
GET THIS WOMAN PREPPED FOR IMMEDIATE NANOFLEET DEPLOYMENT!
ALSO THERE'S A SLIGHT CHANCE OF HER EXPLODING IF YOU DROP HER, SO BE JUST A HAIR MORE CAREFUL THAN NORMAL--NO, DON'T LOOK AT ME LIKE THAT, YOU'LL BE FINE--

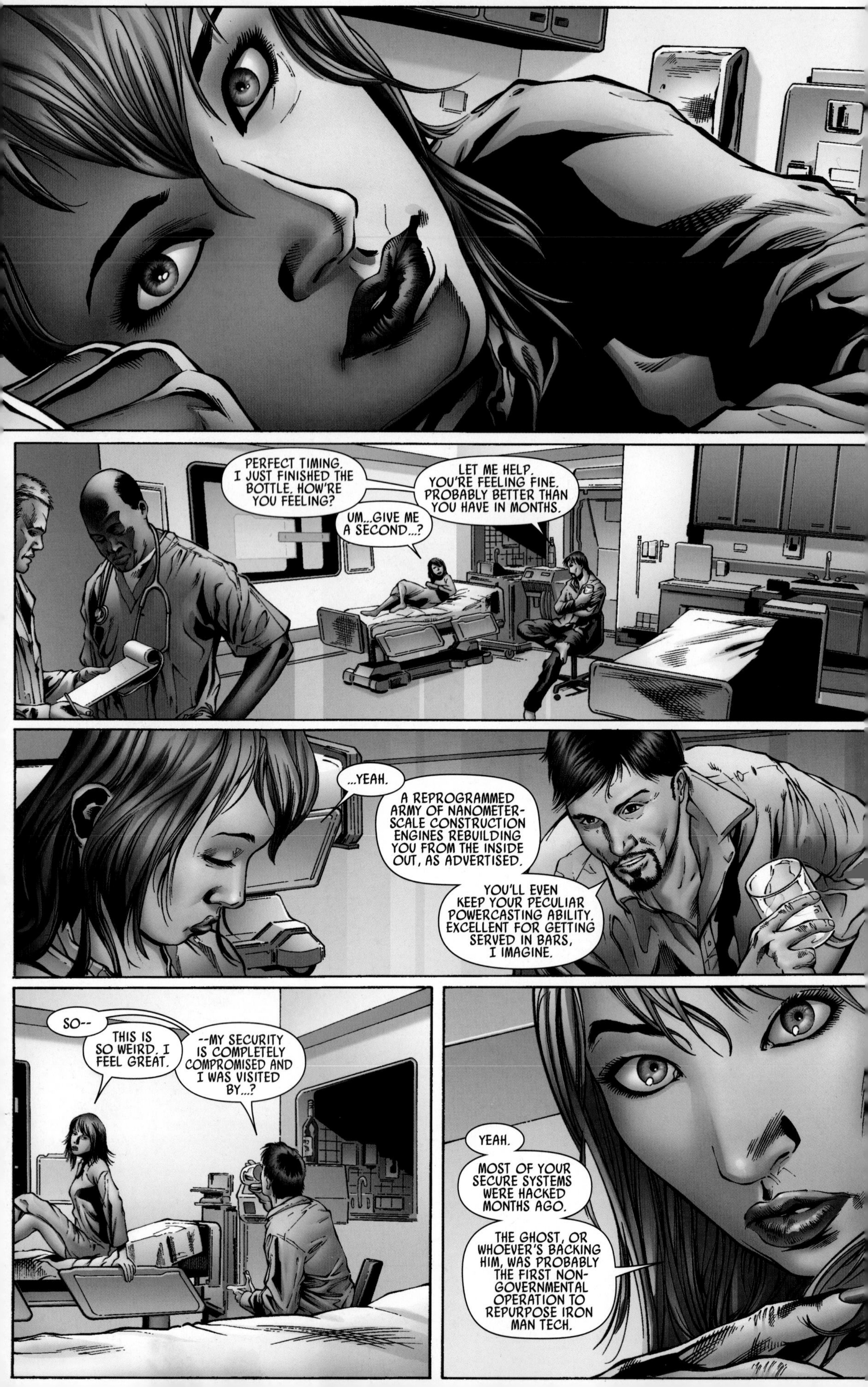
PERFECT TIMING. I JUST FINISHED THE BOTTLE. HOW'RE YOU FEELING?
UM...GIVE ME A SECOND...?
LET ME HELP. YOU'RE FEELING FINE. PROBABLY BETTER THAN YOU HAVE IN MONTHS.
...YEAH.
A REPROGRAMMED ARMY OF NANOMETER-SCALE CONSTRUCTION ENGINES REBUILDING YOU FROM THE INSIDE OUT, AS ADVERTISED.
YOU'LL EVEN KEEP YOUR PECULIAR POWERCASTING ABILITY. EXCELLENT FOR GETTING SERVED IN BARS, I IMAGINE.
SO--
THIS IS SO WEIRD. I FEEL GREAT.
--MY SECURITY IS COMPLETELY COMPROMISED AND I WAS VISITED BY...?
YEAH.
MOST OF YOUR SECURE SYSTEMS WERE HACKED MONTHS AGO.
THE GHOST, OR WHOEVER'S BACKING HIM, WAS PROBABLY THE FIRST NON-GOVERNMENTAL OPERATION TO REPURPOSE IRON MAN TECH.

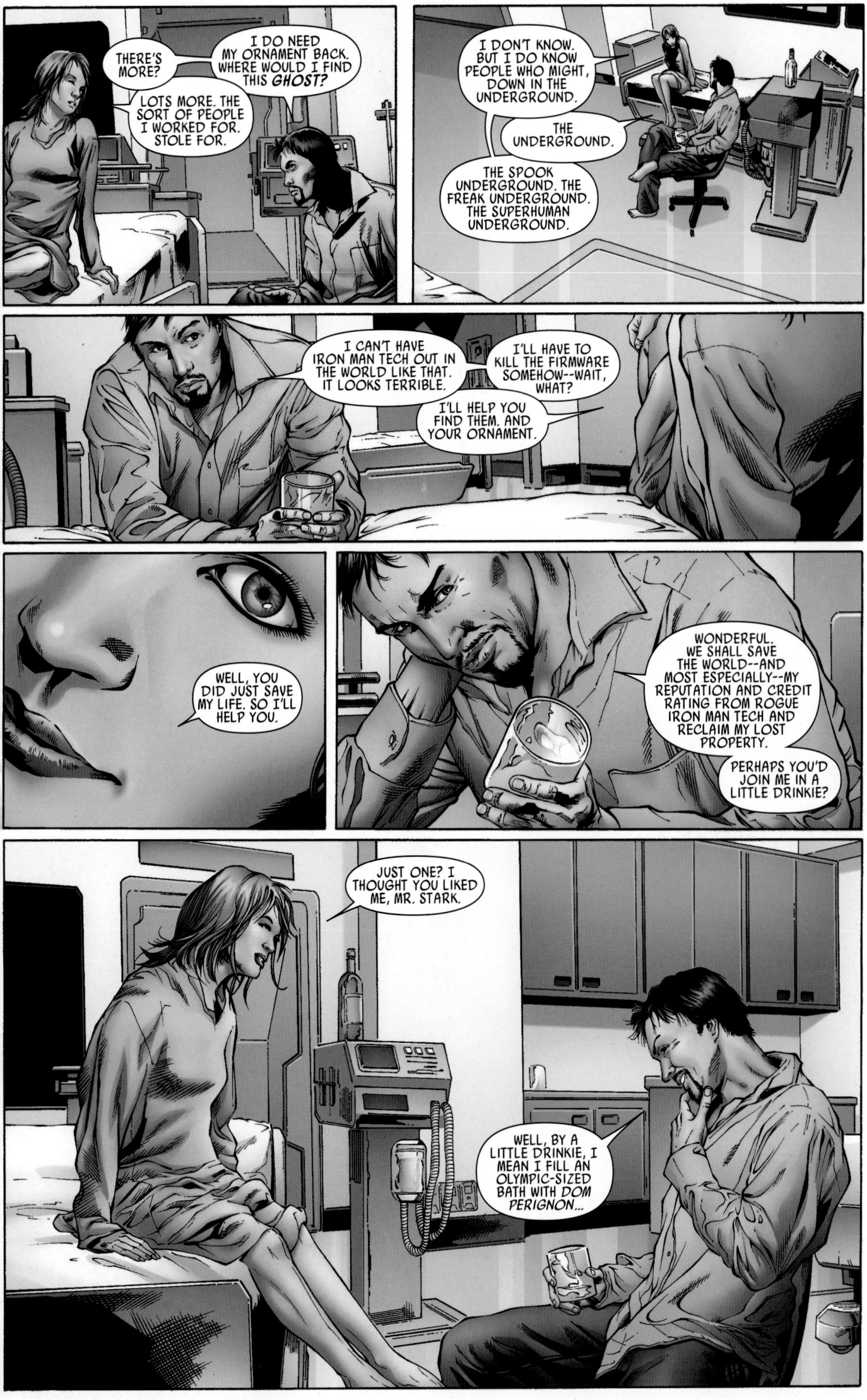
THERE'S MORE?
I DO NEED MY ORNAMENT BACK. WHERE WOULD I FIND THIS GHOST?
LOTS MORE. THE SORT OF PEOPLE I WORKED FOR. STOLE FOR.
I DON'T KNOW. BUT I DO KNOW PEOPLE WHO MIGHT, DOWN IN THE UNDERGROUND.
THE UNDERGROUND.
THE SPOOK UNDERGROUND. THE FREAK UNDERGROUND. THE SUPERHUMAN UNDERGROUND.
I CAN'T HAVE IRON MAN TECH OUT IN THE WORLD LIKE THAT. IT LOOKS TERRIBLE.
I'LL HAVE TO KILL THE FIRMWARE SOMEHOW--WAIT, WHAT?
I'LL HELP YOU FIND THEM. AND YOUR ORNAMENT.
WELL, YOU DID JUST SAVE MY LIFE. SO I'LL HELP YOU.
WONDERFUL. WE SHALL SAVE THE WORLD--AND MOST ESPECIALLY--MY REPUTATION AND CREDIT RATING FROM ROGUE IRON MAN TECH AND RECLAIM MY LOST PROPERTY.
PERHAPS YOU'D JOIN ME IN A LITTLE DRINKIE?
JUST ONE? I THOUGHT YOU LIKED ME, MR. STARK.
WELL, BY A LITTLE DRINKIE, I MEAN I FILL AN OLYMPIC-SIZED BATH WITH DOM PERIGNON...

2

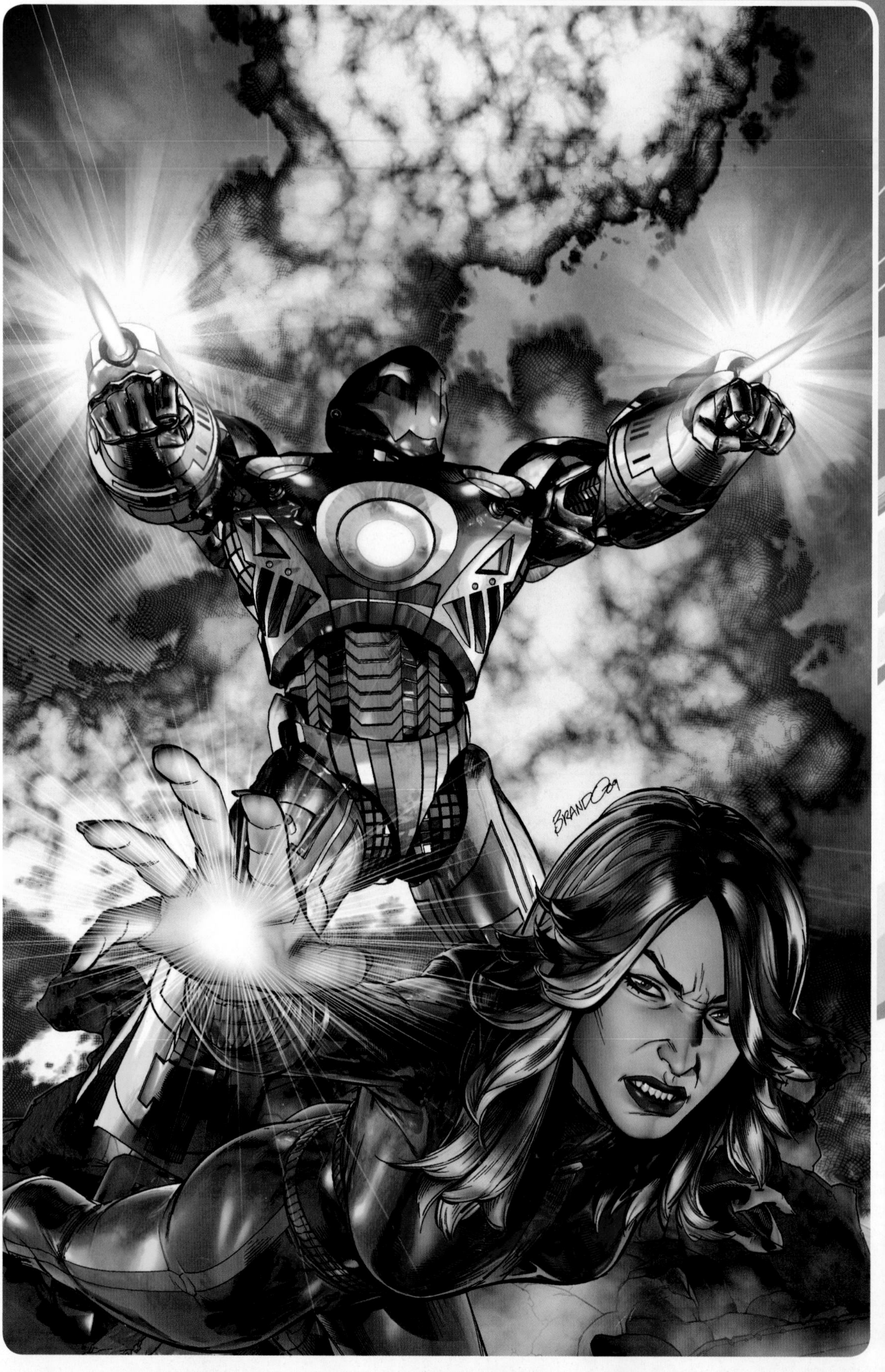

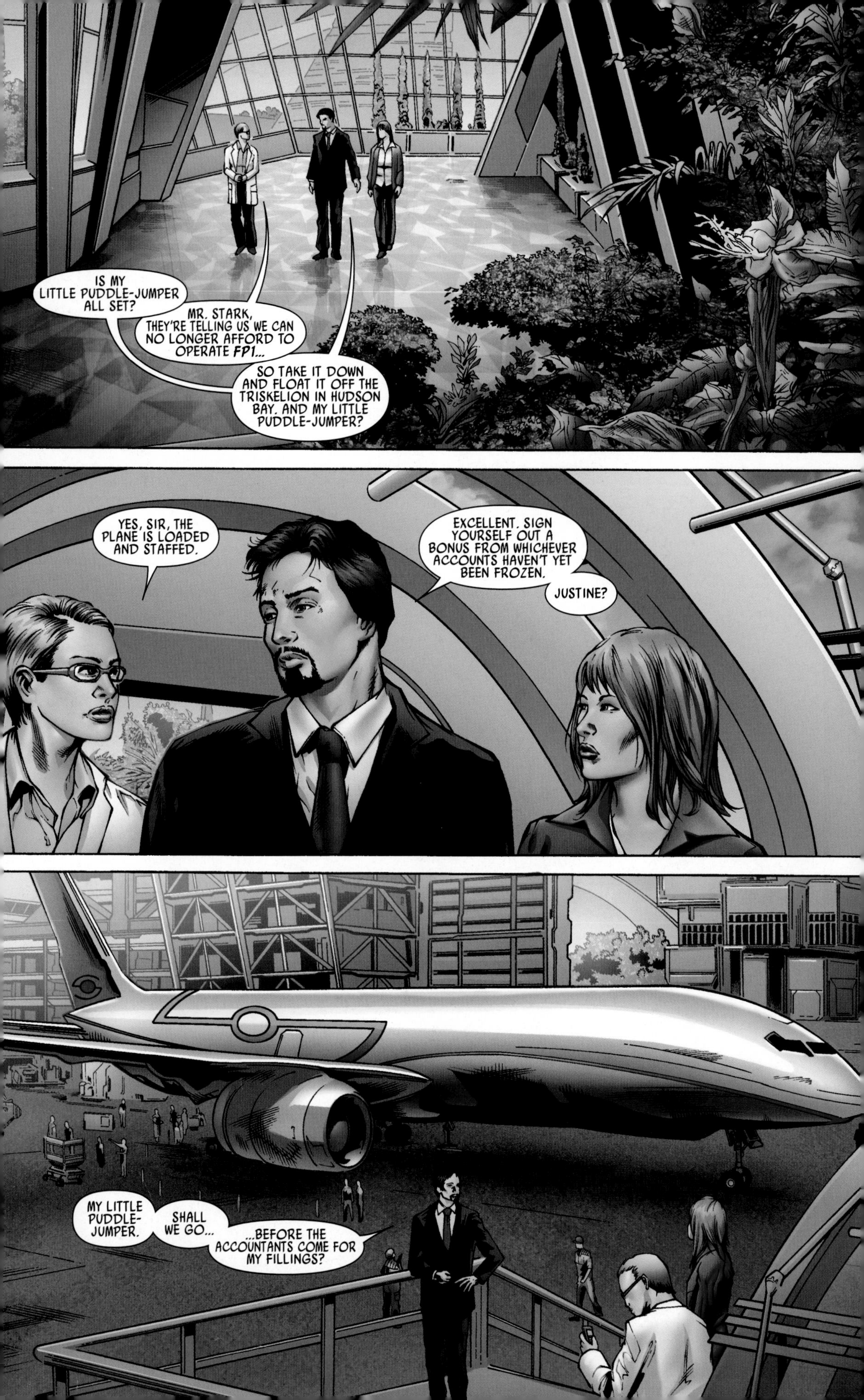
IS MY LITTLE PUDDLE-JUMPER ALL SET?
MR. STARK, THEY'RE TELLING US WE CAN NO LONGER AFFORD TO OPERATE FP1...
SO TAKE IT DOWN AND FLOAT IT OFF THE TRISKELION IN HUDSON BAY. AND MY LITTLE PUDDLE-JUMPER?
YES, SIR, THE PLANE IS LOADED AND STAFFED.
EXCELLENT. SIGN YOURSELF OUT A BONUS FROM WHICHEVER ACCOUNTS HAVEN'T YET BEEN FROZEN.
JUSTINE?
MY LITTLE PUDDLE-JUMPER.
SHALL WE GO...
...BEFORE THE ACCOUNTANTS COME FOR MY FILLINGS?

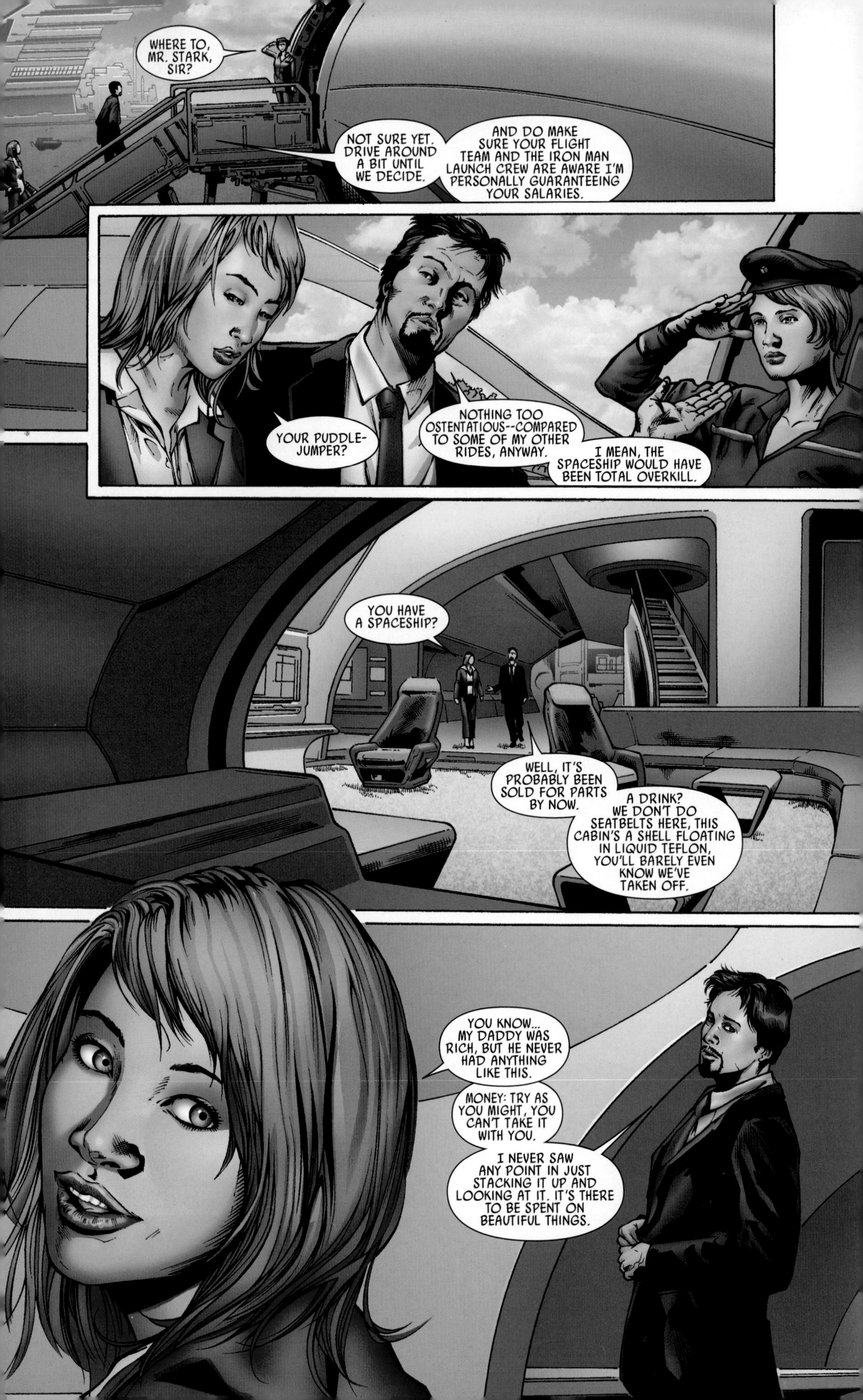

WHERE TO, MR. STARK, SIR?
NOT SURE YET. DRIVE AROUND A BIT UNTIL WE DECIDE.
AND DO MAKE SURE YOUR FLIGHT TEAM AND THE IRON MAN LAUNCH CREW ARE AWARE I'M PERSONALLY GUARANTEEING YOUR SALARIES.
YOUR PUDDLE-JUMPER?
NOTHING TOO OSTENTATIOUS--COMPARED TO SOME OF MY OTHER RIDES, ANYWAY.
I MEAN, THE SPACESHIP WOULD HAVE BEEN TOTAL OVERKILL.
YOU HAVE A SPACESHIP?
WELL, IT'S PROBABLY BEEN SOLD FOR PARTS BY NOW.
A DRINK? WE DON'T DO SEATBELTS HERE, THIS CABIN'S A SHELL FLOATING IN LIQUID TEFLON, YOU'LL BARELY EVEN KNOW WE'VE TAKEN OFF.
YOU KNOW... MY DADDY WAS RICH, BUT HE NEVER HAD ANYTHING LIKE THIS.
MONEY: TRY AS YOU MIGHT, YOU CAN'T TAKE IT WITH YOU.
I NEVER SAW ANY POINT IN JUST STACKING IT UP AND LOOKING AT IT. IT'S THERE TO BE SPENT ON BEAUTIFUL THINGS.

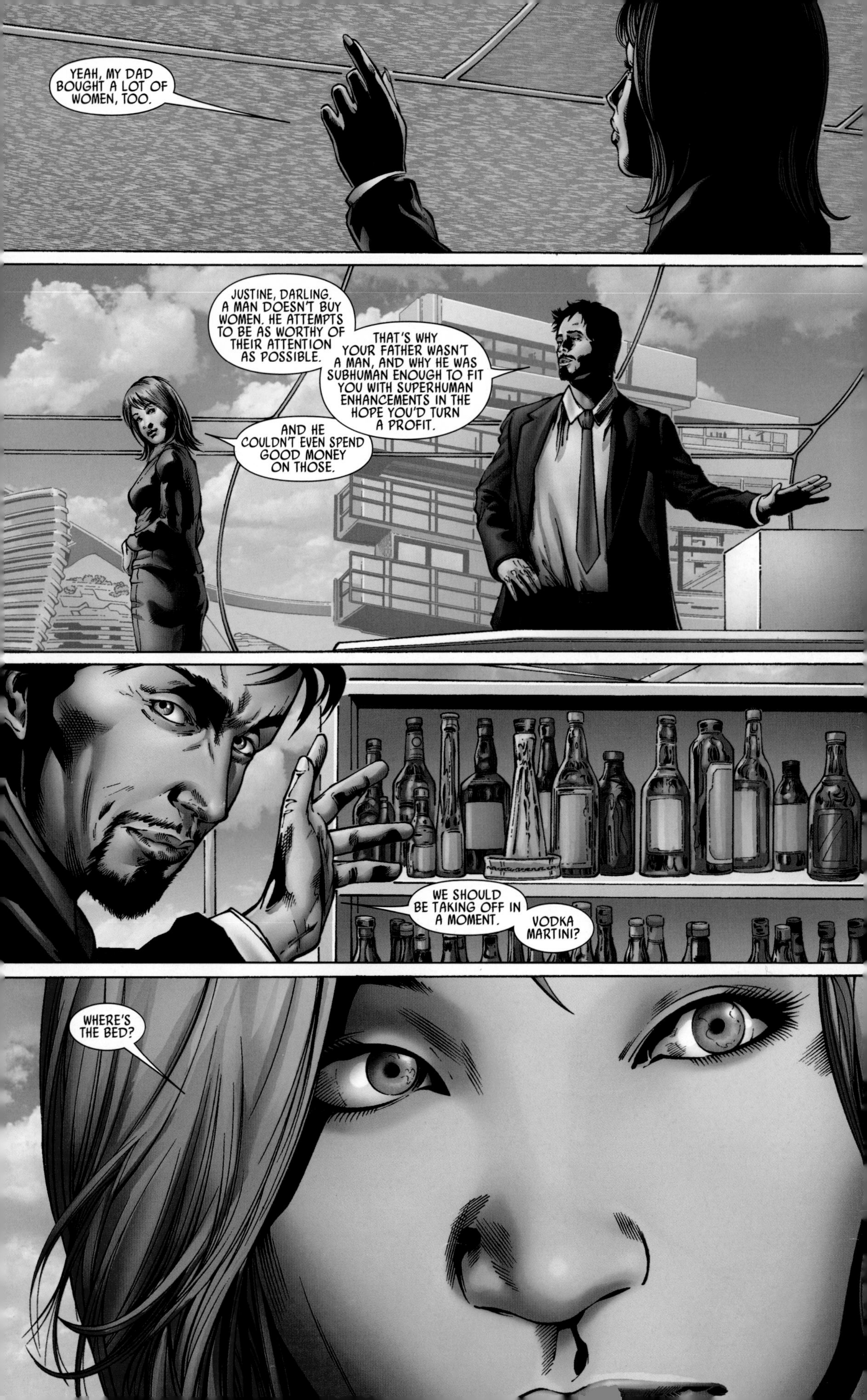
YEAH, MY DAD BOUGHT A LOT OF WOMEN, TOO.
JUSTINE, DARLING. A MAN DOESN'T BUY WOMEN. HE ATTEMPTS TO BE AS WORTHY OF THEIR ATTENTION AS POSSIBLE.
THAT'S WHY YOUR FATHER WASN'T A MAN, AND WHY HE WAS SUBHUMAN ENOUGH TO FIT YOU WITH SUPERHUMAN ENHANCEMENTS IN THE HOPE YOU'D TURN A PROFIT.
AND HE COULDN'T EVEN SPEND GOOD MONEY ON THOSE.
WE SHOULD BE TAKING OFF IN A MOMENT.
VODKA MARTINI?
WHERE'S THE BED?

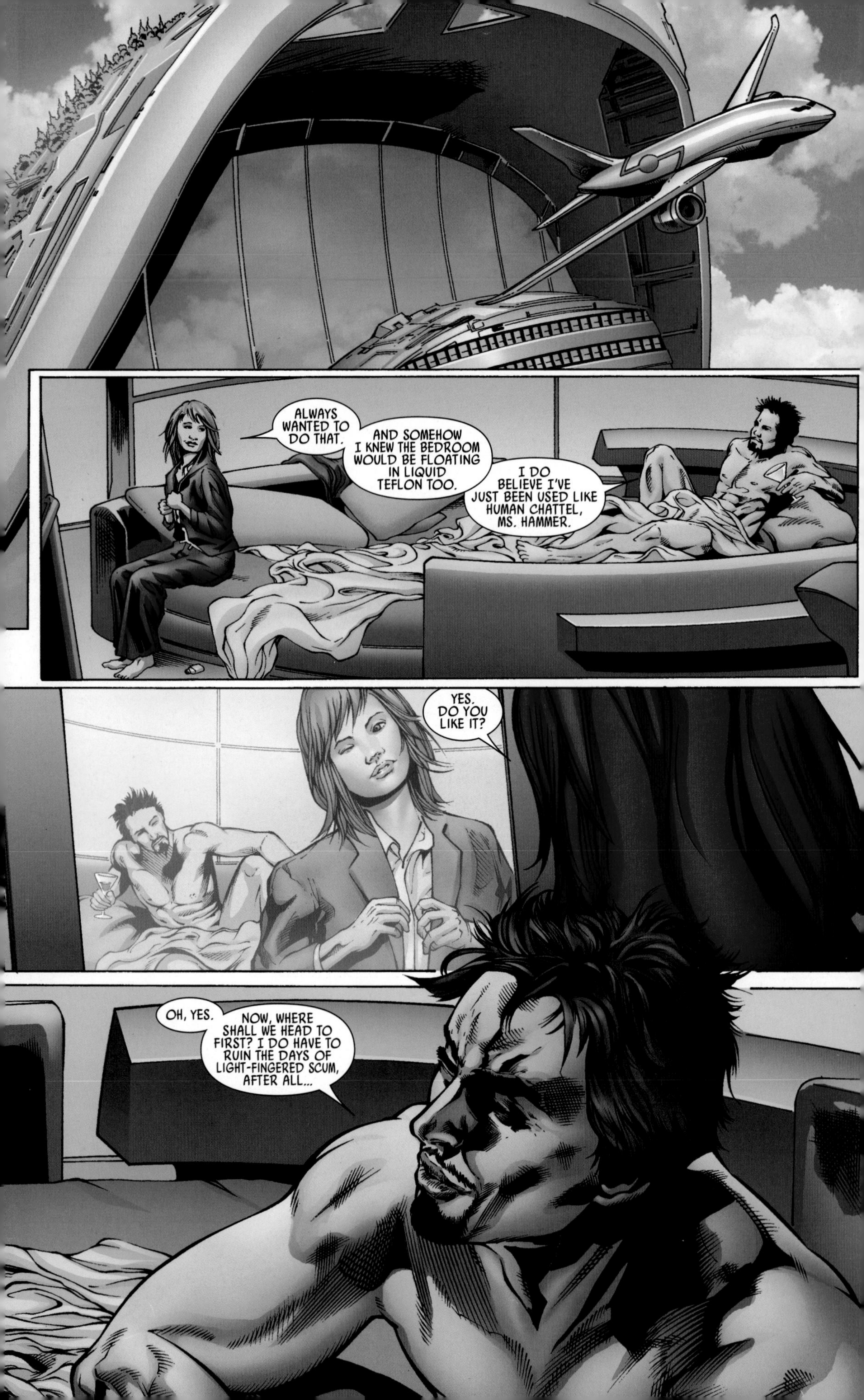
ALWAYS WANTED TO DO THAT.
AND SOMEHOW I KNEW THE BEDROOM WOULD BE FLOATING IN LIQUID TEFLON TOO.
I DO BELIEVE I'VE JUST BEEN USED LIKE HUMAN CHATTEL, MS. HAMMER.
YES. DO YOU LIKE IT?
OH, YES.
NOW, WHERE SHALL WE HEAD TO FIRST? I DO HAVE TO RUIN THE DAYS OF LIGHT-FINGERED SCUM, AFTER ALL...

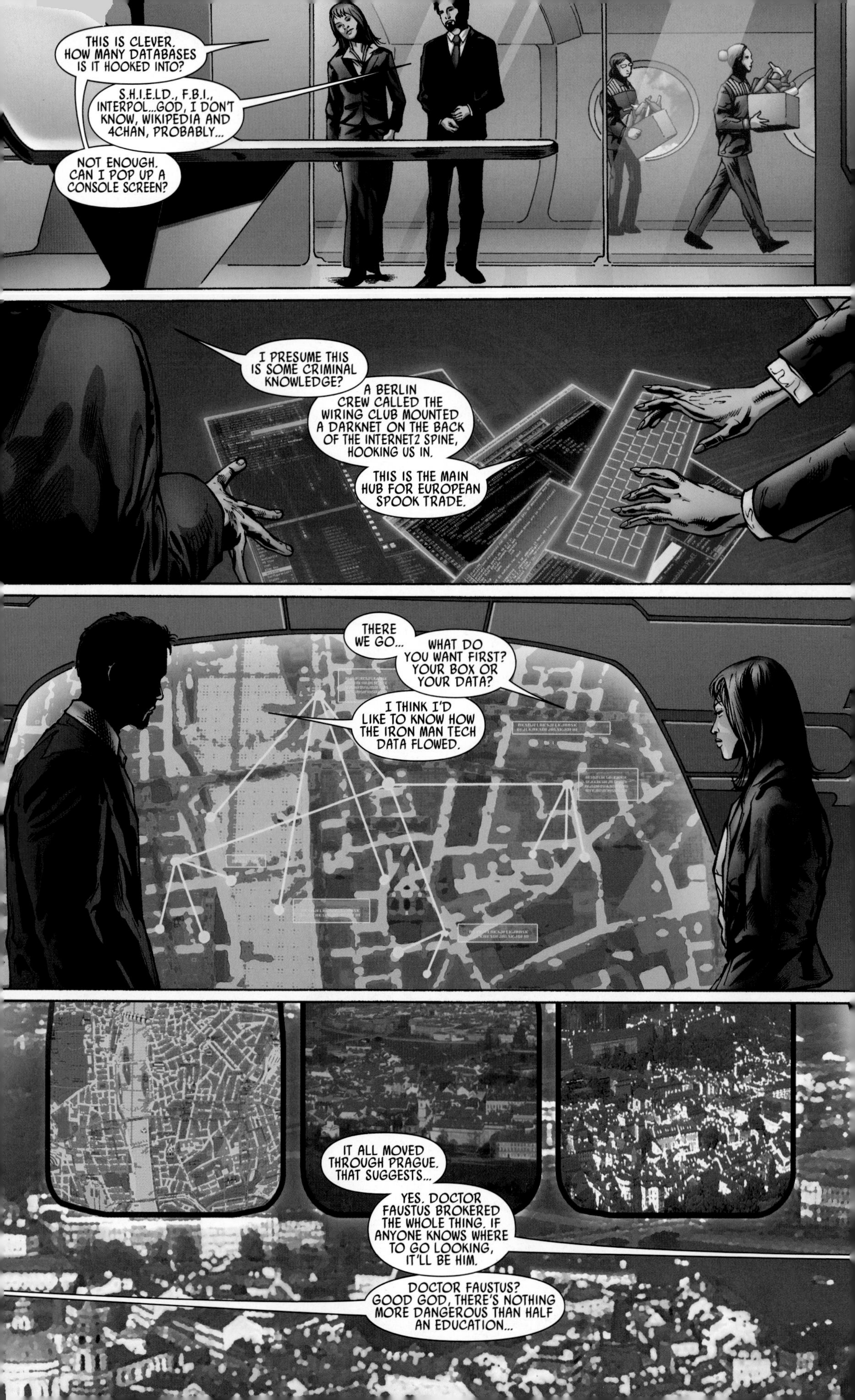
THIS IS CLEVER. HOW MANY DATABASES IS IT HOOKED INTO?
S.H.I.E.L.D., F.B.I., INTERPOL...GOD, I DON'T KNOW, WIKIPEDIA AND 4CHAN, PROBABLY...
NOT ENOUGH. CAN I POP UP A CONSOLE SCREEN?
I PRESUME THIS IS SOME CRIMINAL KNOWLEDGE?
A BERLIN CREW CALLED THE WIRING CLUB MOUNTED A DARKNET ON THE BACK OF THE INTERNET2 SPINE, HOOKING US IN.
THIS IS THE MAIN HUB FOR EUROPEAN SPOOK TRADE.
THERE WE GO...
WHAT DO YOU WANT FIRST? YOUR BOX OR YOUR DATA?
I THINK I'D LIKE TO KNOW HOW THE IRON MAN TECH DATA FLOWED.
IT ALL MOVED THROUGH PRAGUE. THAT SUGGESTS...
YES. DOCTOR FAUSTUS BROKERED THE WHOLE THING. IF ANYONE KNOWS WHERE TO GO LOOKING, IT'LL BE HIM.
DOCTOR FAUSTUS? GOOD GOD, THERE'S NOTHING MORE DANGEROUS THAN HALF AN EDUCATION...

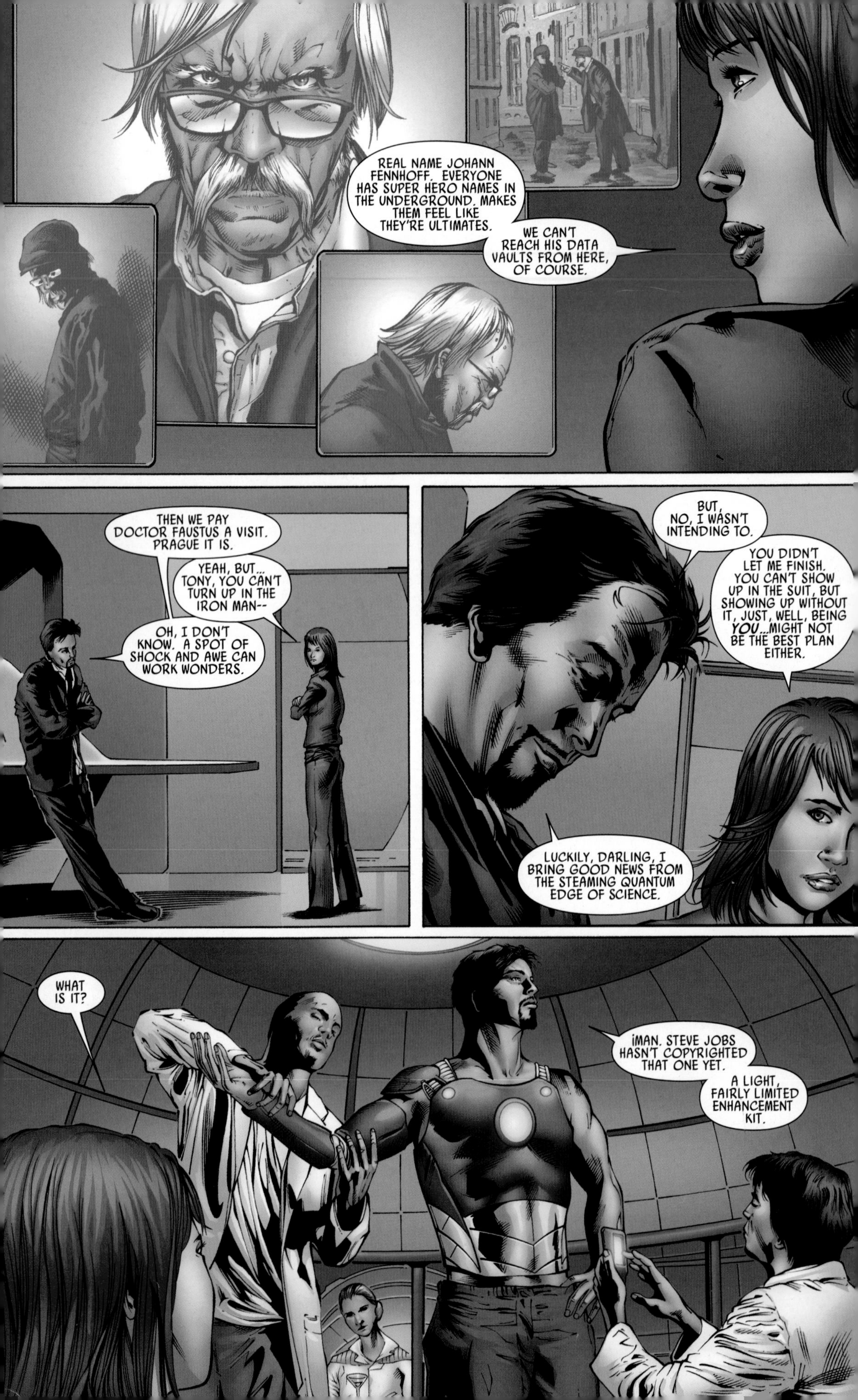
REAL NAME JOHANN FENNHOFF. EVERYONE HAS SUPER HERO NAMES IN THE UNDERGROUND. MAKES THEM FEEL LIKE THEY'RE ULTIMATES.
WE CAN'T REACH HIS DATA VAULTS FROM HERE, OF COURSE.
THEN WE PAY DOCTOR FAUSTUS A VISIT. PRAGUE IT IS.
YEAH, BUT... TONY, YOU CAN'T TURN UP IN THE IRON MAN--
OH, I DON'T KNOW. A SPOT OF SHOCK AND AWE CAN WORK WONDERS.
BUT, NO, I WASN'T INTENDING TO.
YOU DIDN'T LET ME FINISH. YOU CAN'T SHOW UP IN THE SUIT, BUT SHOWING UP WITHOUT IT, JUST, WELL, BEING *YOU*...MIGHT NOT BE THE BEST PLAN EITHER.
LUCKILY, DARLING, I BRING GOOD NEWS FROM THE STEAMING QUANTUM EDGE OF SCIENCE.
WHAT IS IT?
iMAN. STEVE JOBS HASN'T COPYRIGHTED THAT ONE YET.
A LIGHT, FAIRLY LIMITED ENHANCEMENT KIT.

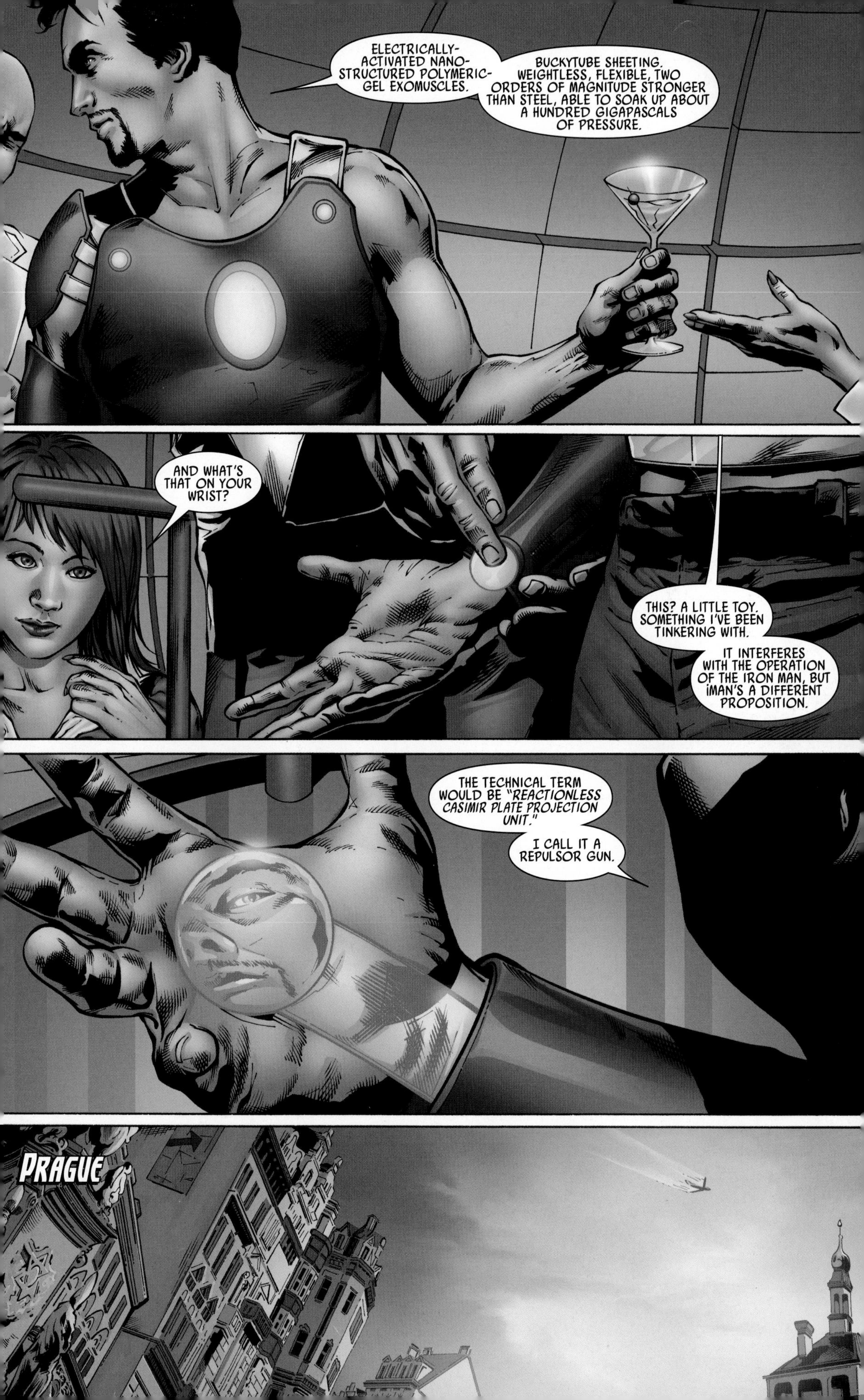
ELECTRICALLY-ACTIVATED NANO-STRUCTURED POLYMERIC-GEL EXOMUSCLES.
BUCKYTUBE SHEETING. WEIGHTLESS, FLEXIBLE, TWO ORDERS OF MAGNITUDE STRONGER THAN STEEL, ABLE TO SOAK UP ABOUT A HUNDRED GIGAPASCALS OF PRESSURE.
AND WHAT'S THAT ON YOUR WRIST?
THIS? A LITTLE TOY. SOMETHING I'VE BEEN TINKERING WITH.
IT INTERFERES WITH THE OPERATION OF THE IRON MAN, BUT iMAN'S A DIFFERENT PROPOSITION.
THE TECHNICAL TERM WOULD BE "REACTIONLESS CASIMIR PLATE PROJECTION UNIT."
I CALL IT A REPULSOR GUN.
PRAGUE

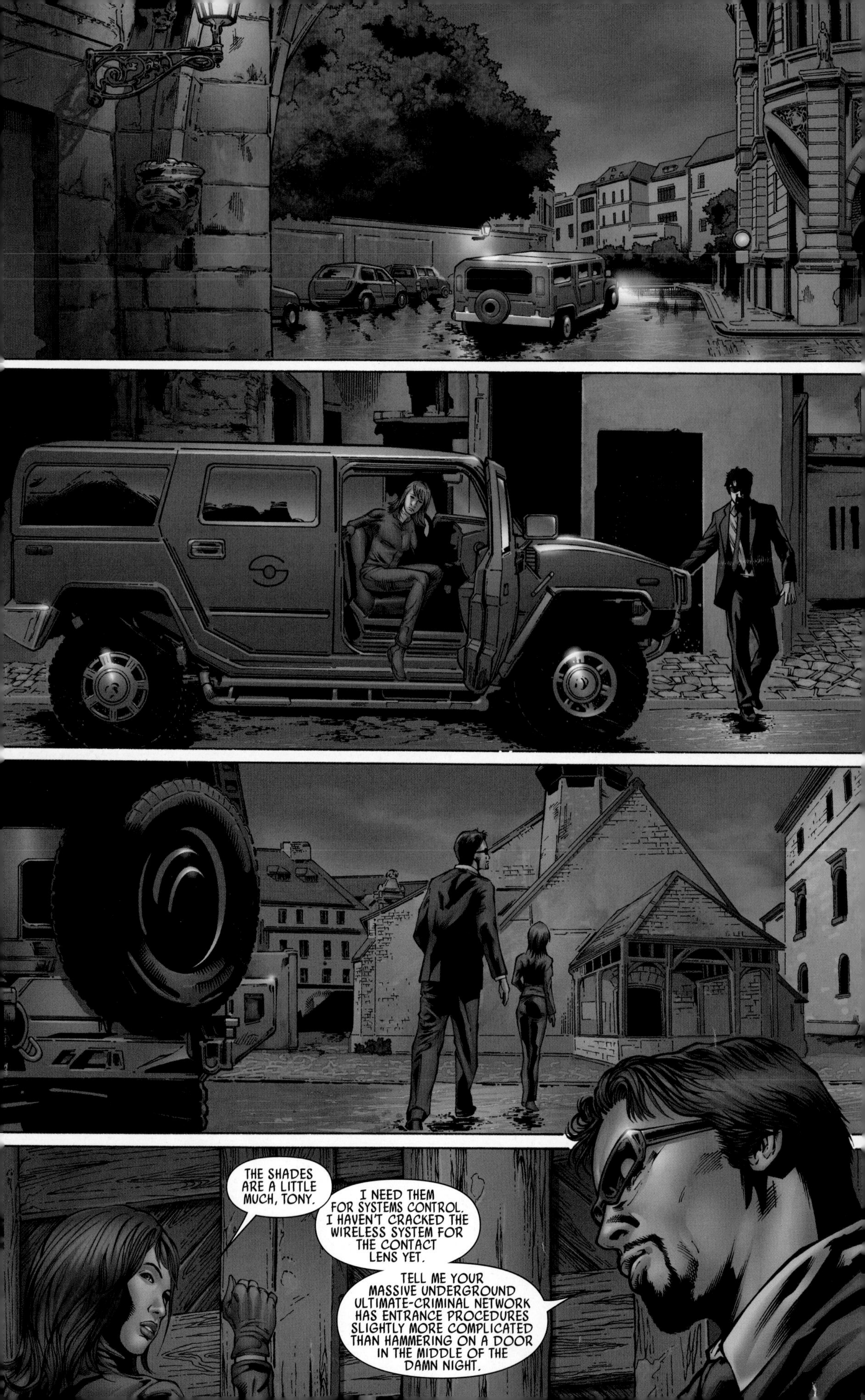
THE SHADES ARE A LITTLE MUCH, TONY.
I NEED THEM FOR SYSTEMS CONTROL. I HAVEN'T CRACKED THE WIRELESS SYSTEM FOR THE CONTACT LENS YET.
TELL ME YOUR MASSIVE UNDERGROUND ULTIMATE-CRIMINAL NETWORK HAS ENTRANCE PROCEDURES SLIGHTLY MORE COMPLICATED THAN HAMMERING ON A DOOR IN THE MIDDLE OF THE DAMN NIGHT.

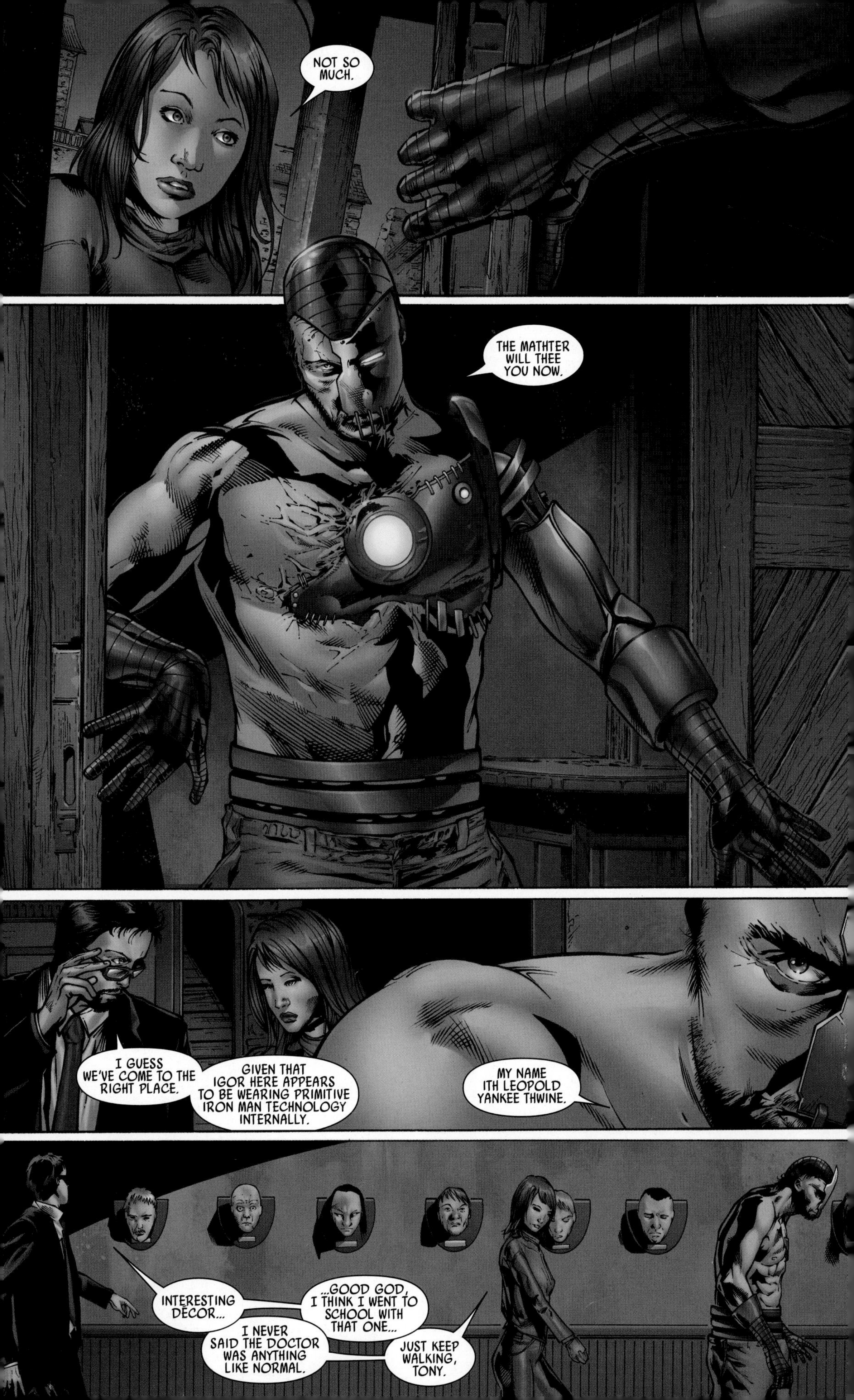
NOT SO MUCH.
THE MATHTER WILL THEE YOU NOW.
I GUESS WE'VE COME TO THE RIGHT PLACE.
GIVEN THAT IGOR HERE APPEARS TO BE WEARING PRIMITIVE IRON MAN TECHNOLOGY INTERNALLY.
MY NAME ITH LEOPOLD YANKEE THWINE.
INTERESTING DÉCOR...
...GOOD GOD, I THINK I WENT TO SCHOOL WITH THAT ONE...
I NEVER SAID THE DOCTOR WAS ANYTHING LIKE NORMAL.
JUST KEEP WALKING, TONY.

THESE ARE WORSE THAN THOSE PAINTING WITH EYES THAT FOLLOW YOU AROUND THE ROOM...

WHY ISN'T THERE ANY SECURITY HAPPENING? NO SCANS, NO SWEEPS, NOT EVEN A FRIENDLY PAT-DOWN...

BECAUSE, MY DEAR MR. STARK, WE ARE ALL SO VASTLY MORE THAN HUMAN THAT I EXPECT NOTHING SHORT OF GODS AND GODDESSES TO ENTER THIS ROOM.

PEOPLE WHO CANNOT BE DEFENDED FROM OR SECURED MUST SIMPLY BE ENJOYED, DON'T YOU THINK?

WELCOME TO MY HOME. MS. HAMMER, A PLEASURE TO SEE YOU AGAIN.

I LIKE YOUR ATTITUDE. YOU WOULD BE DOCTOR FAUSTUS?

AND YOU, OF COURSE, ARE TONY STARK, THE FAMOUS IRON MAN. DO YOU KNOW WHAT I LIKE BEST ABOUT YOU, MR. STARK?

OH, GO ON, FLATTER ME.

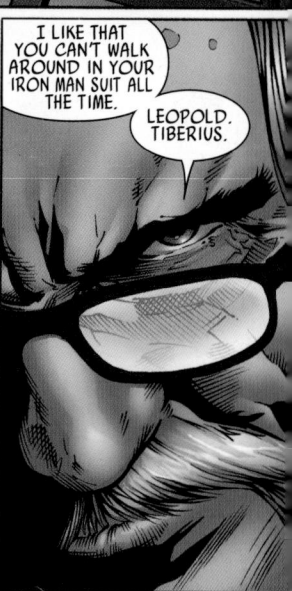

I LIKE THAT YOU CAN'T WALK AROUND IN YOUR IRON MAN SUIT ALL THE TIME.

LEOPOLD. TIBERIUS.

WELL...IN HINDSIGHT, THAT WAS KIND OF OBVIOUS.

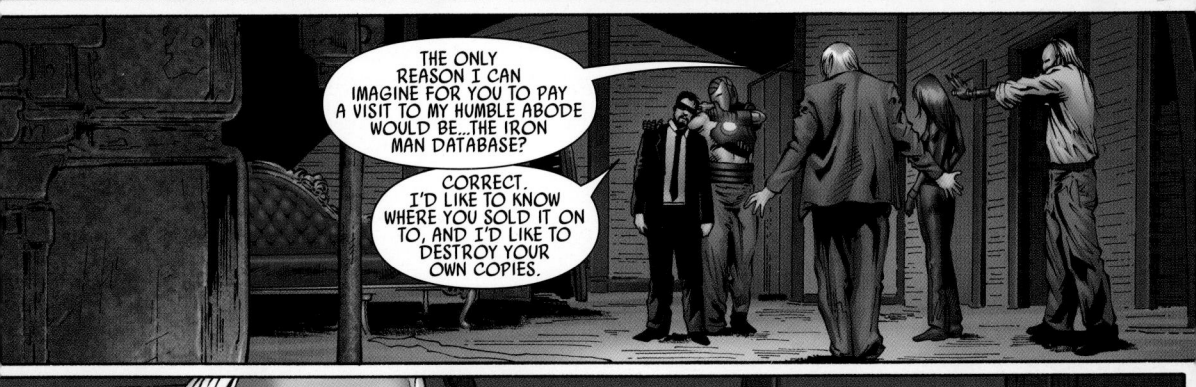

THE ONLY REASON I CAN IMAGINE FOR YOU TO PAY A VISIT TO MY HUMBLE ABODE WOULD BE...THE IRON MAN DATABASE?

CORRECT. I'D LIKE TO KNOW WHERE YOU SOLD IT ON TO, AND I'D LIKE TO DESTROY YOUR OWN COPIES.

I'M SURE YOU WOULD. HOWEVER, I THINK IT MORE PRUDENT THAT YOUR BODY BE DISCOVERED STRIPPED IN A DITCH.

SAD END TO THE DRUNKEN SUPER HERO PLAYBOY, BUT NOT AN UNEXPECTED ONE.

YOUR DEATH IN MY CITY WOULD DO WONDERS FOR MY STANDING IN THE REPUTATION ECONOMY. I SHOULD THANK YOU.

AH, WELL.

I'M AFRAID I DON'T HAVE ALL NIGHT, SO...

VOICECODE: JAZZLER.

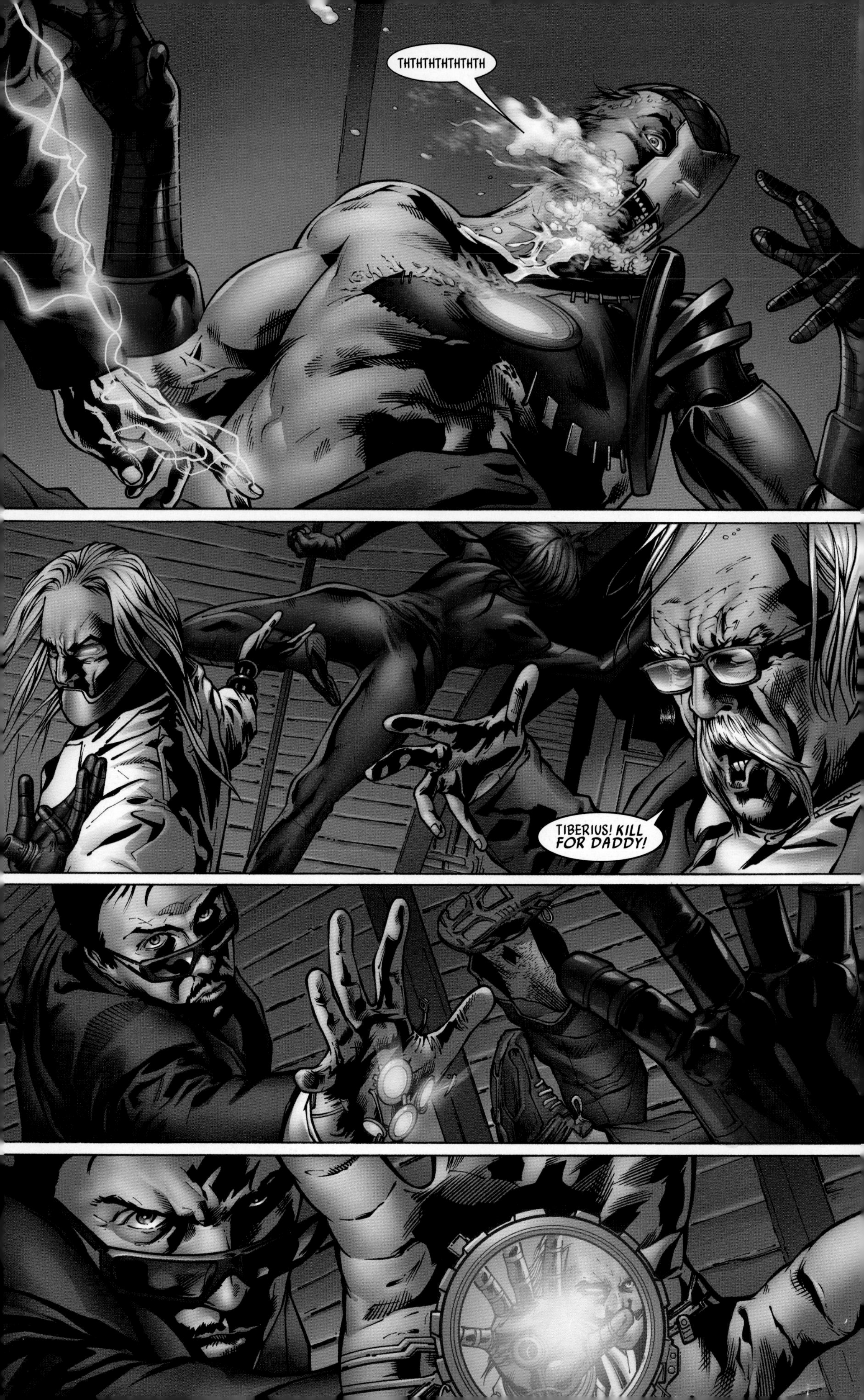
THTHTHTHTHTHTH
TIBERIUS! KILL FOR DADDY!

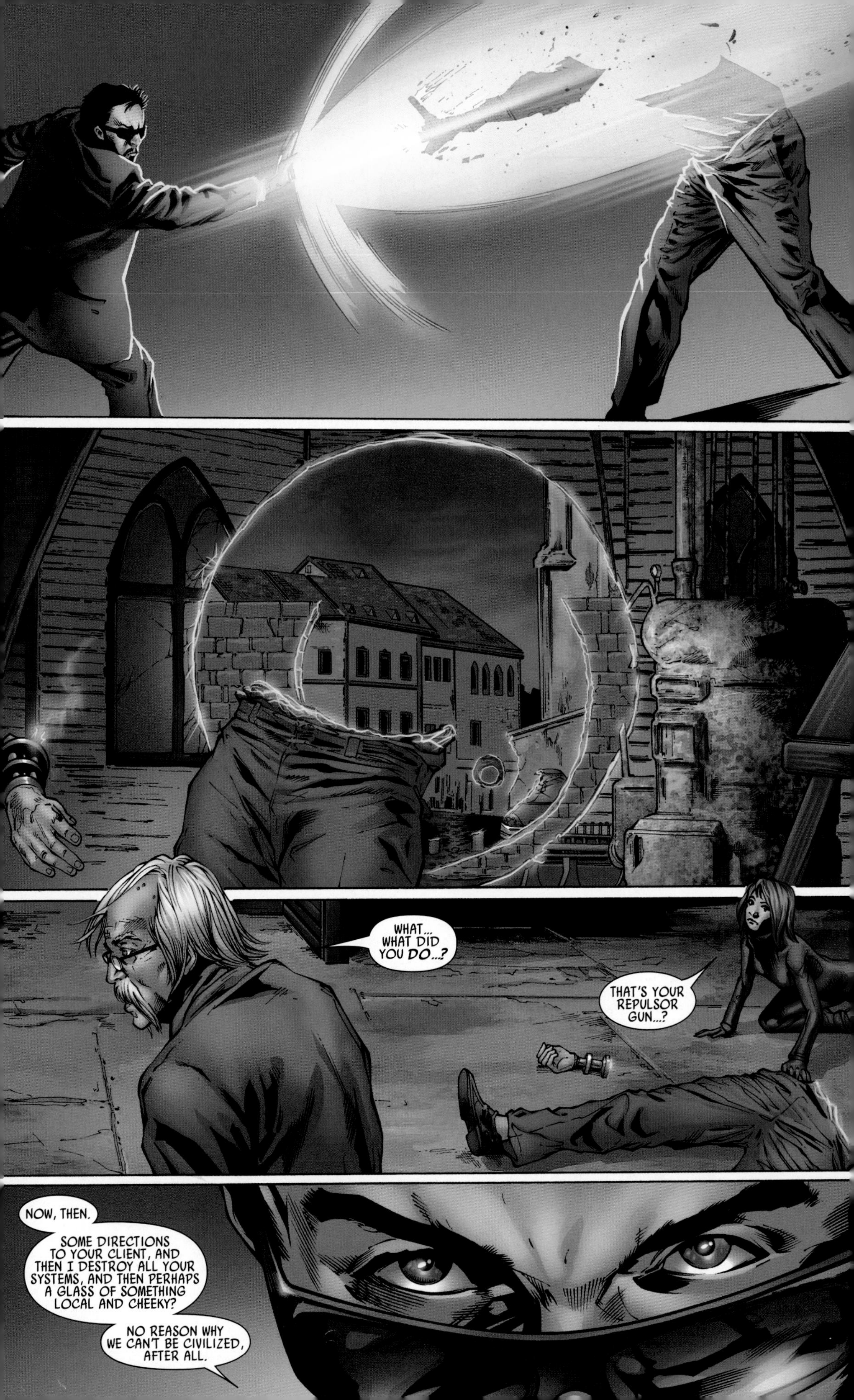
WHAT... WHAT DID YOU DO...?
THAT'S YOUR REPULSOR GUN...?
NOW, THEN.
SOME DIRECTIONS TO YOUR CLIENT, AND THEN I DESTROY ALL YOUR SYSTEMS, AND THEN PERHAPS A GLASS OF SOMETHING LOCAL AND CHEEKY?
NO REASON WHY WE CAN'T BE CIVILIZED, AFTER ALL.

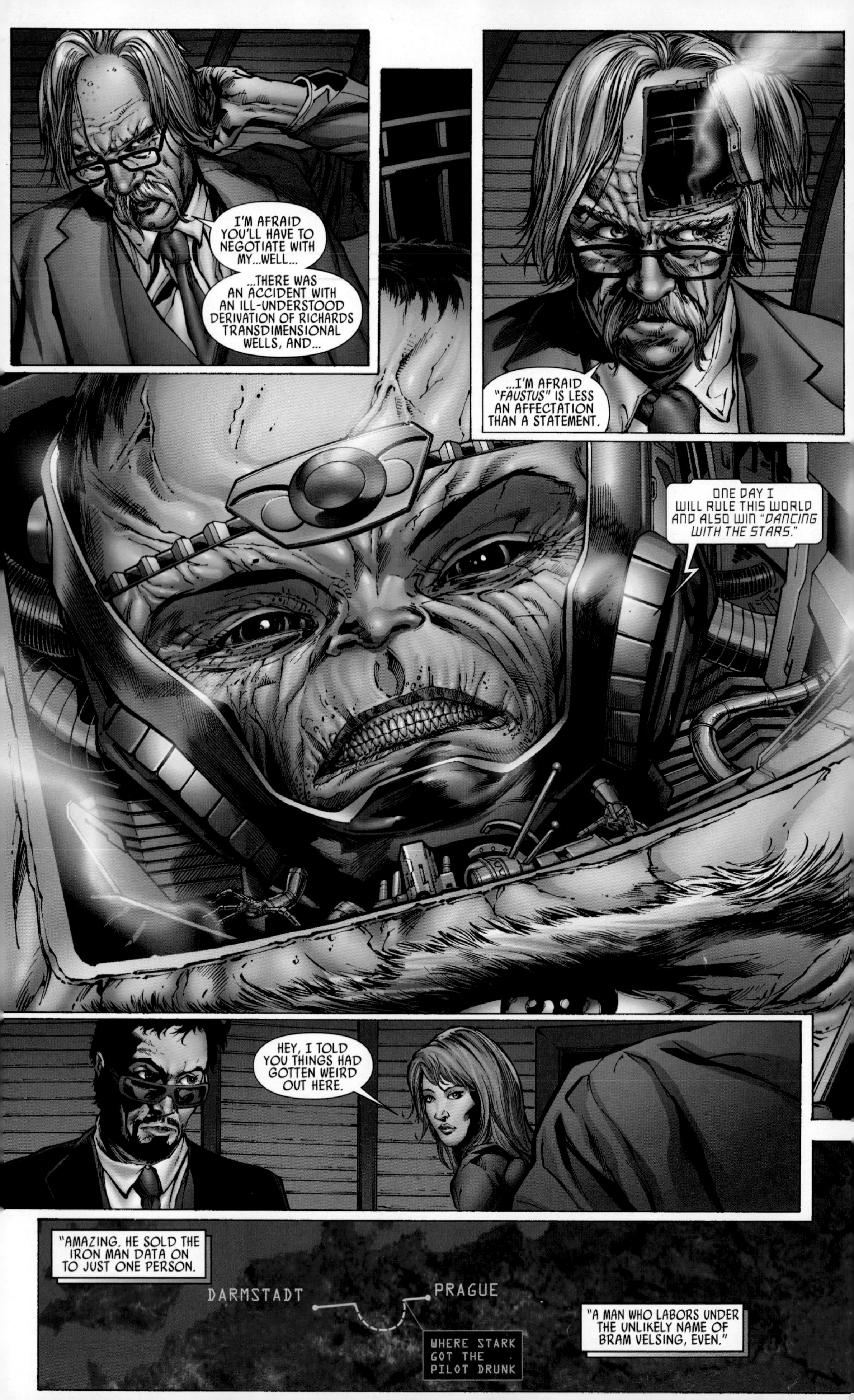
I'M AFRAID YOU'LL HAVE TO NEGOTIATE WITH MY...WELL...
...THERE WAS AN ACCIDENT WITH AN ILL-UNDERSTOOD DERIVATION OF RICHARDS TRANSDIMENSIONAL WELLS, AND...
...I'M AFRAID "FAUSTUS" IS LESS AN AFFECTATION THAN A STATEMENT.
ONE DAY I WILL RULE THIS WORLD AND ALSO WIN "DANCING WITH THE STARS."
HEY, I TOLD YOU THINGS HAD GOTTEN WEIRD OUT HERE.
"AMAZING. HE SOLD THE IRON MAN DATA ON TO JUST ONE PERSON.
DARMSTADT
PRAGUE
WHERE STARK GOT THE PILOT DRUNK
"A MAN WHO LABORS UNDER THE UNLIKELY NAME OF BRAM VELSING, EVEN."

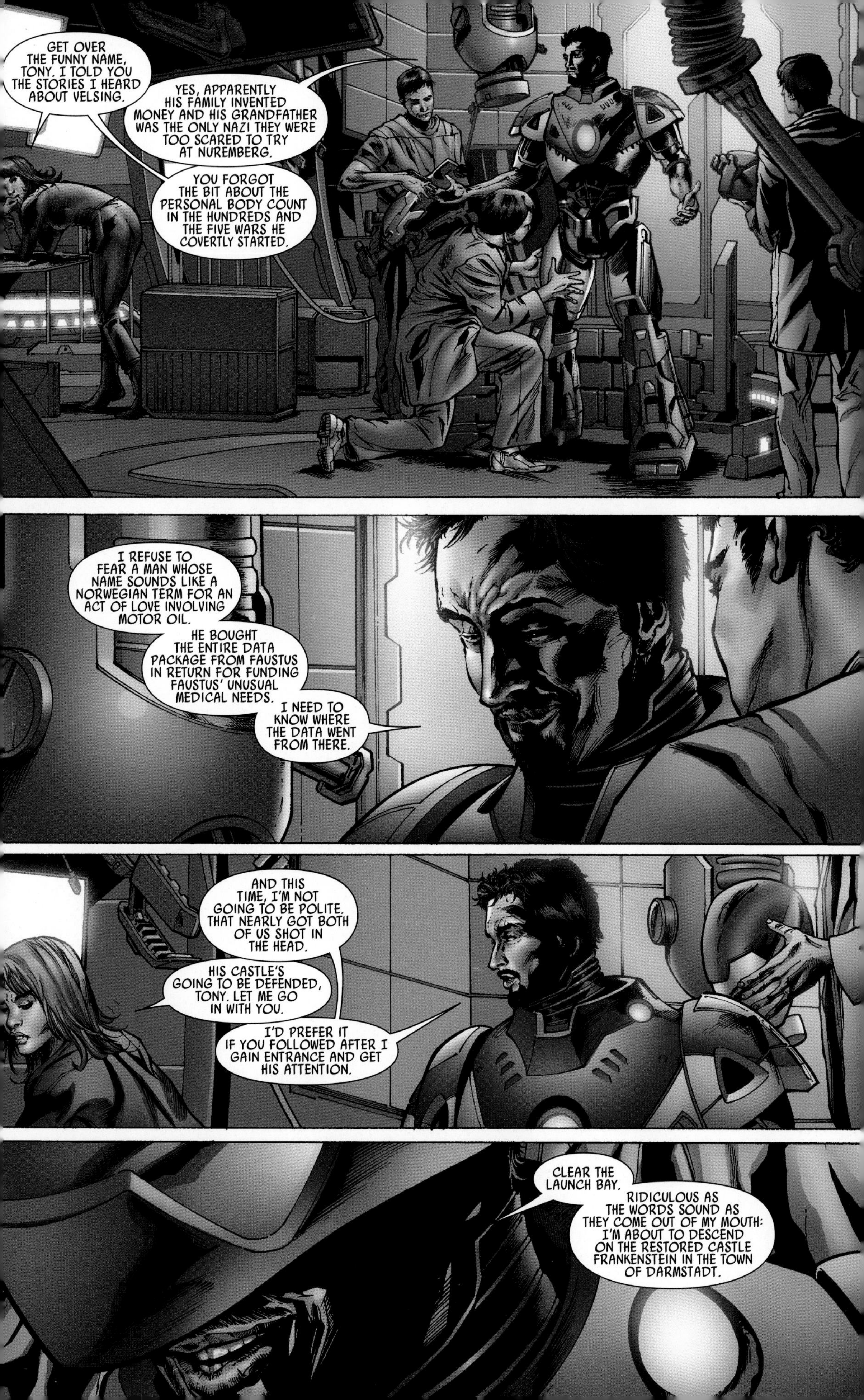
GET OVER THE FUNNY NAME, TONY. I TOLD YOU THE STORIES I HEARD ABOUT VELSING.
YES, APPARENTLY HIS FAMILY INVENTED MONEY AND HIS GRANDFATHER WAS THE ONLY NAZI THEY WERE TOO SCARED TO TRY AT NUREMBERG.
YOU FORGOT THE BIT ABOUT THE PERSONAL BODY COUNT IN THE HUNDREDS AND THE FIVE WARS HE COVERTLY STARTED.
I REFUSE TO FEAR A MAN WHOSE NAME SOUNDS LIKE A NORWEGIAN TERM FOR AN ACT OF LOVE INVOLVING MOTOR OIL.
HE BOUGHT THE ENTIRE DATA PACKAGE FROM FAUSTUS IN RETURN FOR FUNDING FAUSTUS' UNUSUAL MEDICAL NEEDS.
I NEED TO KNOW WHERE THE DATA WENT FROM THERE.
AND THIS TIME, I'M NOT GOING TO BE POLITE. THAT NEARLY GOT BOTH OF US SHOT IN THE HEAD.
HIS CASTLE'S GOING TO BE DEFENDED, TONY. LET ME GO IN WITH YOU.
I'D PREFER IT IF YOU FOLLOWED AFTER I GAIN ENTRANCE AND GET HIS ATTENTION.
CLEAR THE LAUNCH BAY.
RIDICULOUS AS THE WORDS SOUND AS THEY COME OUT OF MY MOUTH: I'M ABOUT TO DESCEND ON THE RESTORED CASTLE FRANKENSTEIN IN THE TOWN OF DARMSTADT.

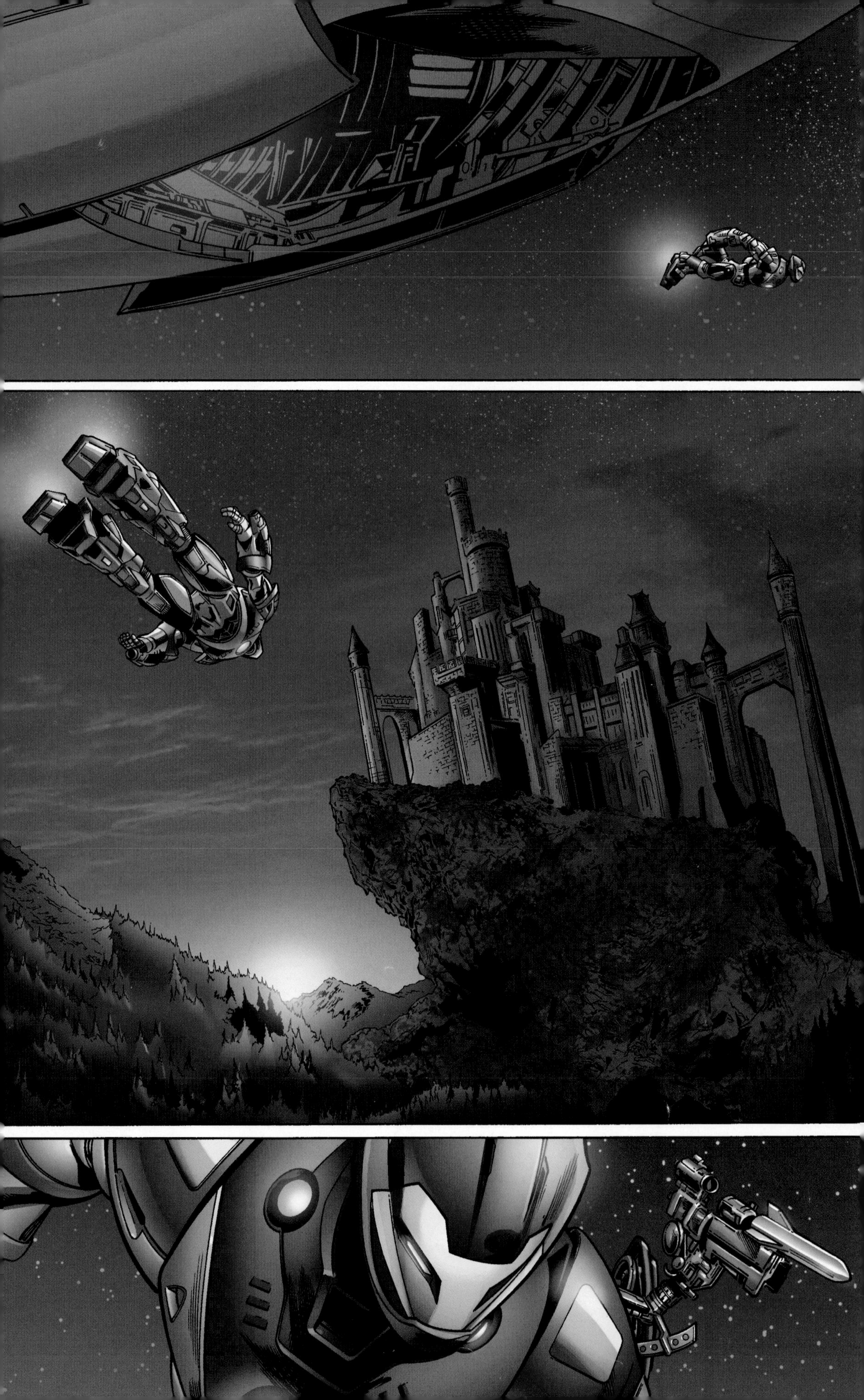

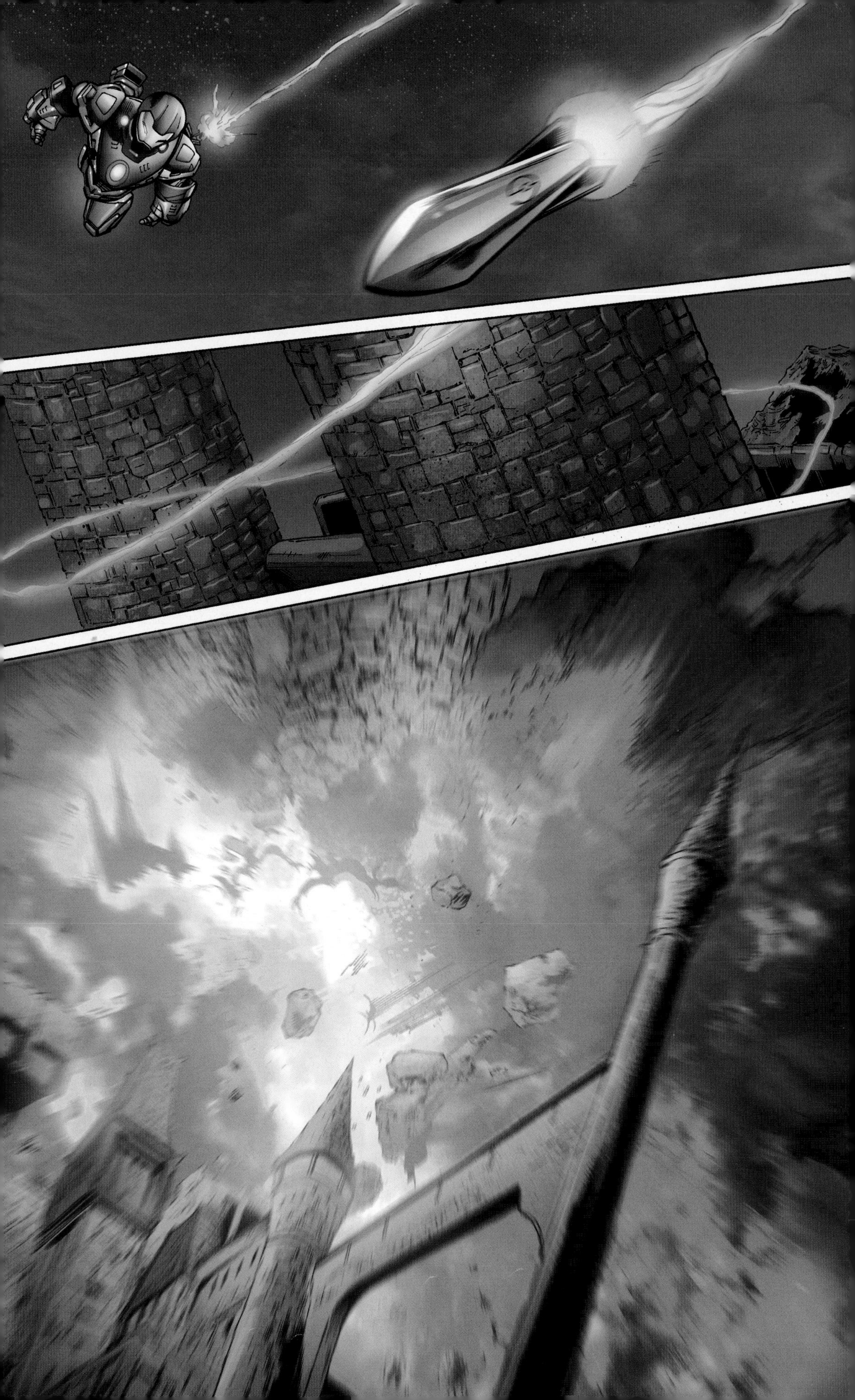

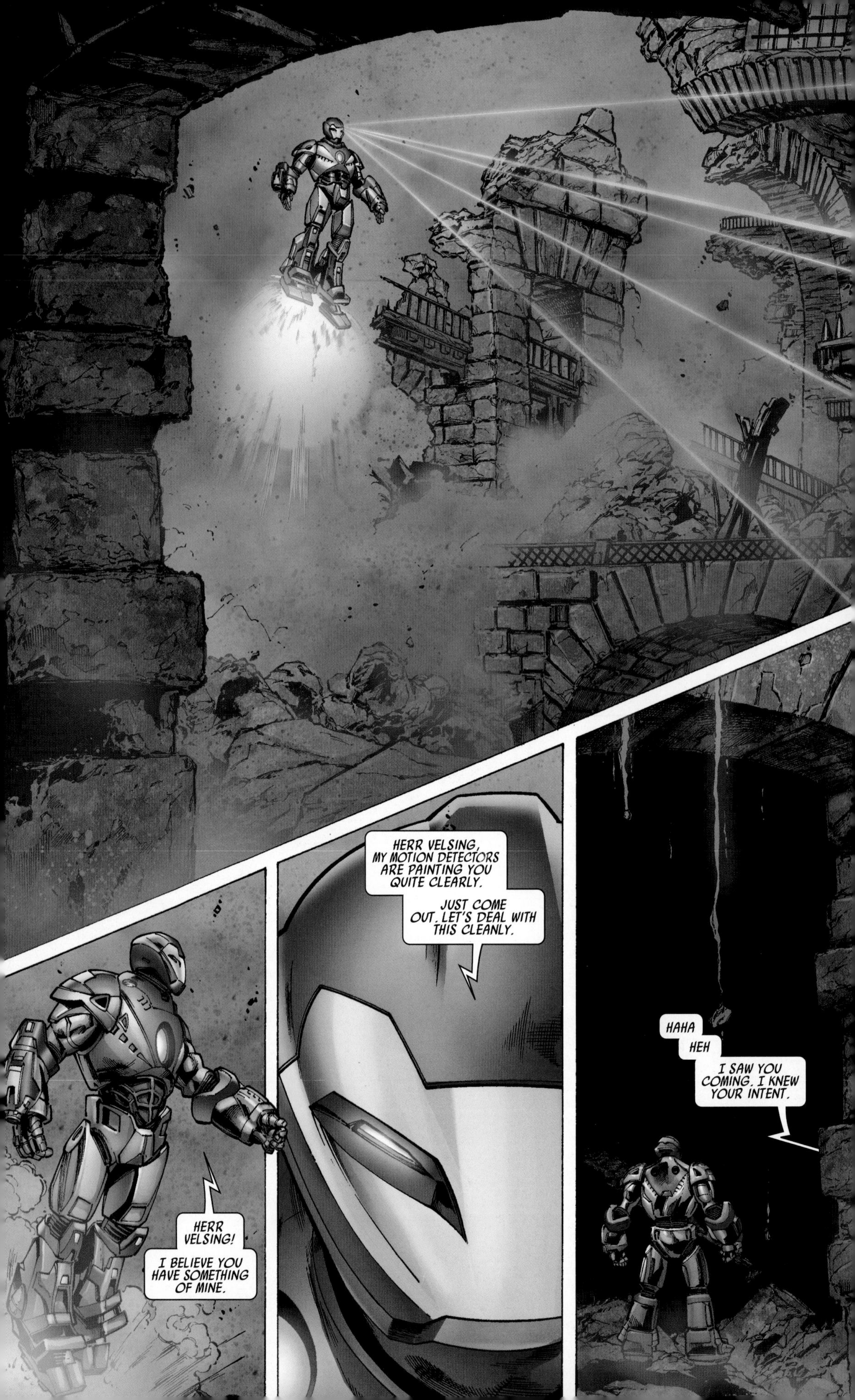
HERR VELSING!
I BELIEVE YOU HAVE SOMETHING OF MINE.
HERR VELSING, MY MOTION DETECTORS ARE PAINTING YOU QUITE CLEARLY.
JUST COME OUT. LET'S DEAL WITH THIS CLEANLY.
HAHA
HEH
I SAW YOU COMING. I KNEW YOUR INTENT.

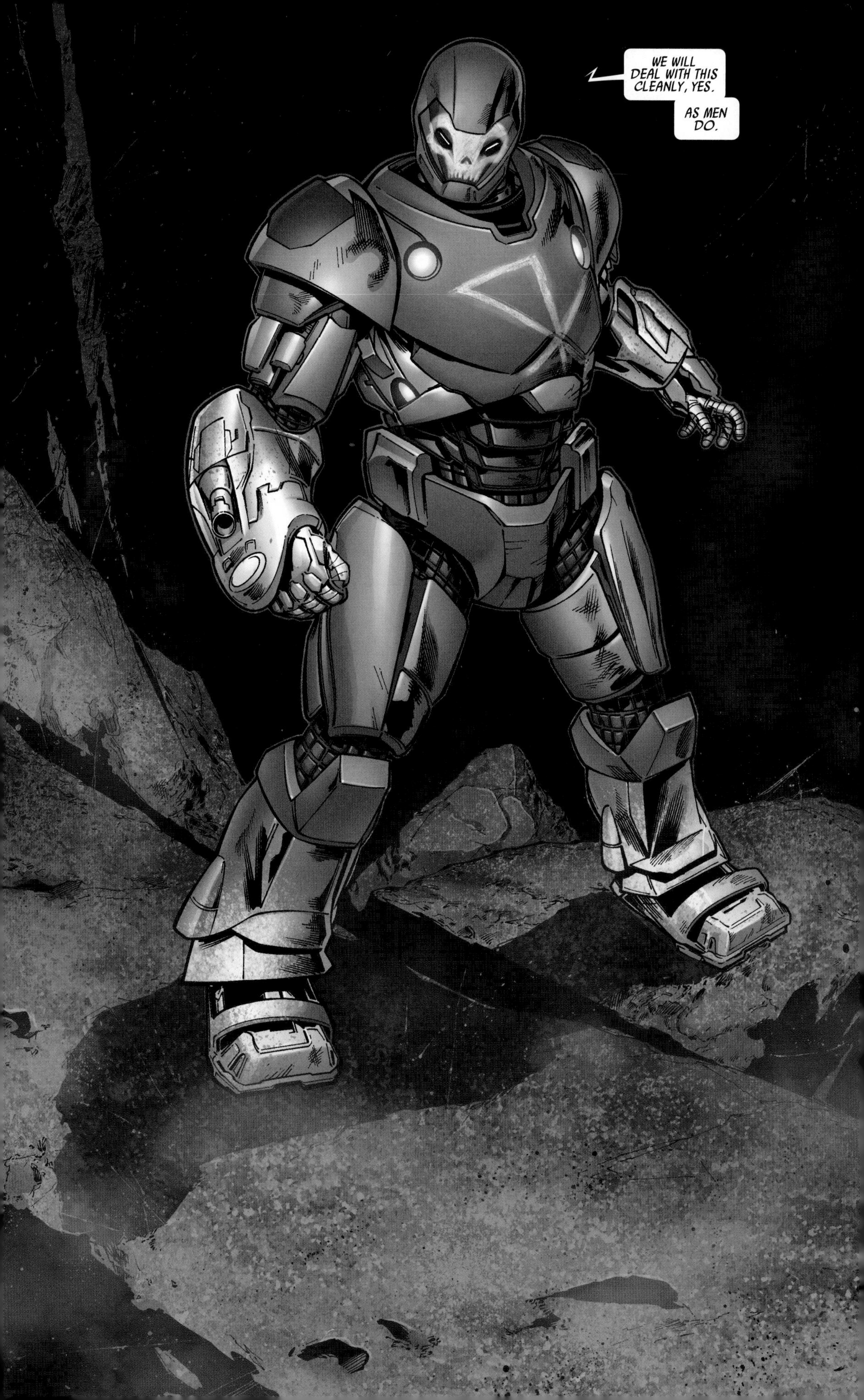
WE WILL DEAL WITH THIS CLEANLY, YES.
AS MEN DO.

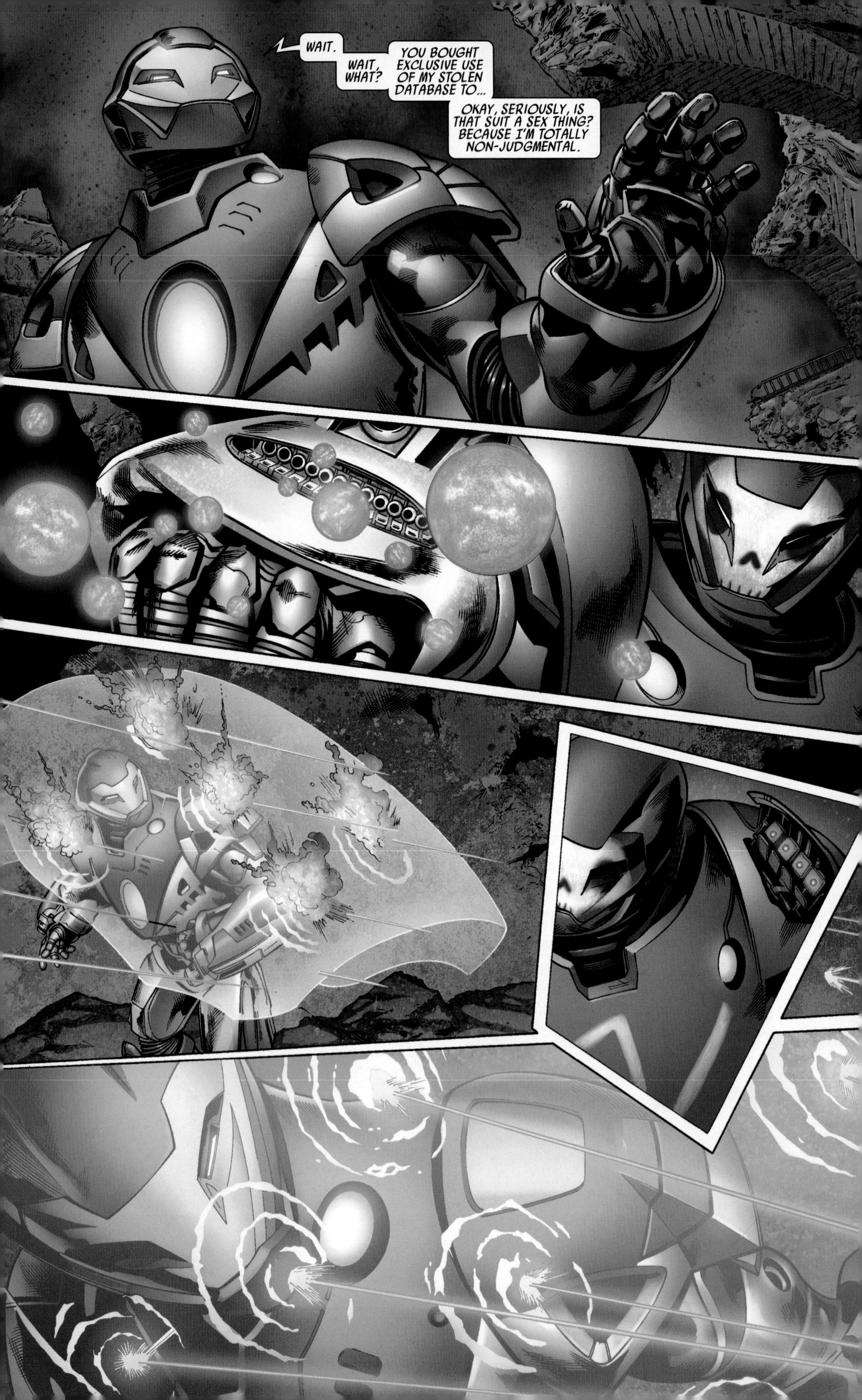
WAIT.
WAIT, WHAT?
YOU BOUGHT EXCLUSIVE USE OF MY STOLEN DATABASE TO...
OKAY, SERIOUSLY, IS THAT SUIT A SEX THING? BECAUSE I'M TOTALLY NON-JUDGMENTAL.

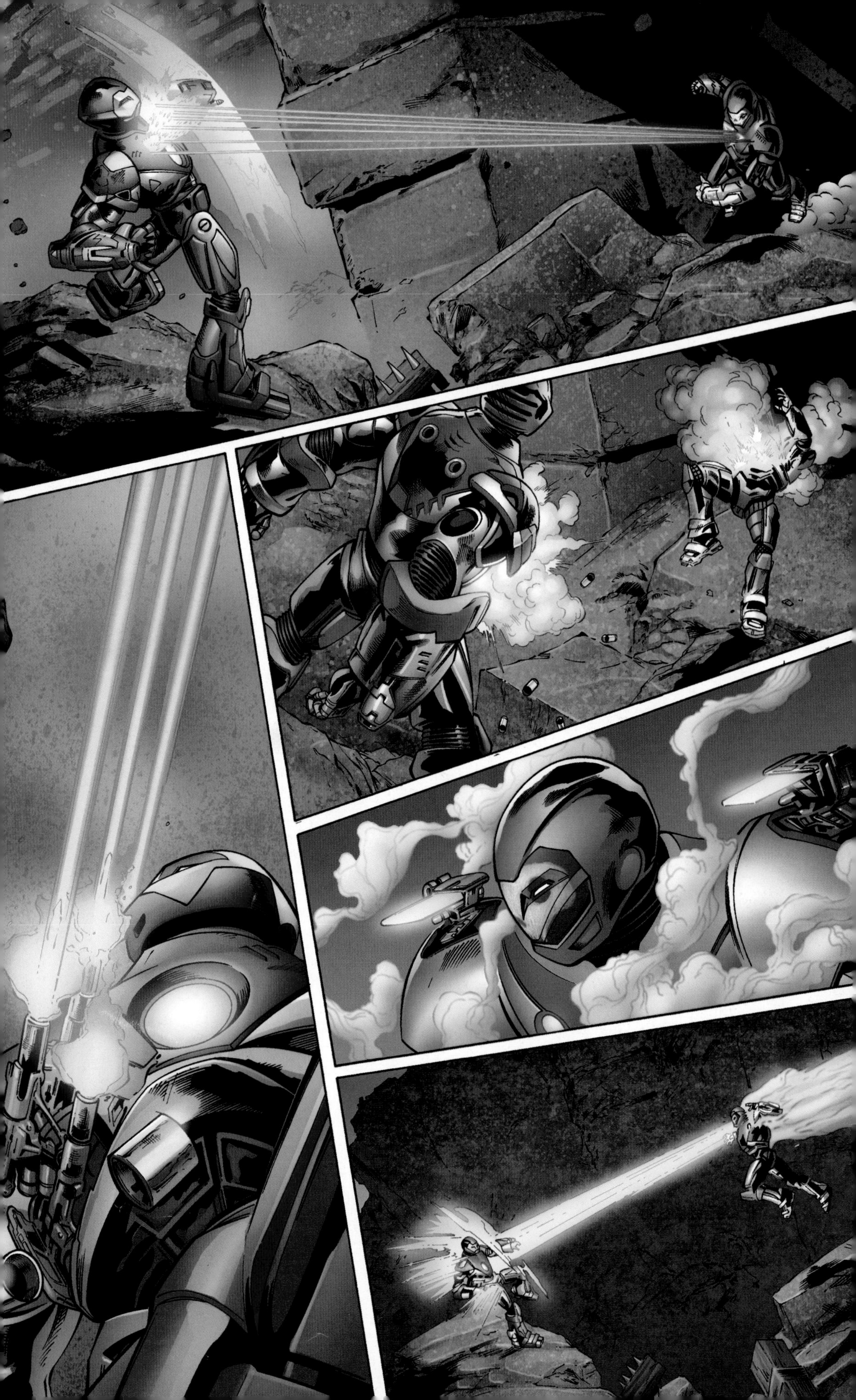

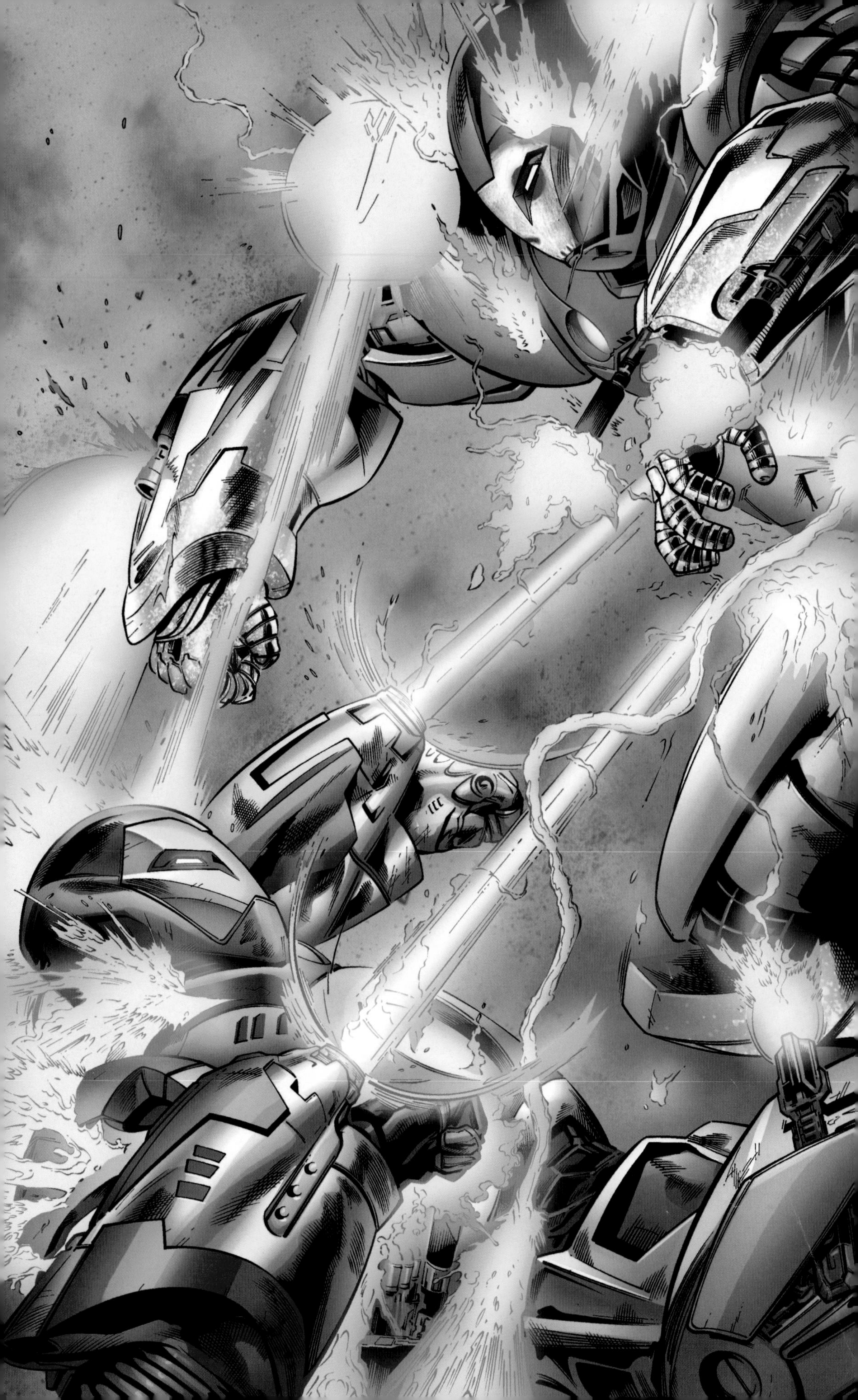

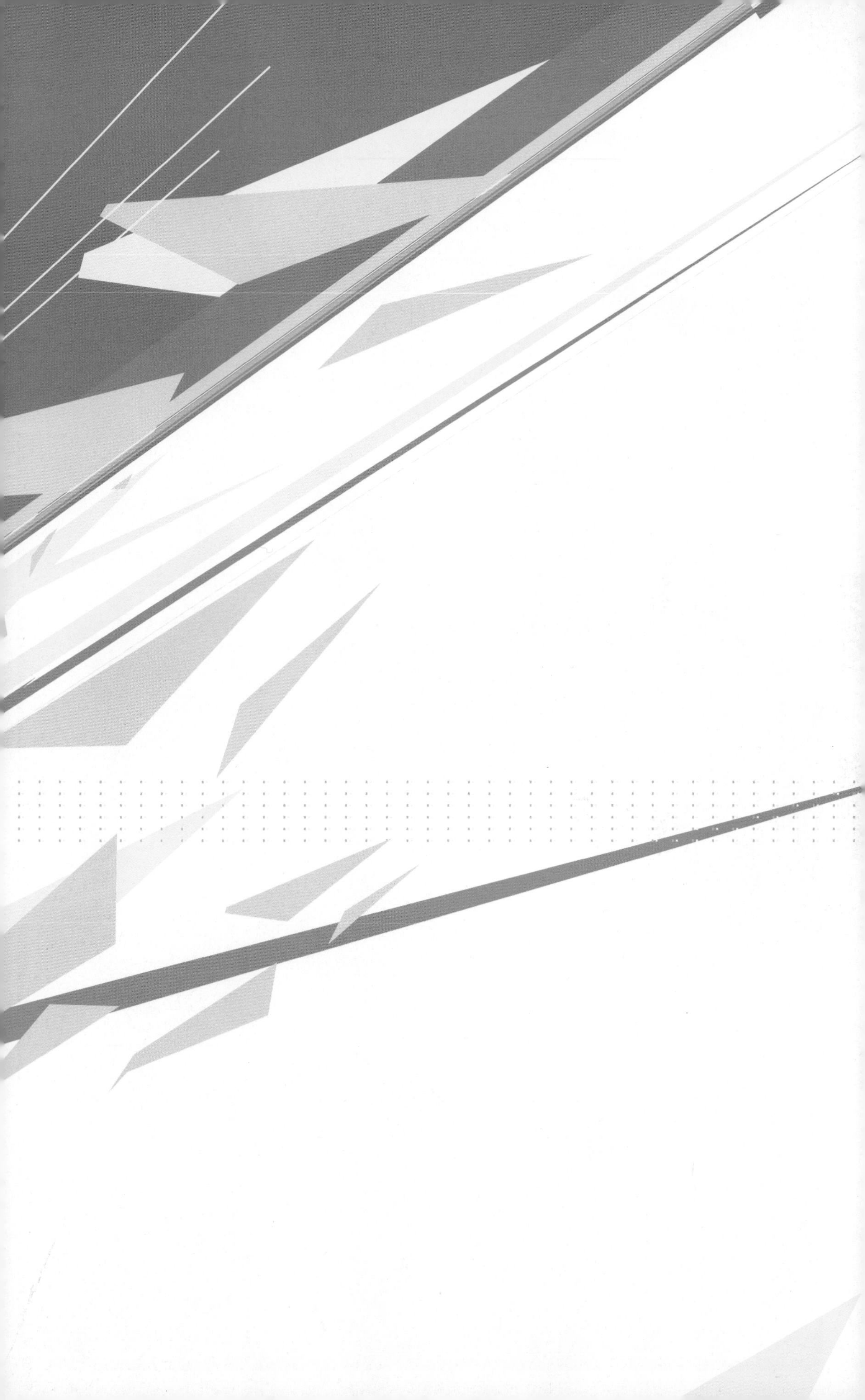

3

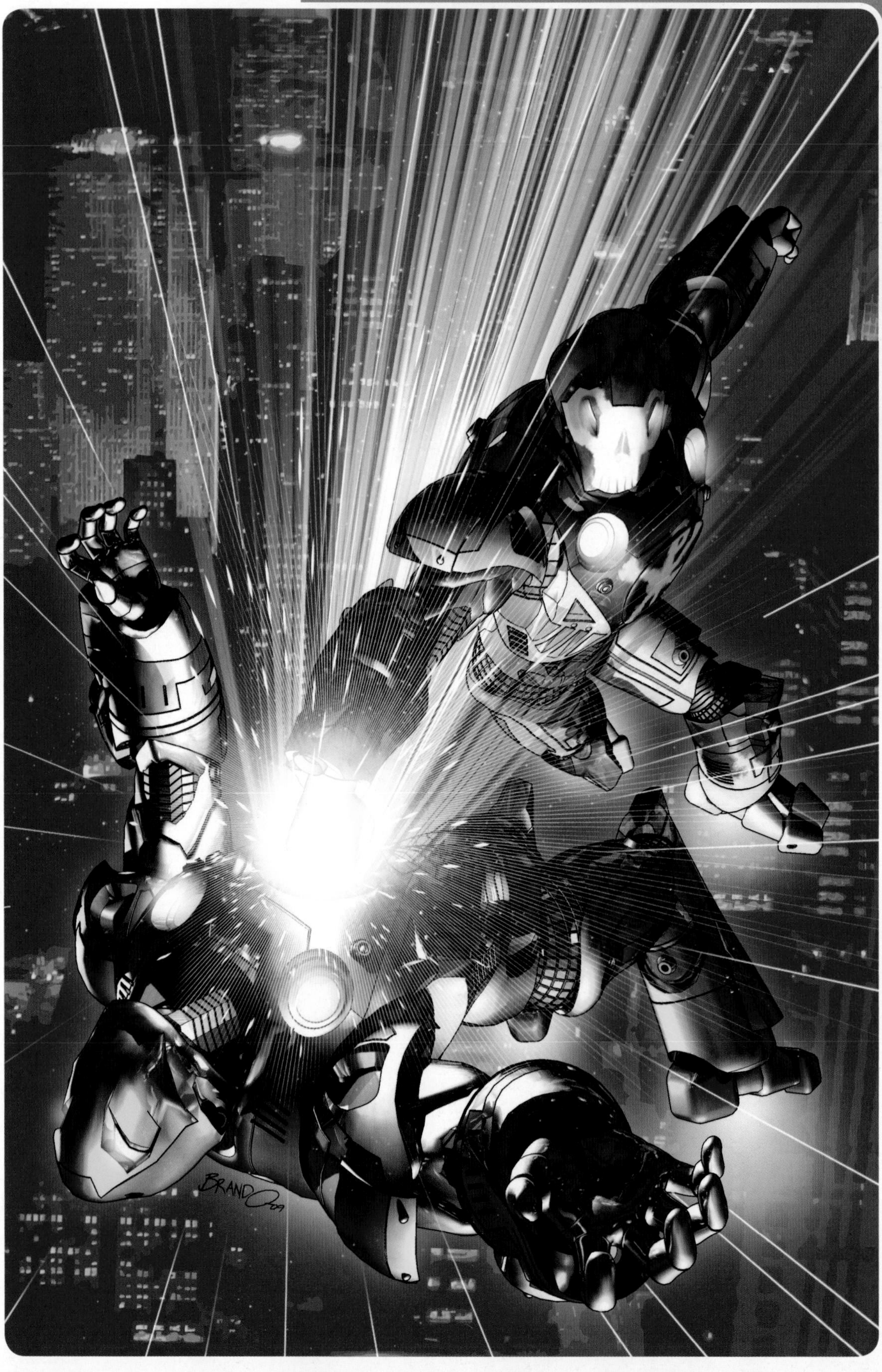

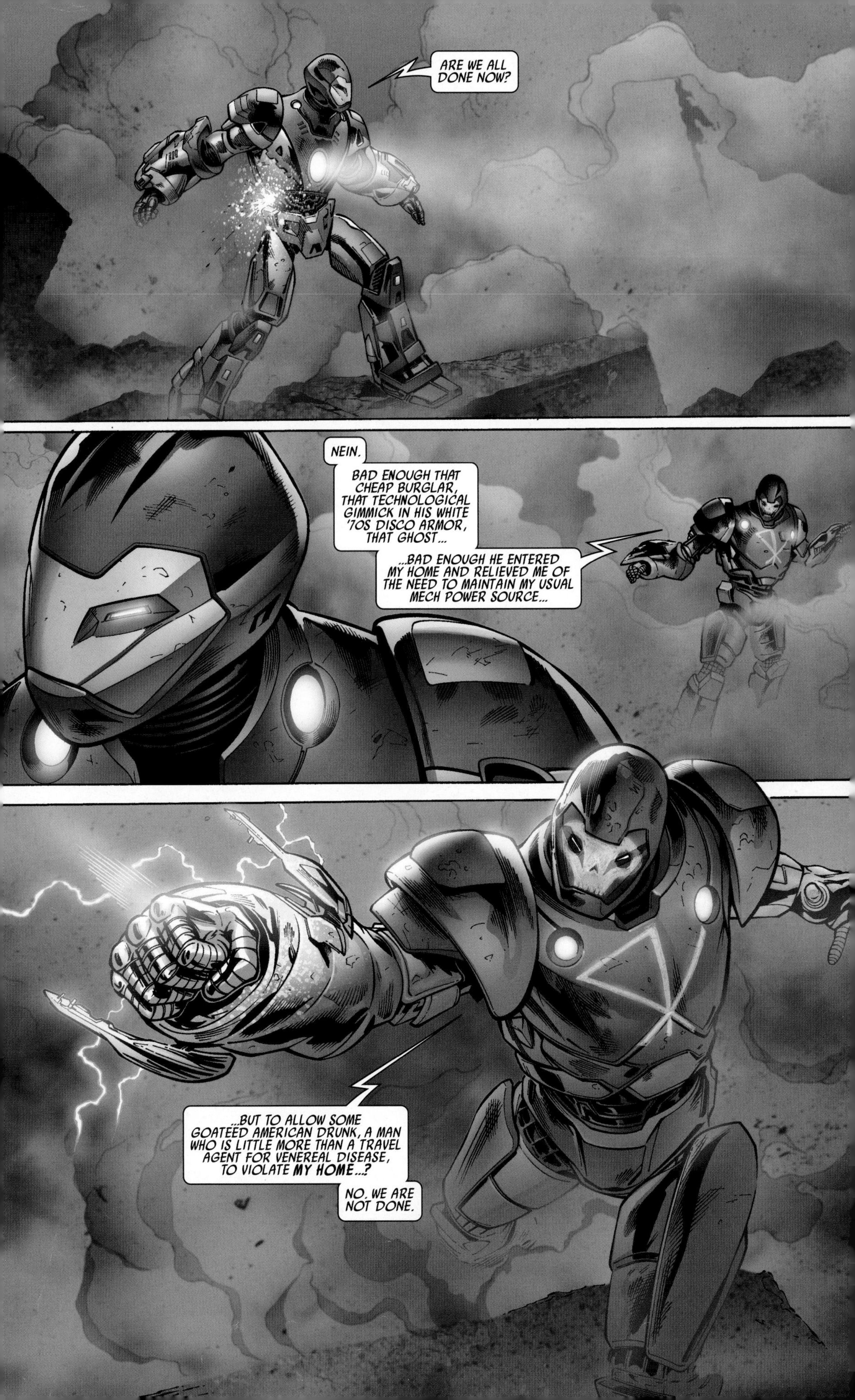
ARE WE ALL DONE NOW?
NEIN.
BAD ENOUGH THAT CHEAP BURGLAR, THAT TECHNOLOGICAL GIMMICK IN HIS WHITE '70S DISCO ARMOR, THAT GHOST...
...BAD ENOUGH HE ENTERED MY HOME AND RELIEVED ME OF THE NEED TO MAINTAIN MY USUAL MECH POWER SOURCE...
...BUT TO ALLOW SOME GOATEED AMERICAN DRUNK, A MAN WHO IS LITTLE MORE THAN A TRAVEL AGENT FOR VENEREAL DISEASE, TO VIOLATE MY HOME...?
NO. WE ARE NOT DONE.

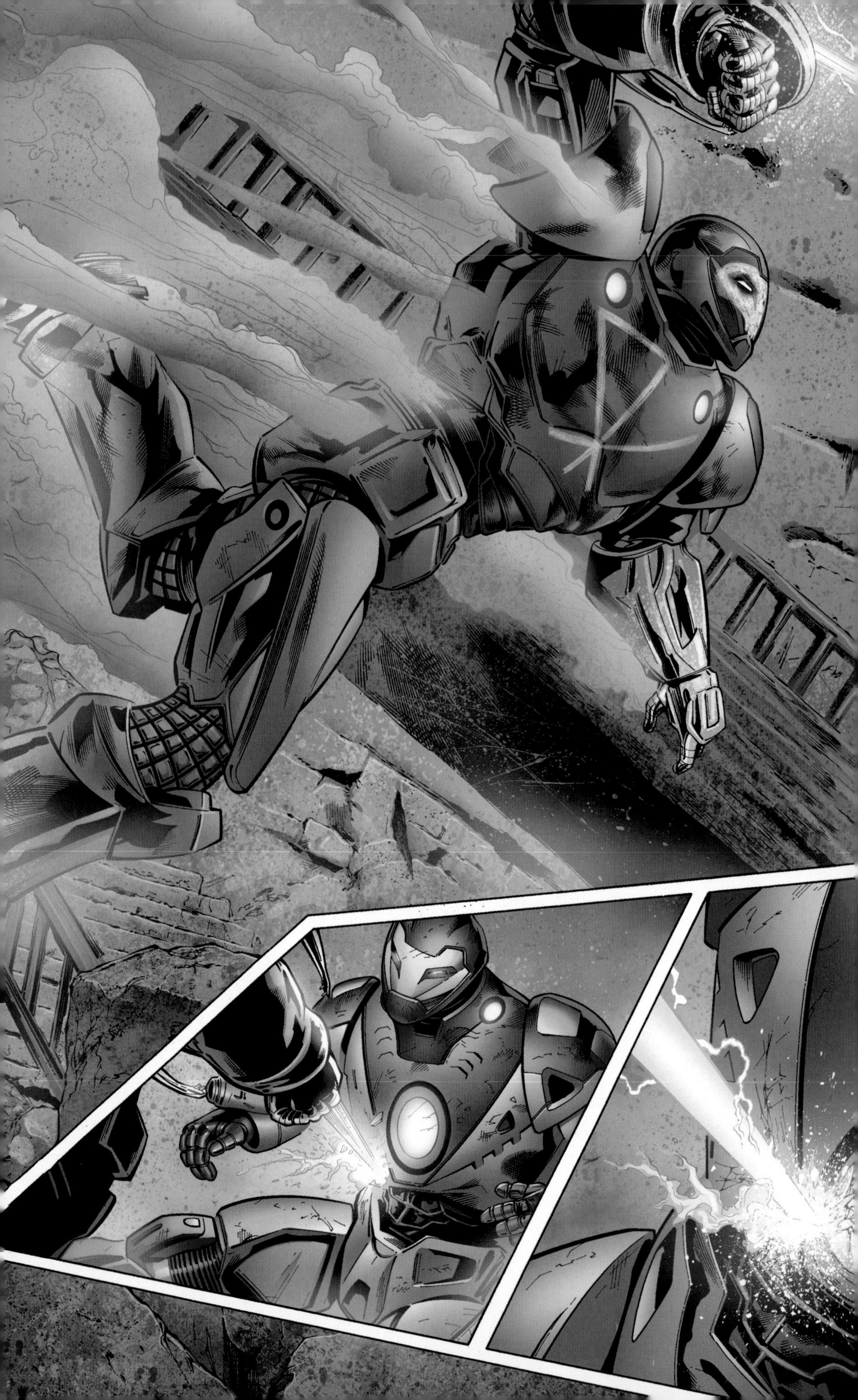

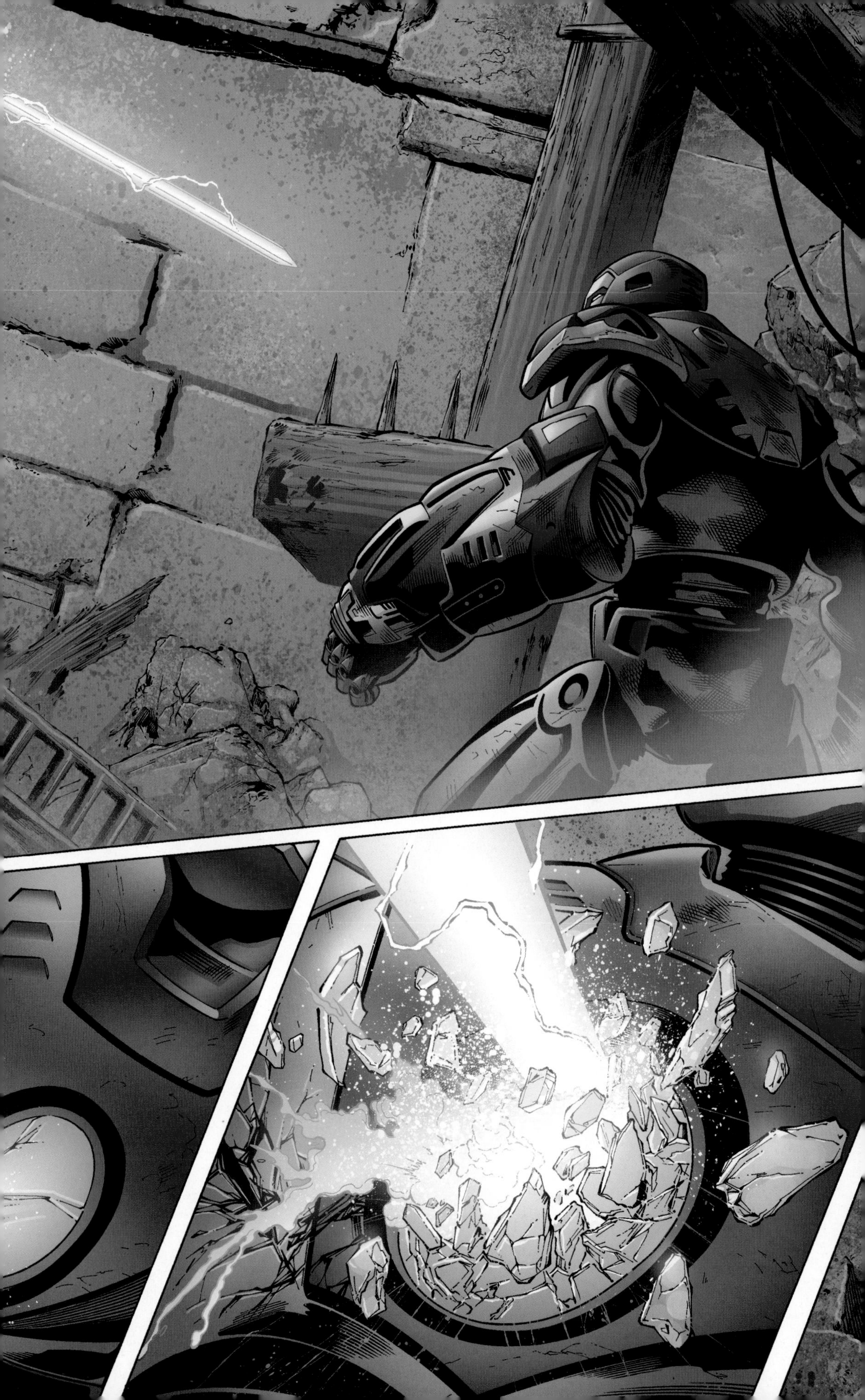

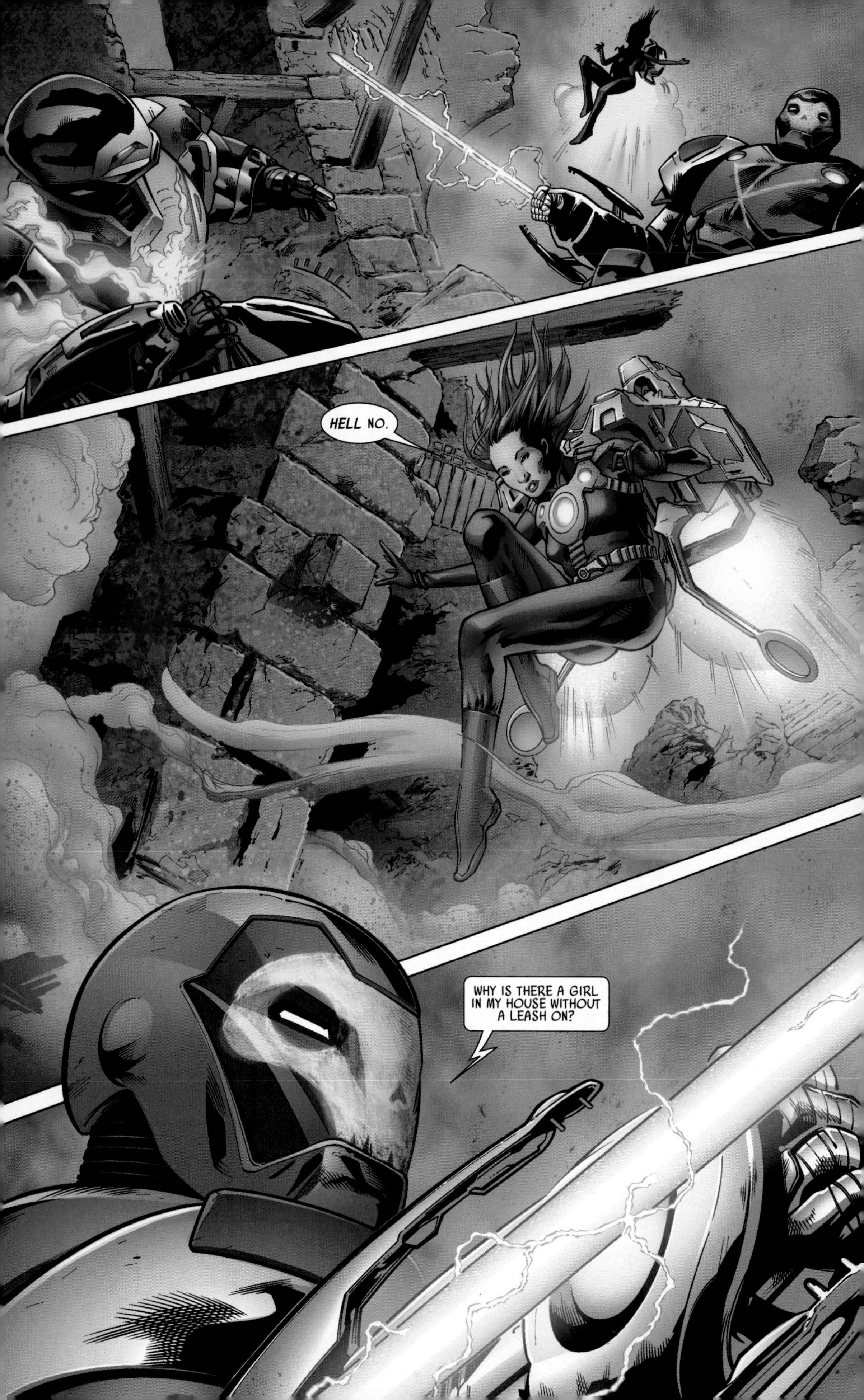
HELL NO.
WHY IS THERE A GIRL IN MY HOUSE WITHOUT A LEASH ON?

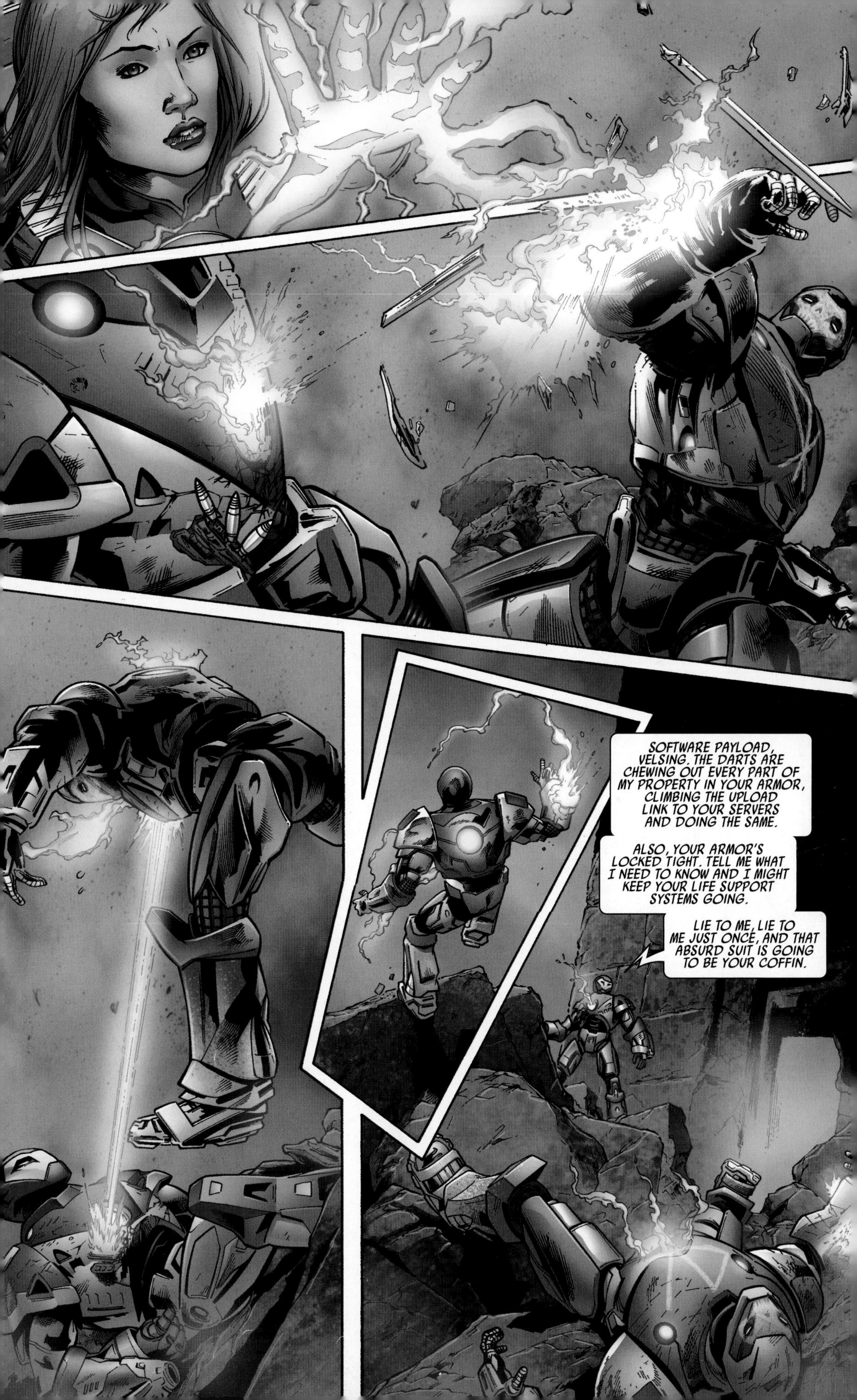
SOFTWARE PAYLOAD, VELSING. THE DARTS ARE CHEWING OUT EVERY PART OF MY PROPERTY IN YOUR ARMOR, CLIMBING THE UPLOAD LINK TO YOUR SERVERS AND DOING THE SAME.
ALSO, YOUR ARMOR'S LOCKED TIGHT. TELL ME WHAT I NEED TO KNOW AND I MIGHT KEEP YOUR LIFE SUPPORT SYSTEMS GOING.
LIE TO ME, LIE TO ME JUST ONCE, AND THAT ABSURD SUIT IS GOING TO BE YOUR COFFIN.

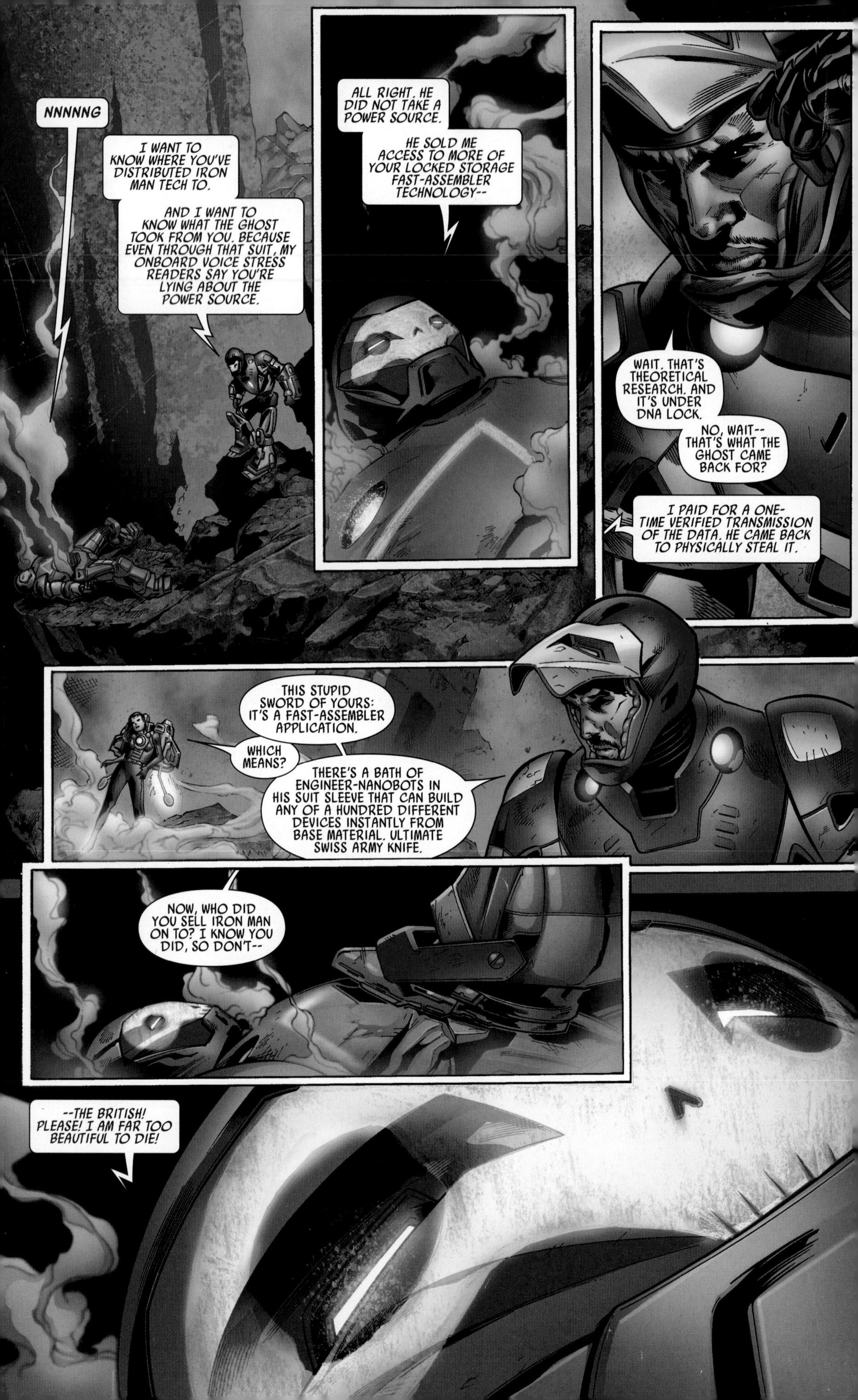
NNNNNG
I WANT TO KNOW WHERE YOU'VE DISTRIBUTED IRON MAN TECH TO.
AND I WANT TO KNOW WHAT THE GHOST TOOK FROM YOU. BECAUSE EVEN THROUGH THAT SUIT, MY ONBOARD VOICE STRESS READERS SAY YOU'RE LYING ABOUT THE POWER SOURCE.
ALL RIGHT. HE DID NOT TAKE A POWER SOURCE.
HE SOLD ME ACCESS TO MORE OF YOUR LOCKED STORAGE FAST-ASSEMBLER TECHNOLOGY--
WAIT. THAT'S THEORETICAL RESEARCH. AND IT'S UNDER DNA LOCK.
NO, WAIT-- THAT'S WHAT THE GHOST CAME BACK FOR?
I PAID FOR A ONE-TIME VERIFIED TRANSMISSION OF THE DATA. HE CAME BACK TO PHYSICALLY STEAL IT.
THIS STUPID SWORD OF YOURS: IT'S A FAST-ASSEMBLER APPLICATION.
WHICH MEANS?
THERE'S A BATH OF ENGINEER-NANOBOTS IN HIS SUIT SLEEVE THAT CAN BUILD ANY OF A HUNDRED DIFFERENT DEVICES INSTANTLY FROM BASE MATERIAL. ULTIMATE SWISS ARMY KNIFE.
NOW, WHO DID YOU SELL IRON MAN ON TO? I KNOW YOU DID, SO DON'T--
--THE BRITISH! PLEASE! I AM FAR TOO BEAUTIFUL TO DIE!

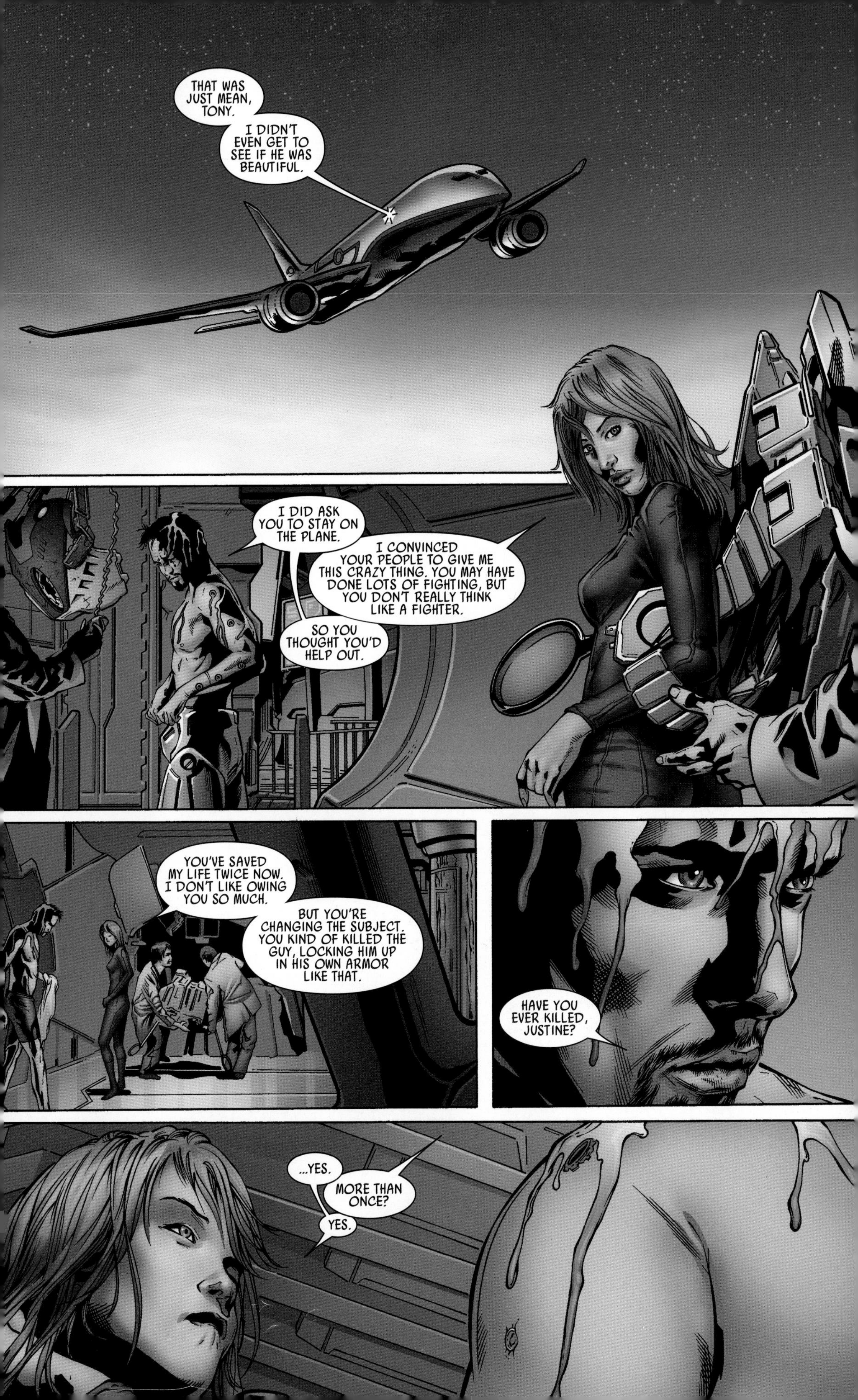
THAT WAS JUST MEAN, TONY.
I DIDN'T EVEN GET TO SEE IF HE WAS BEAUTIFUL.
I DID ASK YOU TO STAY ON THE PLANE.
I CONVINCED YOUR PEOPLE TO GIVE ME THIS CRAZY THING. YOU MAY HAVE DONE LOTS OF FIGHTING, BUT YOU DON'T REALLY THINK LIKE A FIGHTER.
SO YOU THOUGHT YOU'D HELP OUT.
YOU'VE SAVED MY LIFE TWICE NOW. I DON'T LIKE OWING YOU SO MUCH.
BUT YOU'RE CHANGING THE SUBJECT. YOU KIND OF KILLED THE GUY, LOCKING HIM UP IN HIS OWN ARMOR LIKE THAT.
HAVE YOU EVER KILLED, JUSTINE?
...YES.
MORE THAN ONCE?
YES.

IT'S ONLY HARD THE FIRST TIME, ISN'T IT?
THAT WASN'T MY FIRST TIME.
NOW THEN. ON TO LONDON TO SEE WHAT THE JOLLY OLD ENGLISH DID WITH MY TECHNOLOGY.
HOW THE HELL ARE PEOPLE OPENING MY LOCKBOXES?

I SWEAR YOU'RE MAKING ME INTO AN ALCOHOLIC JUST LIKE YOU.

I AM NOT AN ALCOHOLIC. I SIMPLY HAVE A TERRIBLE DRINKS DEFICIENCY.

MR. STARK, YOU NEED TO SEE THIS.

CALM DOWN, JASPER. YOU'LL CLIP YEARS OFF YOUR LIFE IF YOU DON'T LEARN HOW TO--

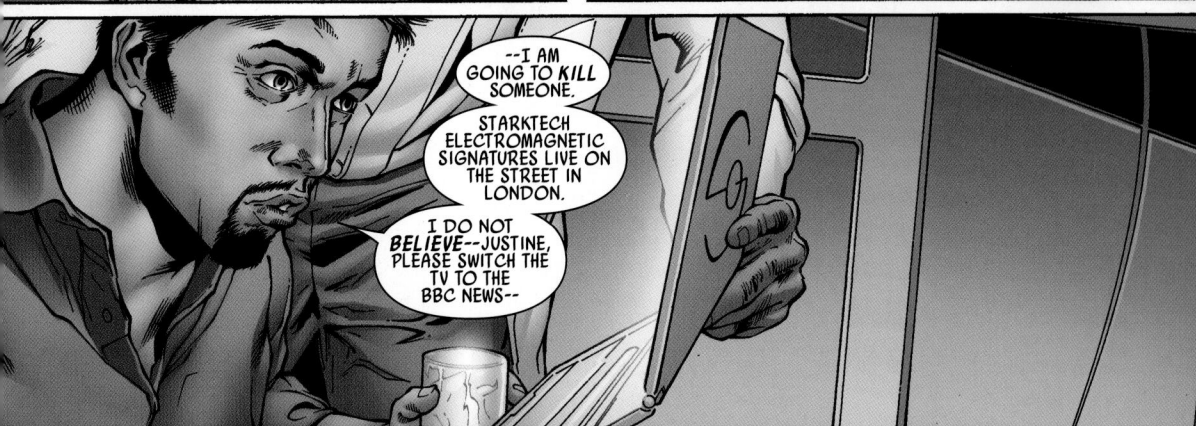

--I AM GOING TO KILL SOMEONE.

STARKTECH ELECTROMAGNETIC SIGNATURES LIVE ON THE STREET IN LONDON.

I DO NOT BELIEVE--JUSTINE, PLEASE SWITCH THE TV TO THE BBC NEWS--

--THROUGHOUT CENTRAL LONDON, PROTESTS IGNITED BY THE GOVERNMENT'S CONTROVERSIAL RESPONSE TO THE CLIMATE CRISIS IN EUROPE...

RENEW ENGLAND WITH RENEWABLE ENERGY

STOP GLOBAL WARMING

GREEN NOW!!

ARE NOW BEING CONTAINED BY THE METROPOLITAN POLICE'S NEW ANTI-RIOT SQUAD, WHICH THE BBC HAS LEARNED IS CODENAMED OPERATION FIREPOWER--

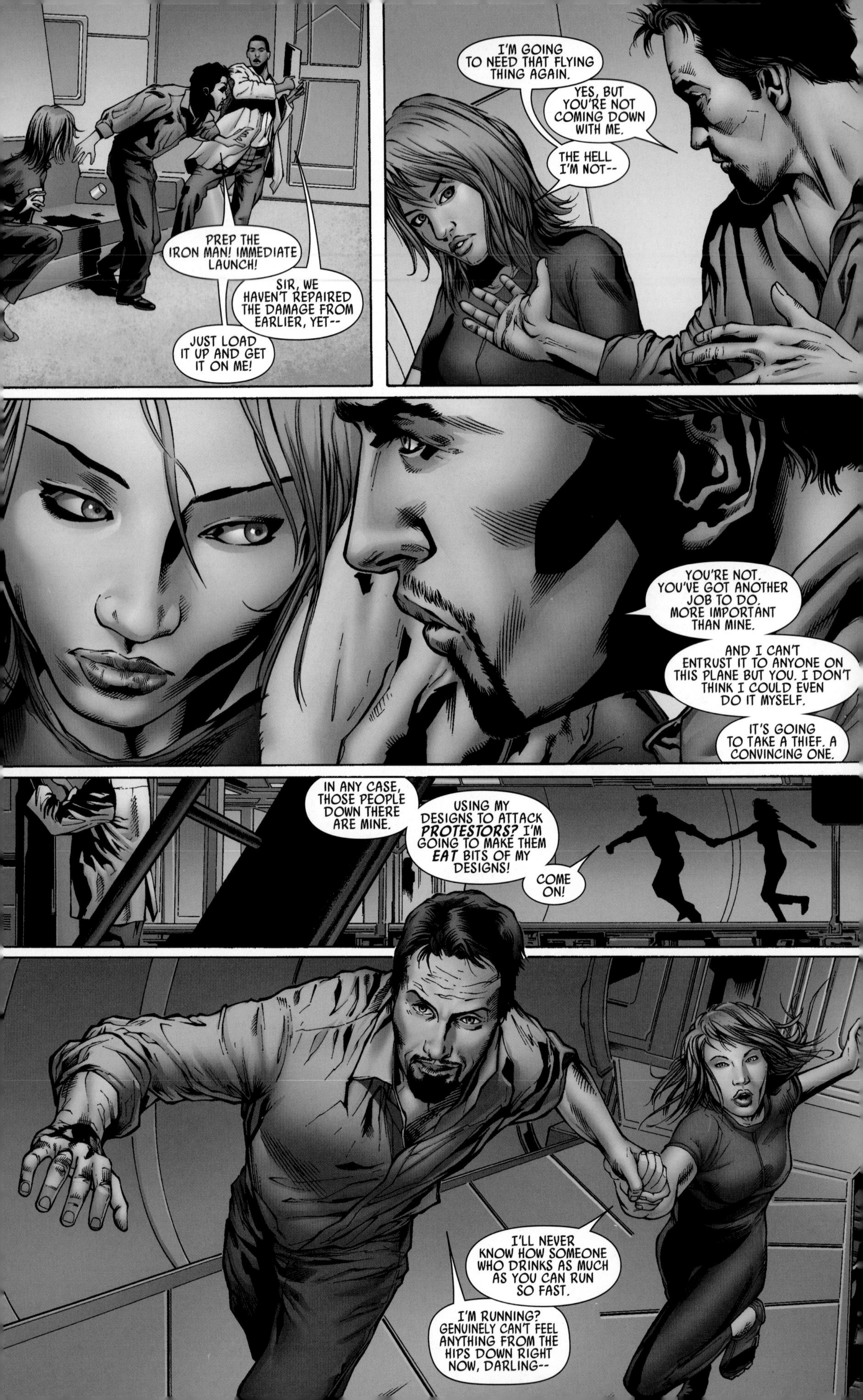
PREP THE IRON MAN! IMMEDIATE LAUNCH!
SIR, WE HAVEN'T REPAIRED THE DAMAGE FROM EARLIER, YET--
JUST LOAD IT UP AND GET IT ON ME!
I'M GOING TO NEED THAT FLYING THING AGAIN.
YES, BUT YOU'RE NOT COMING DOWN WITH ME.
THE HELL I'M NOT--
YOU'RE NOT. YOU'VE GOT ANOTHER JOB TO DO. MORE IMPORTANT THAN MINE.
AND I CAN'T ENTRUST IT TO ANYONE ON THIS PLANE BUT YOU. I DON'T THINK I COULD EVEN DO IT MYSELF.
IT'S GOING TO TAKE A THIEF. A CONVINCING ONE.
IN ANY CASE, THOSE PEOPLE DOWN THERE ARE MINE.
USING MY DESIGNS TO ATTACK *PROTESTORS?* I'M GOING TO MAKE THEM *EAT* BITS OF MY DESIGNS!
COME ON!
I'LL NEVER KNOW HOW SOMEONE WHO DRINKS AS MUCH AS YOU CAN RUN SO FAST.
I'M RUNNING? GENUINELY CAN'T FEEL ANYTHING FROM THE HIPS DOWN RIGHT NOW, DARLING--

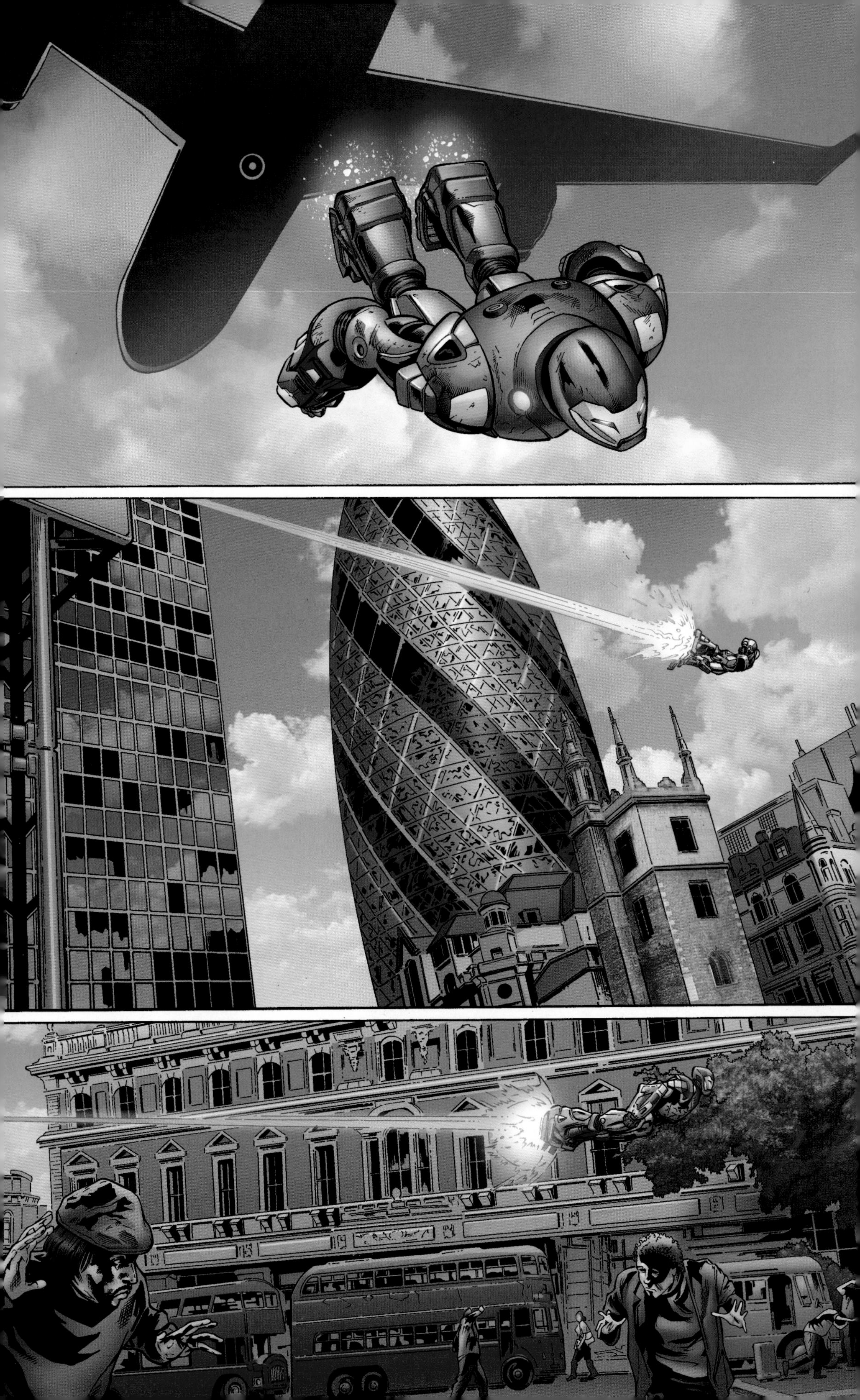

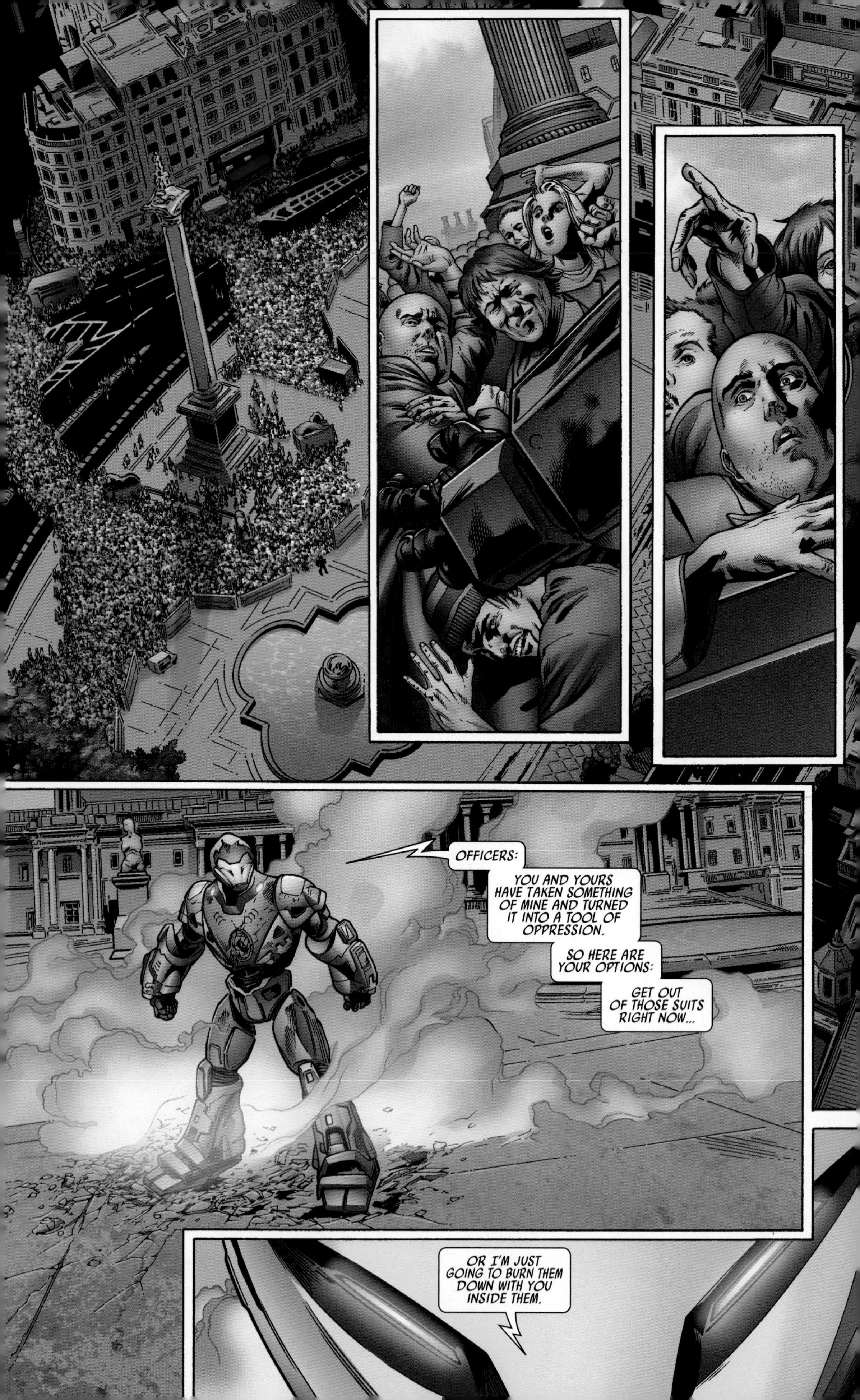
OFFICERS:
YOU AND YOURS HAVE TAKEN SOMETHING OF MINE AND TURNED IT INTO A TOOL OF OPPRESSION.
SO HERE ARE YOUR OPTIONS:
GET OUT OF THOSE SUITS RIGHT NOW...
OR I'M JUST GOING TO BURN THEM DOWN WITH YOU INSIDE THEM.

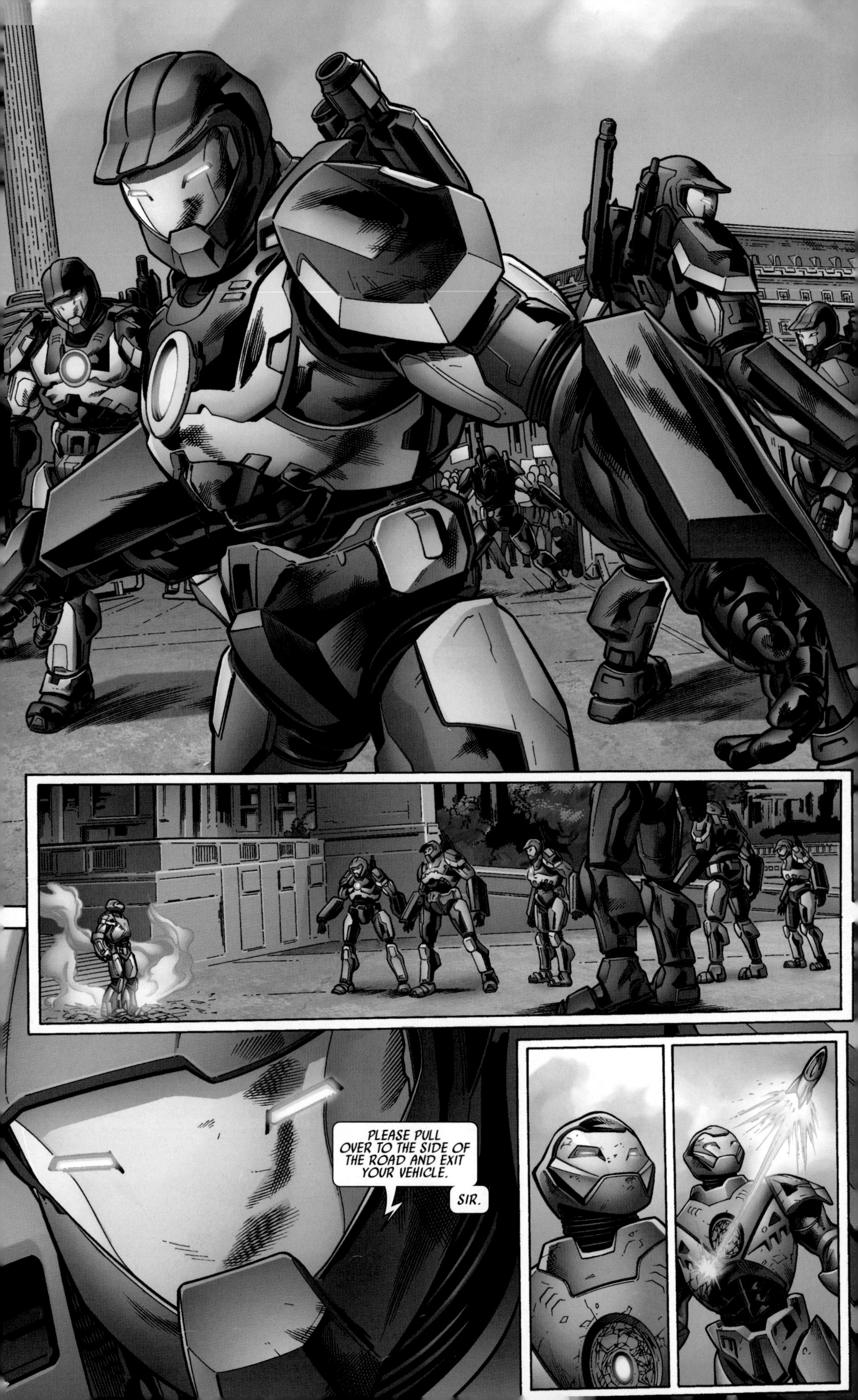
PLEASE PULL OVER TO THE SIDE OF THE ROAD AND EXIT YOUR VEHICLE.
SIR.

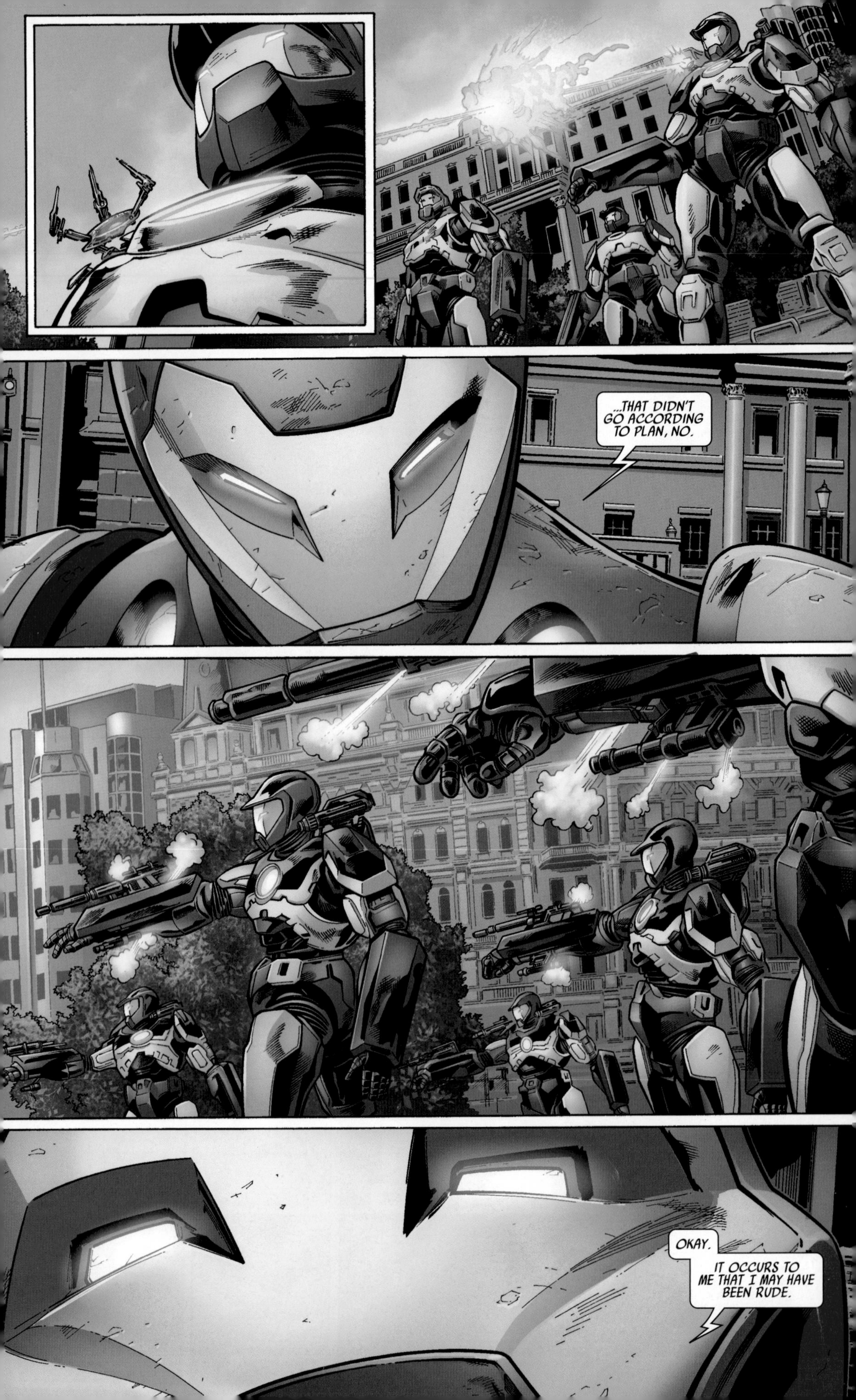
...THAT DIDN'T GO ACCORDING TO PLAN, NO.
OKAY.
IT OCCURS TO ME THAT I MAY HAVE BEEN RUDE.

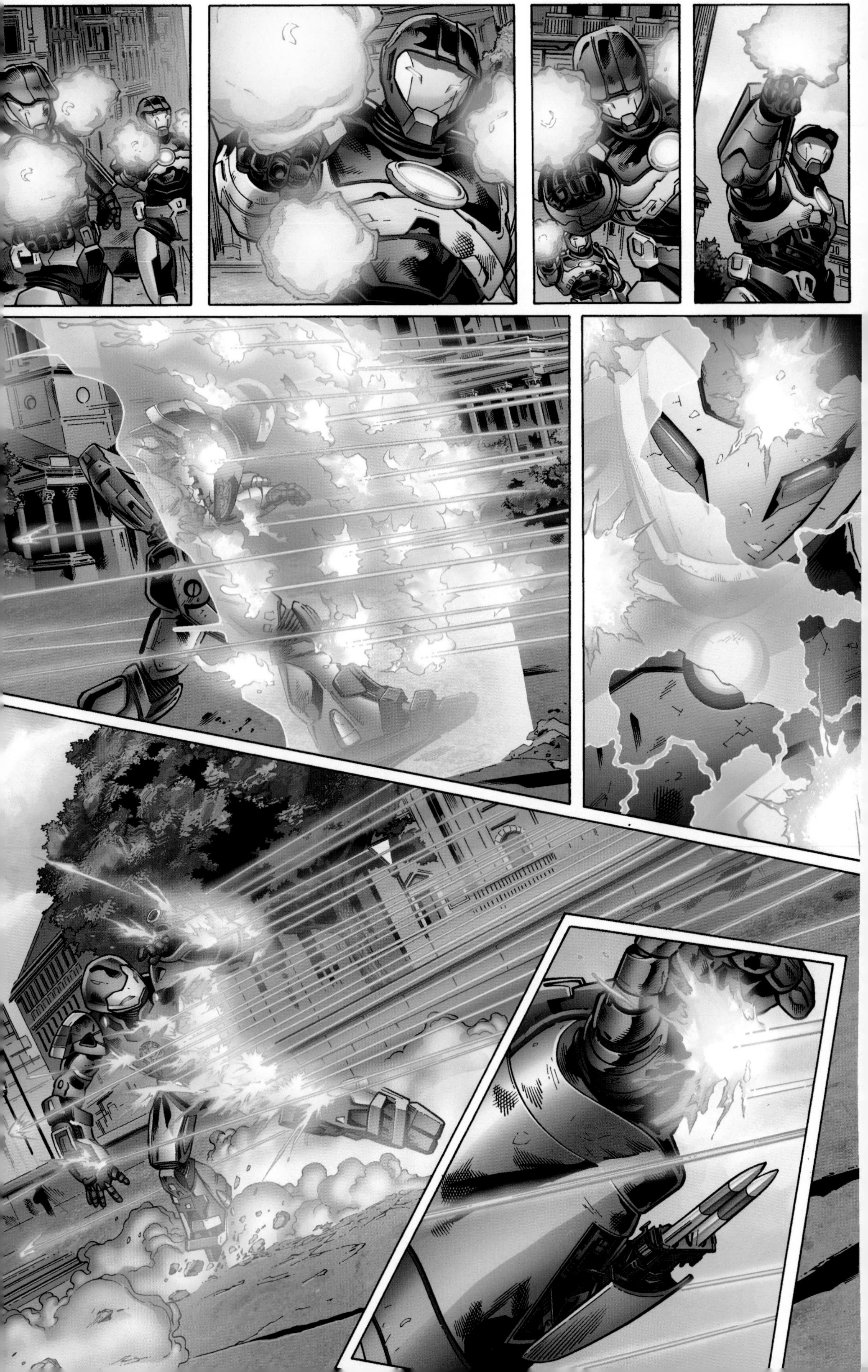

THAT'S RIGHT. I CAN BLOW YOUR SUITS APART IF NEED BE.

NOW, ARE YOU GOING TO STAND DOWN?

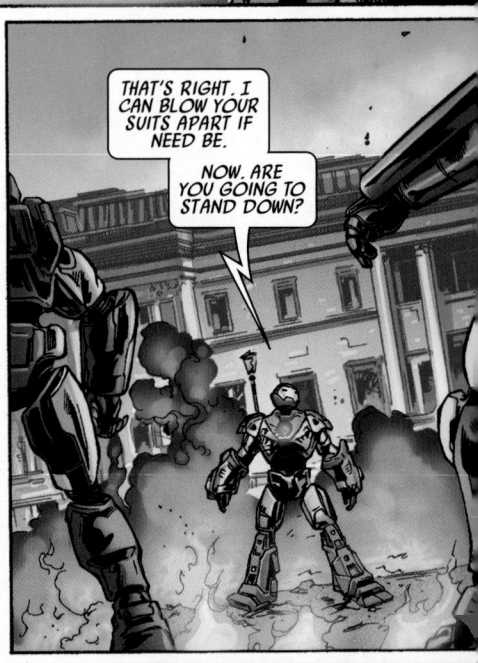

BECAUSE I ONLY HAD TWO OF THOSE ROCKETS ONBOARD, ACTUALLY.

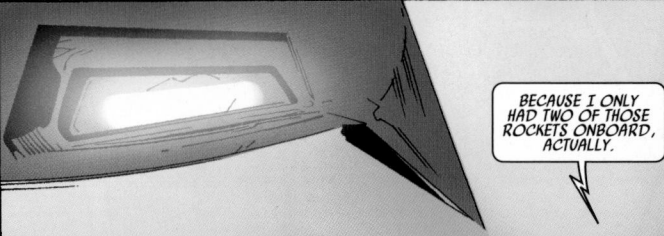

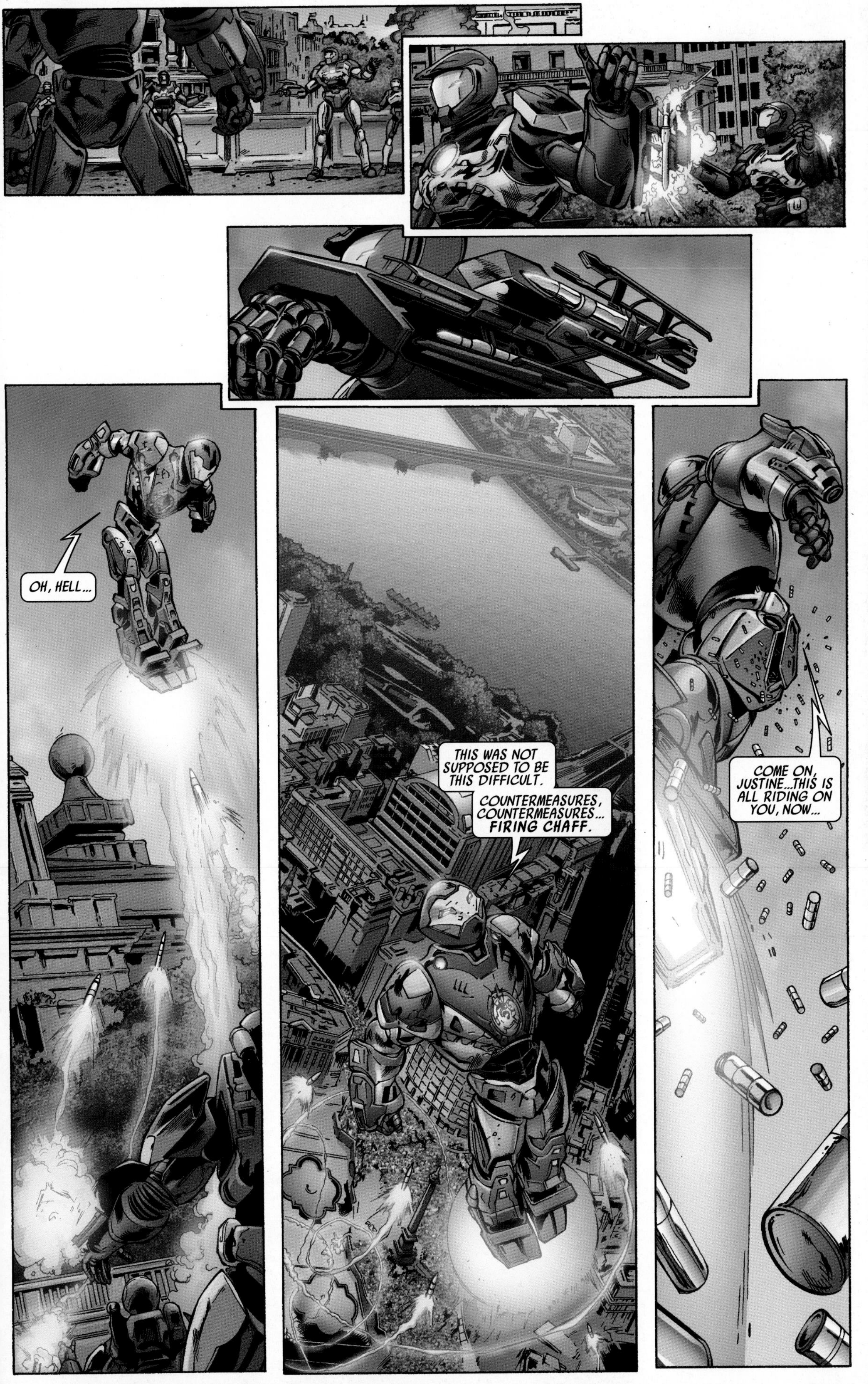
OH, HELL...
THIS WAS NOT SUPPOSED TO BE THIS DIFFICULT.
COUNTERMEASURES, COUNTERMEASURES... FIRING CHAFF.
COME ON, JUSTINE...THIS IS ALL RIDING ON YOU, NOW...

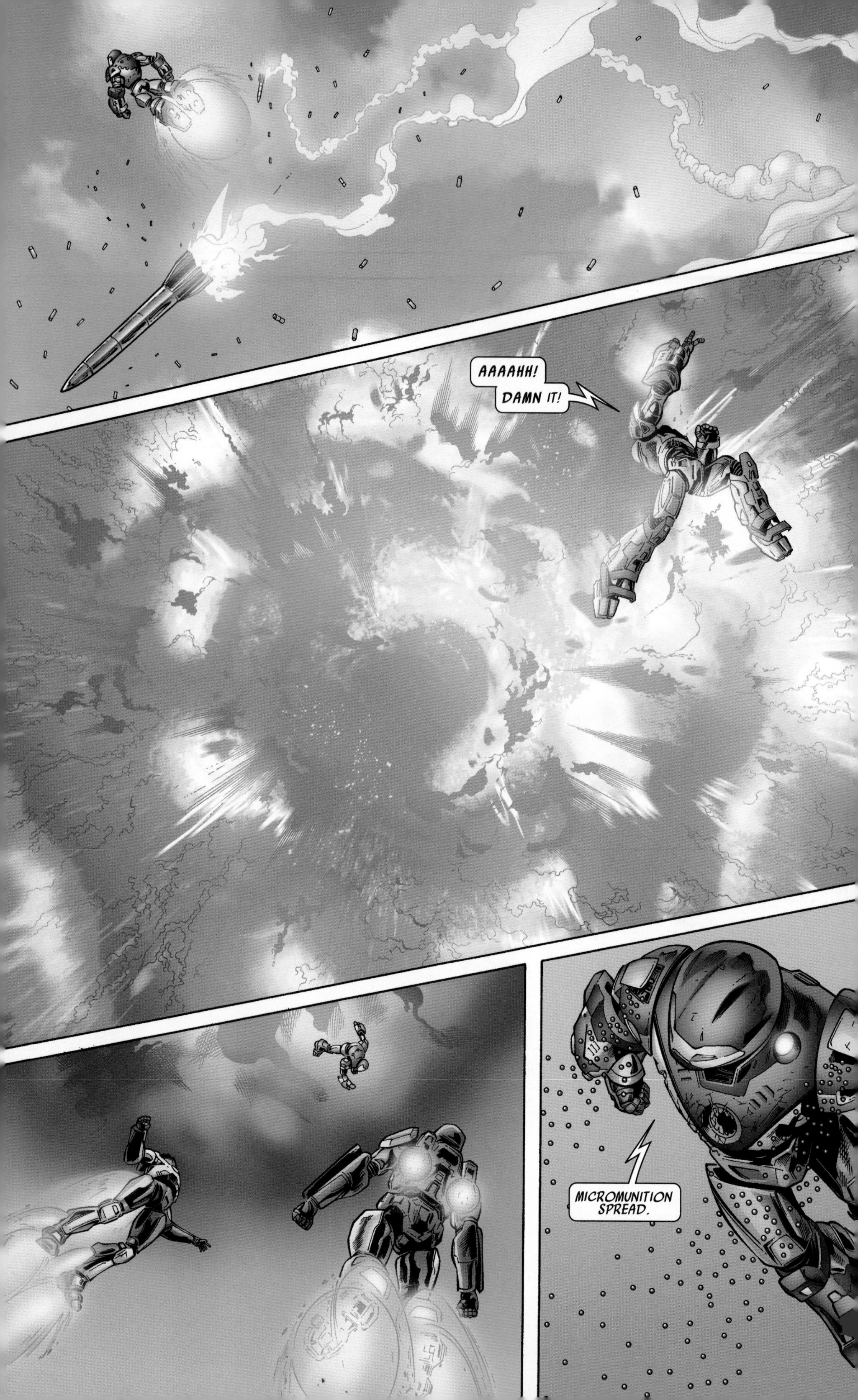
AAAAHH!
DAMN IT!
MICROMUNITION SPREAD.

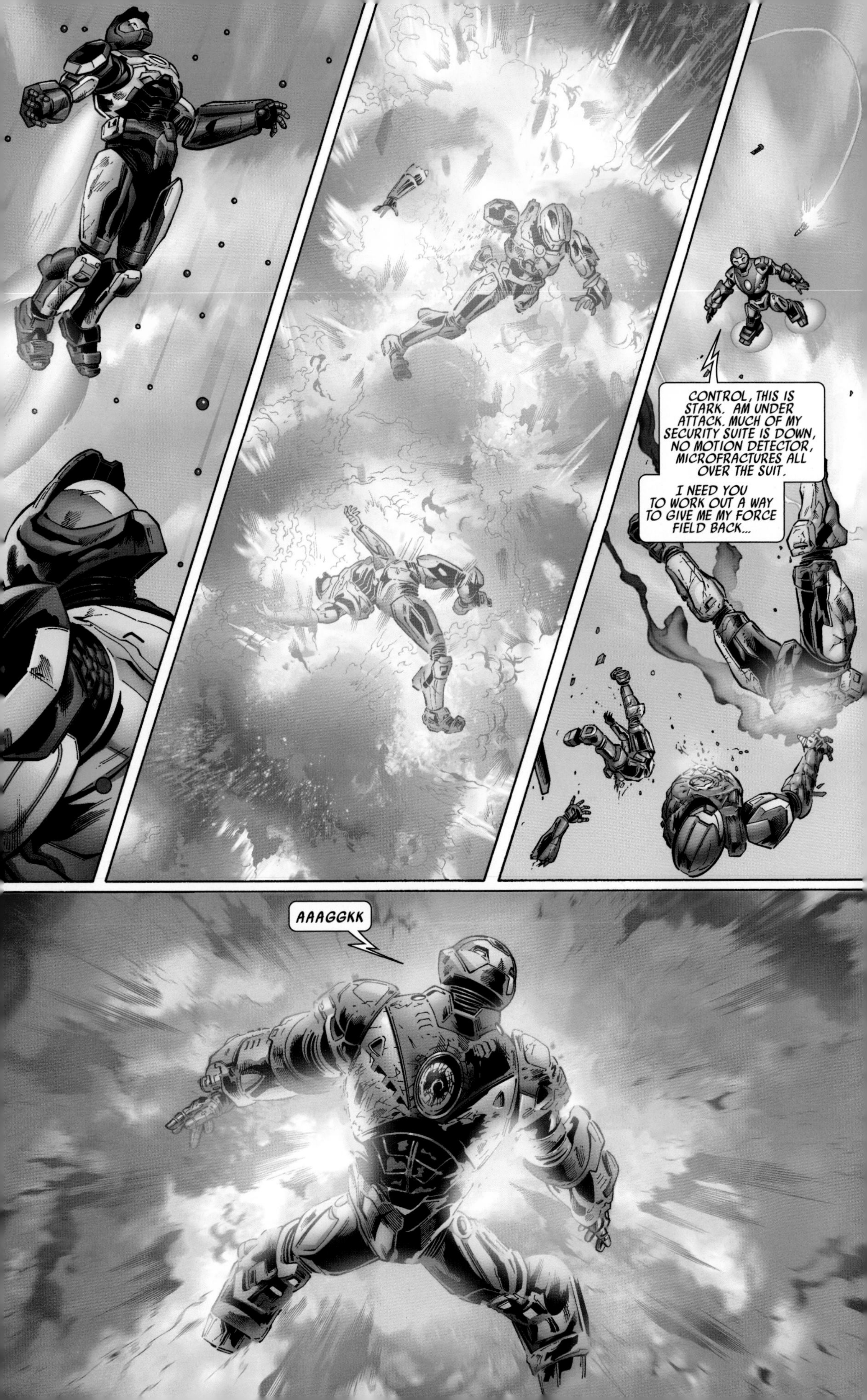
CONTROL, THIS IS STARK. AM UNDER ATTACK. MUCH OF MY SECURITY SUITE IS DOWN, NO MOTION DETECTOR, MICROFRACTURES ALL OVER THE SUIT.
I NEED YOU TO WORK OUT A WAY TO GIVE ME MY FORCE FIELD BACK...
AAAGGKK

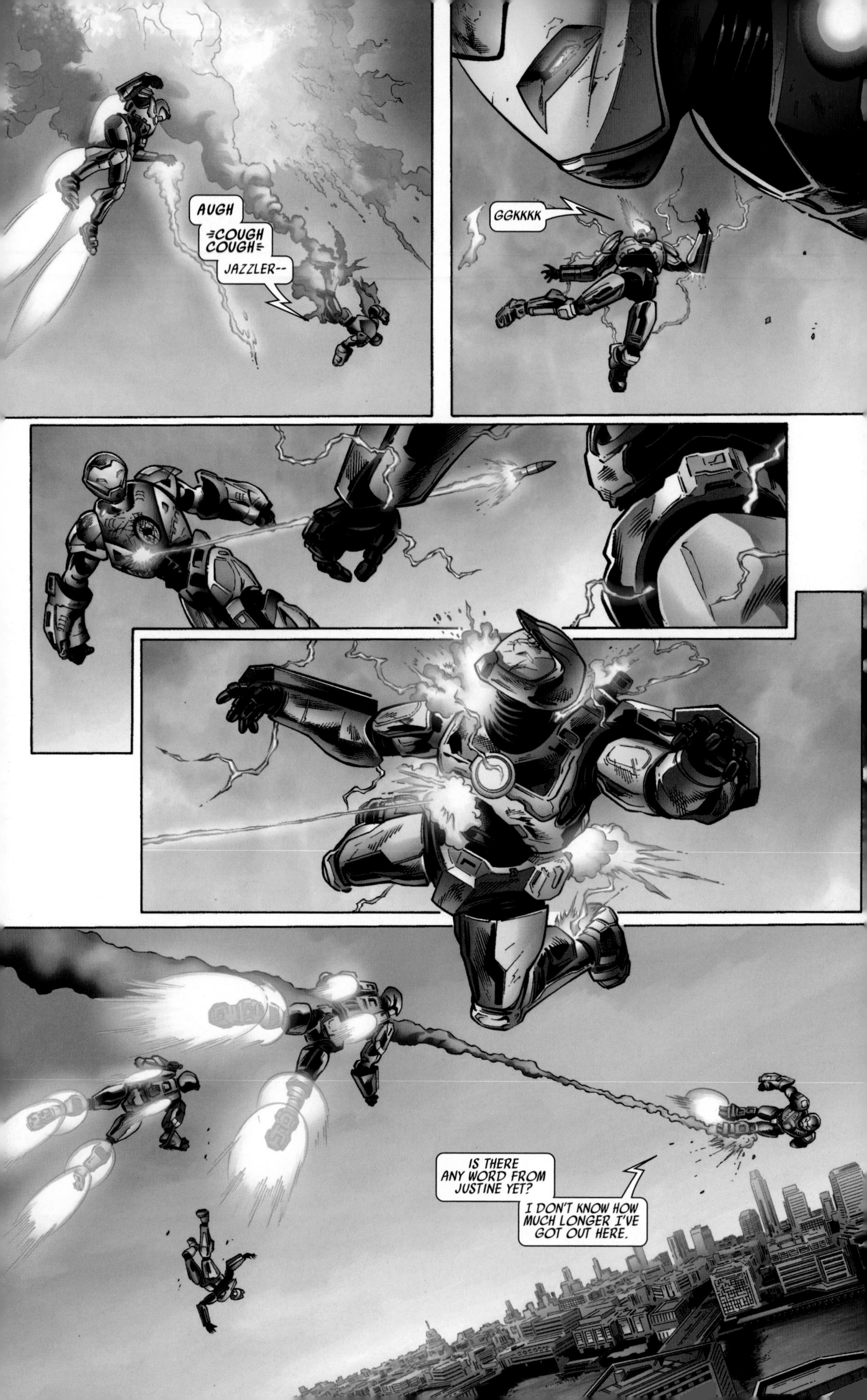
AUGH
COUGH COUGH
JAZZLER--
GGKKKK
IS THERE ANY WORD FROM JUSTINE YET?
I DON'T KNOW HOW MUCH LONGER I'VE GOT OUT HERE.

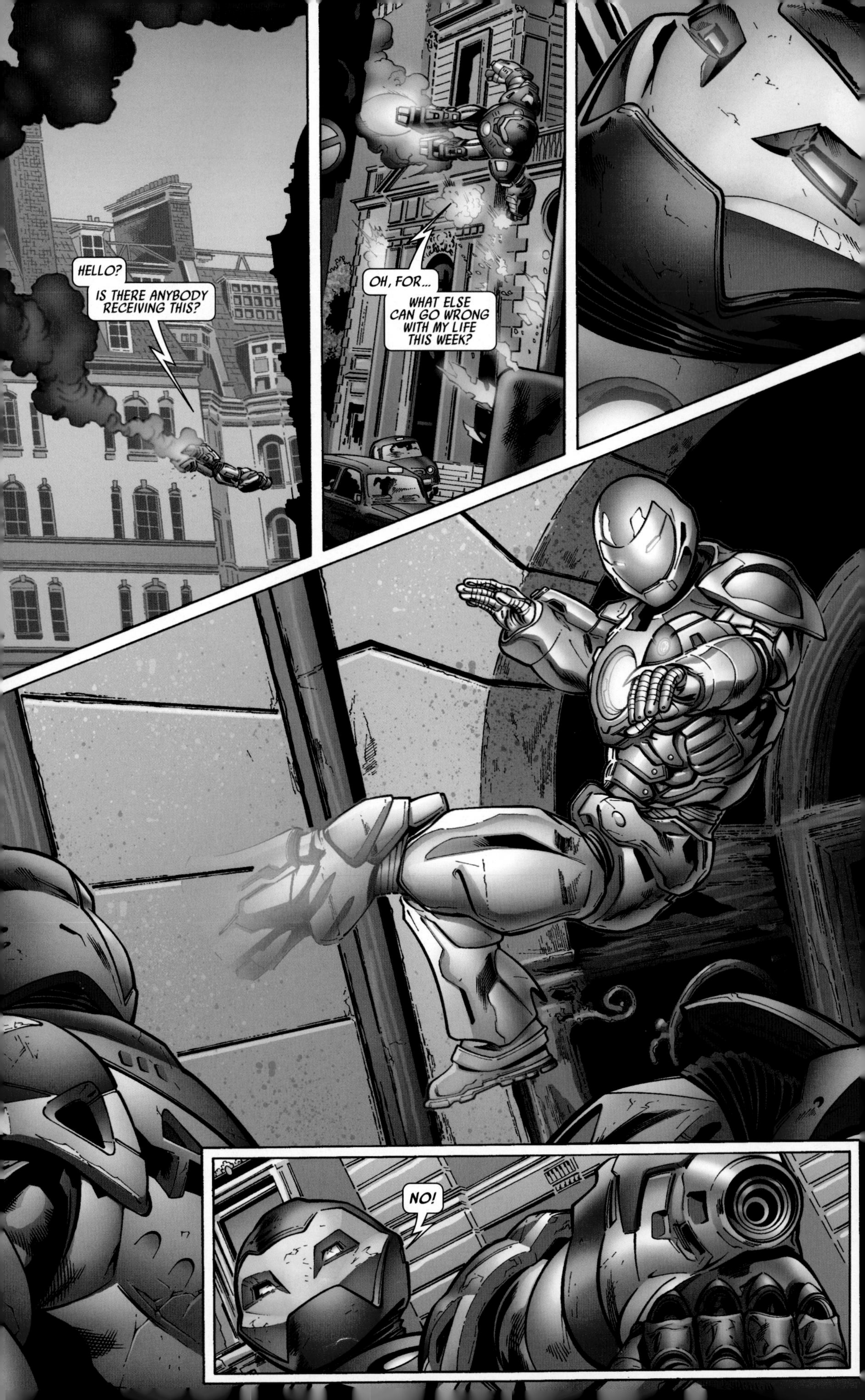
HELLO?
IS THERE ANYBODY RECEIVING THIS?
OH, FOR...
WHAT ELSE CAN GO WRONG WITH MY LIFE THIS WEEK?
NO!

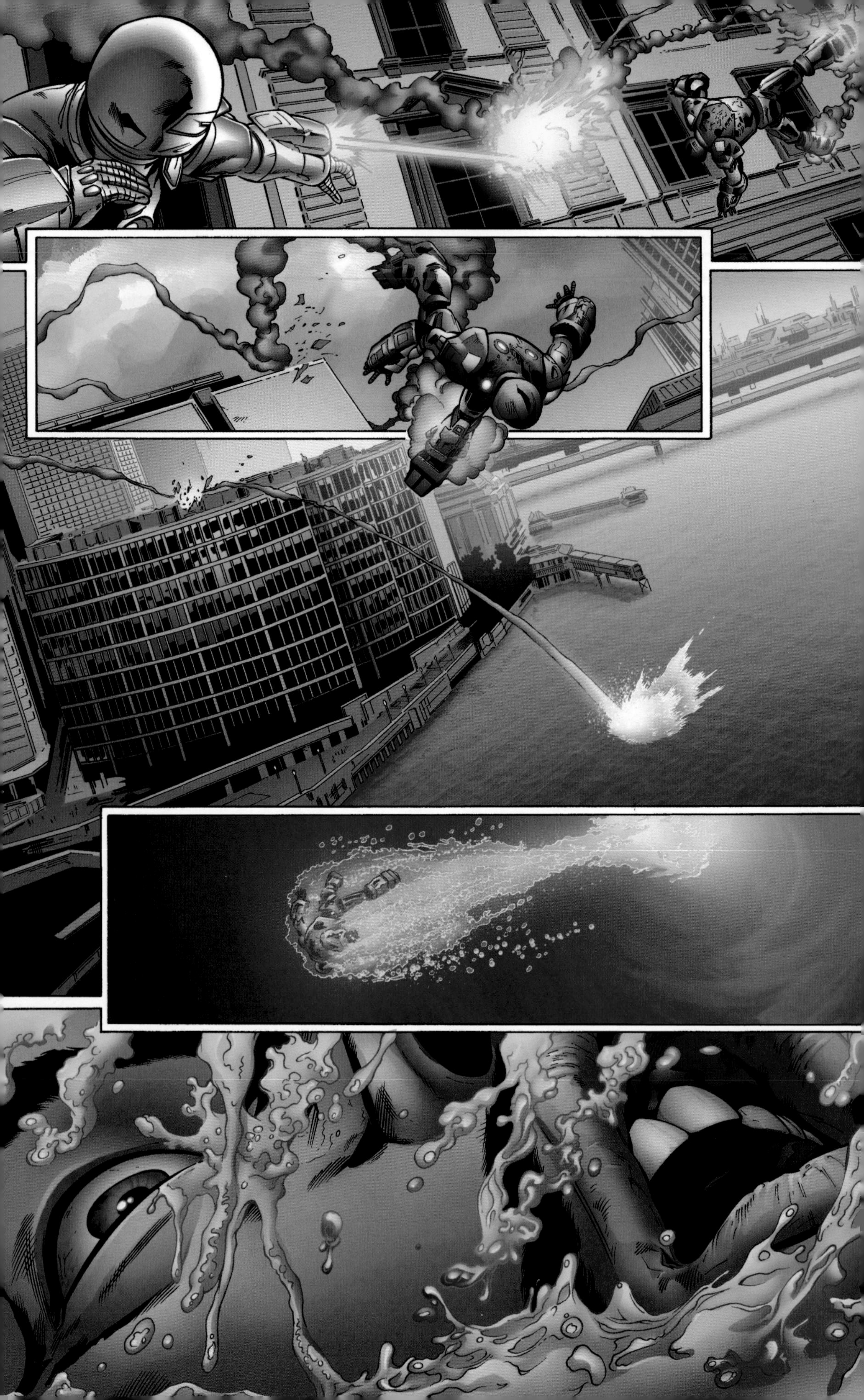

4

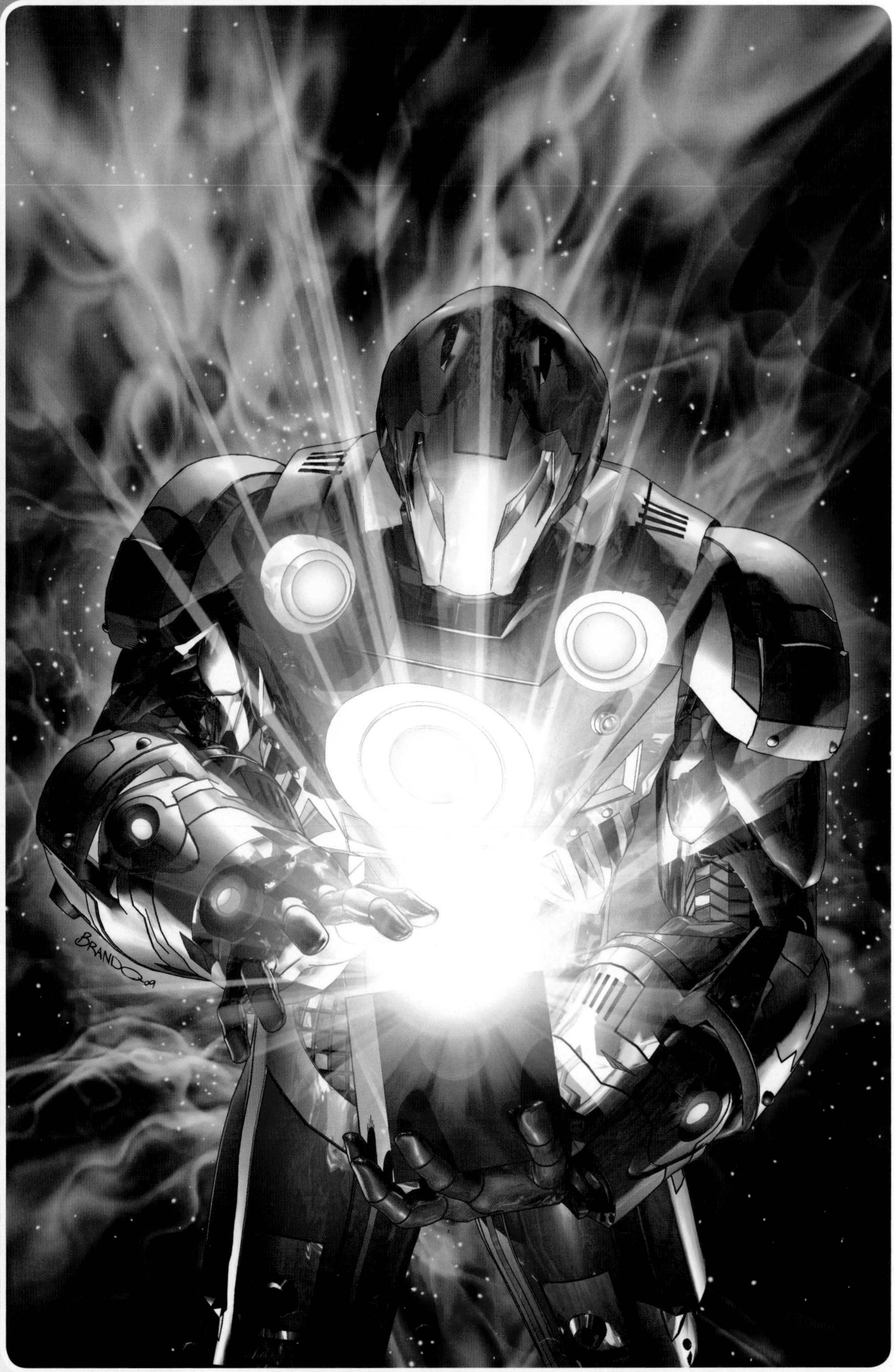

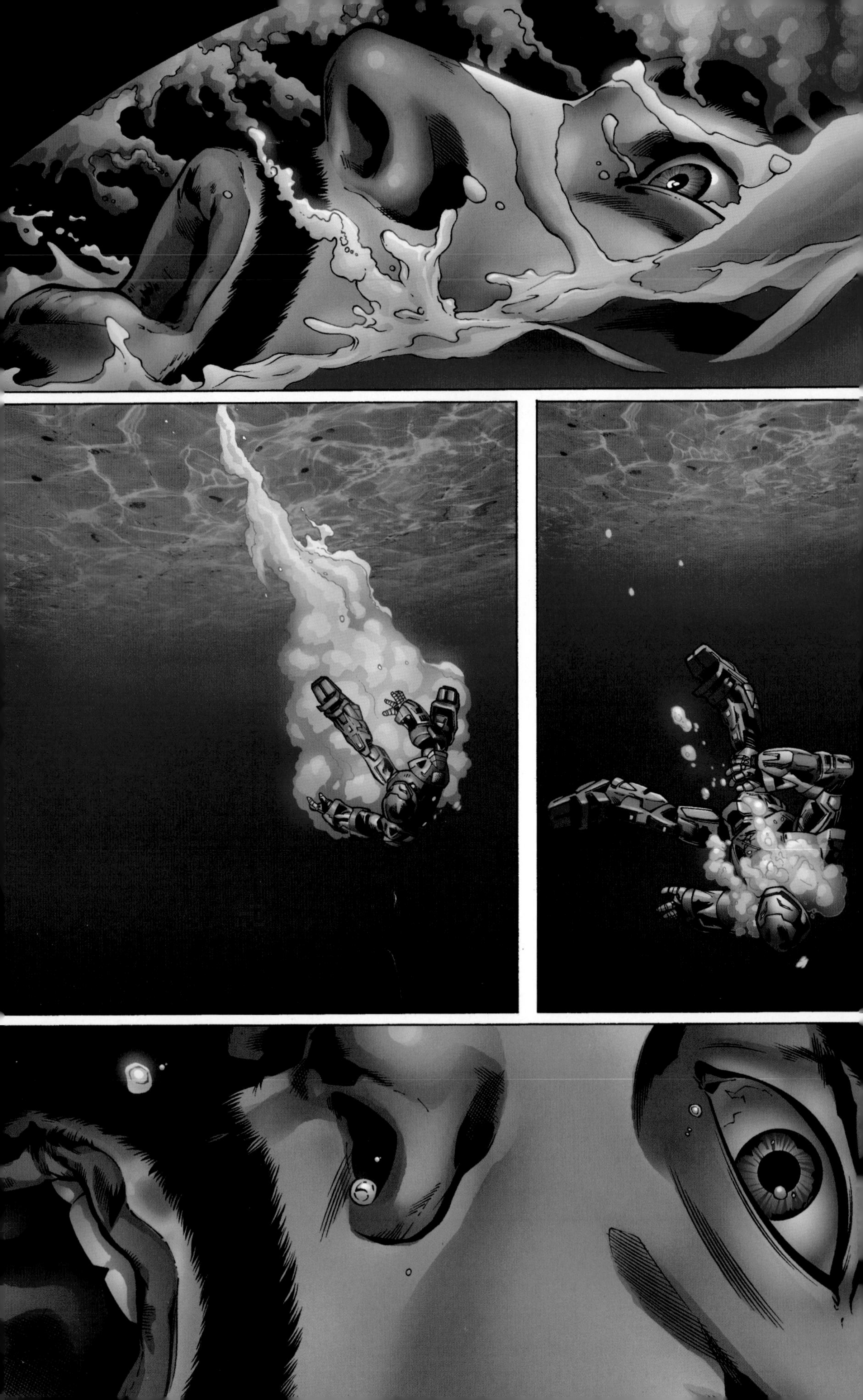

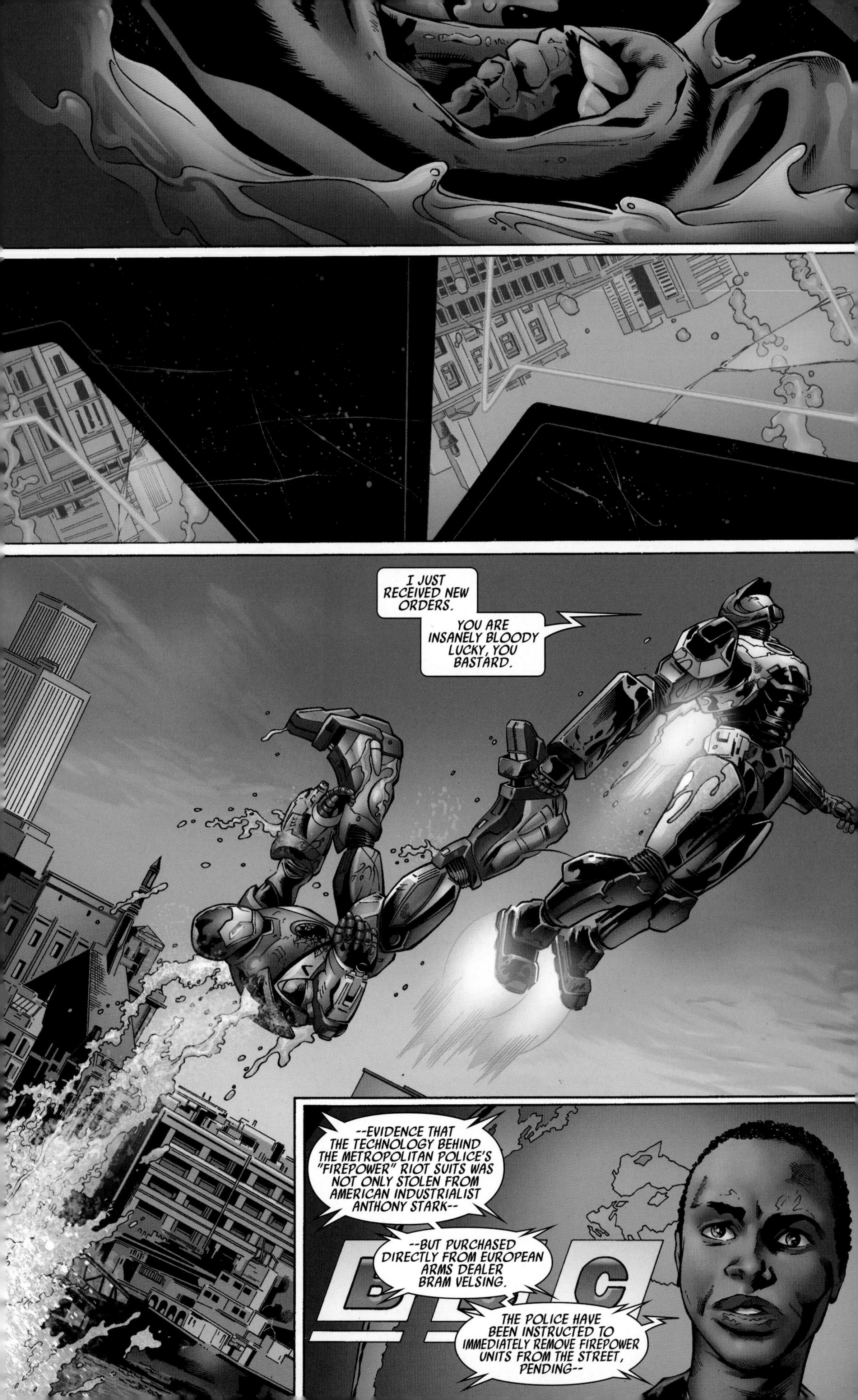
I JUST RECEIVED NEW ORDERS.
YOU ARE INSANELY BLOODY LUCKY, YOU BASTARD.
--EVIDENCE THAT THE TECHNOLOGY BEHIND THE METROPOLITAN POLICE'S "FIREPOWER" RIOT SUITS WAS NOT ONLY STOLEN FROM AMERICAN INDUSTRIALIST ANTHONY STARK--
--BUT PURCHASED DIRECTLY FROM EUROPEAN ARMS DEALER BRAM VELSING.
THE POLICE HAVE BEEN INSTRUCTED TO IMMEDIATELY REMOVE FIREPOWER UNITS FROM THE STREET, PENDING--

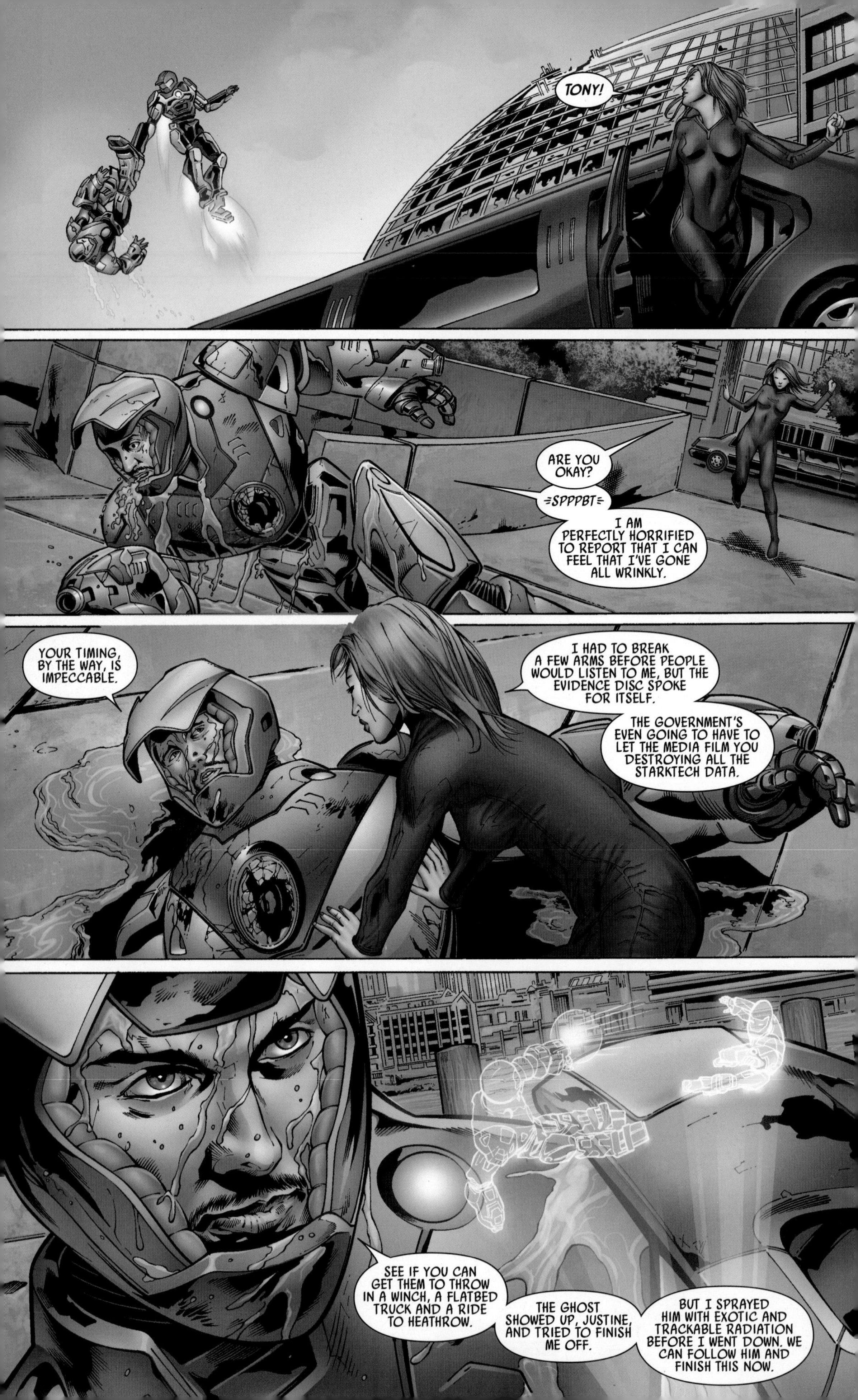
TONY!
ARE YOU OKAY?
SPPPBT
I AM PERFECTLY HORRIFIED TO REPORT THAT I CAN FEEL THAT I'VE GONE ALL WRINKLY.
YOUR TIMING, BY THE WAY, IS IMPECCABLE.
I HAD TO BREAK A FEW ARMS BEFORE PEOPLE WOULD LISTEN TO ME, BUT THE EVIDENCE DISC SPOKE FOR ITSELF.
THE GOVERNMENT'S EVEN GOING TO HAVE TO LET THE MEDIA FILM YOU DESTROYING ALL THE STARKTECH DATA.
SEE IF YOU CAN GET THEM TO THROW IN A WINCH, A FLATBED TRUCK AND A RIDE TO HEATHROW.
THE GHOST SHOWED UP, JUSTINE, AND TRIED TO FINISH ME OFF.
BUT I SPRAYED HIM WITH EXOTIC AND TRACKABLE RADIATION BEFORE I WENT DOWN. WE CAN FOLLOW HIM AND FINISH THIS NOW.

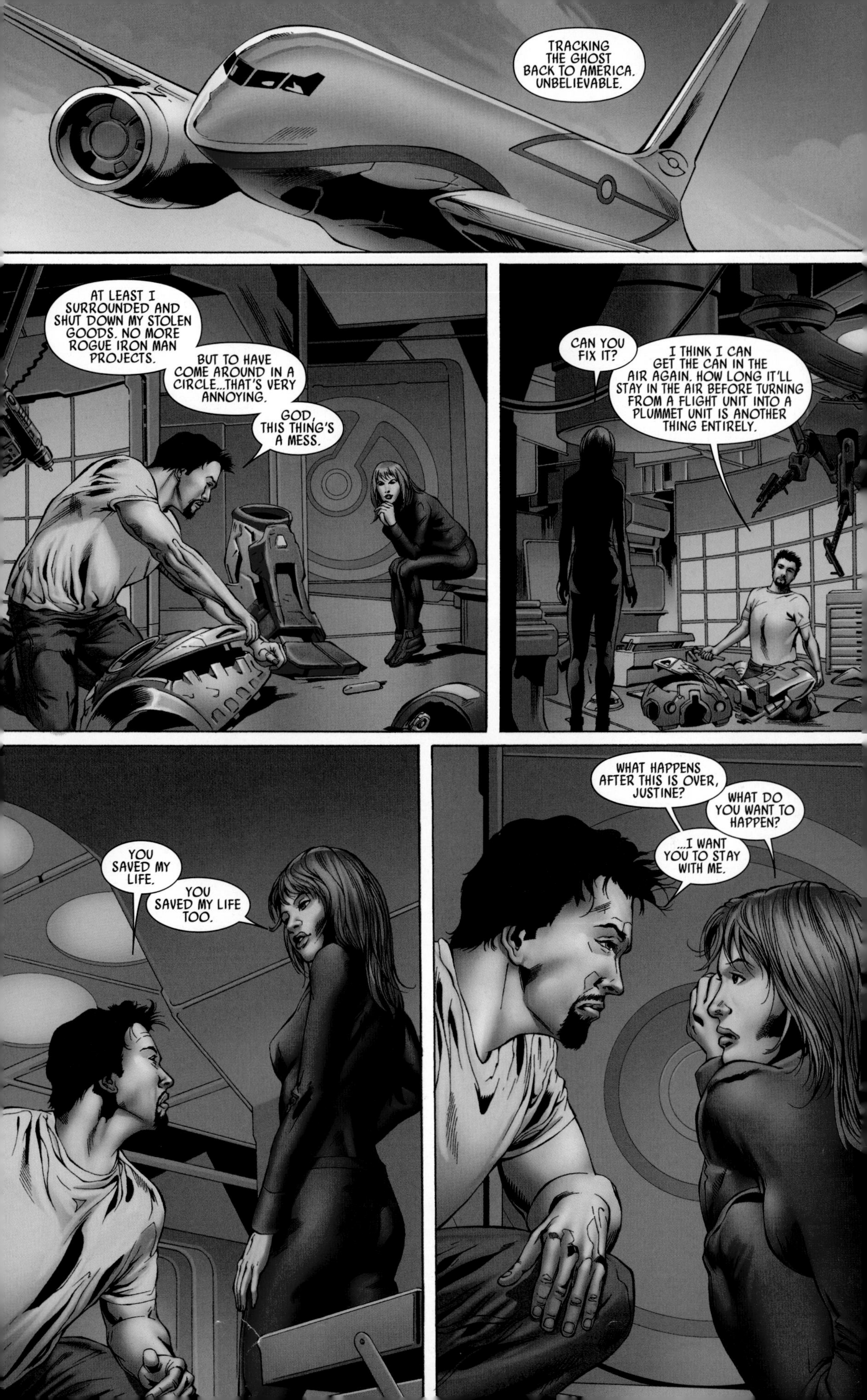
TRACKING THE GHOST BACK TO AMERICA. UNBELIEVABLE.
AT LEAST I SURROUNDED AND SHUT DOWN MY STOLEN GOODS. NO MORE ROGUE IRON MAN PROJECTS.
BUT TO HAVE COME AROUND IN A CIRCLE...THAT'S VERY ANNOYING.
GOD, THIS THING'S A MESS.
CAN YOU FIX IT?
I THINK I CAN GET THE CAN IN THE AIR AGAIN. HOW LONG IT'LL STAY IN THE AIR BEFORE TURNING FROM A FLIGHT UNIT INTO A PLUMMET UNIT IS ANOTHER THING ENTIRELY.
YOU SAVED MY LIFE.
YOU SAVED MY LIFE TOO.
WHAT HAPPENS AFTER THIS IS OVER, JUSTINE?
WHAT DO YOU WANT TO HAPPEN?
...I WANT YOU TO STAY WITH ME.

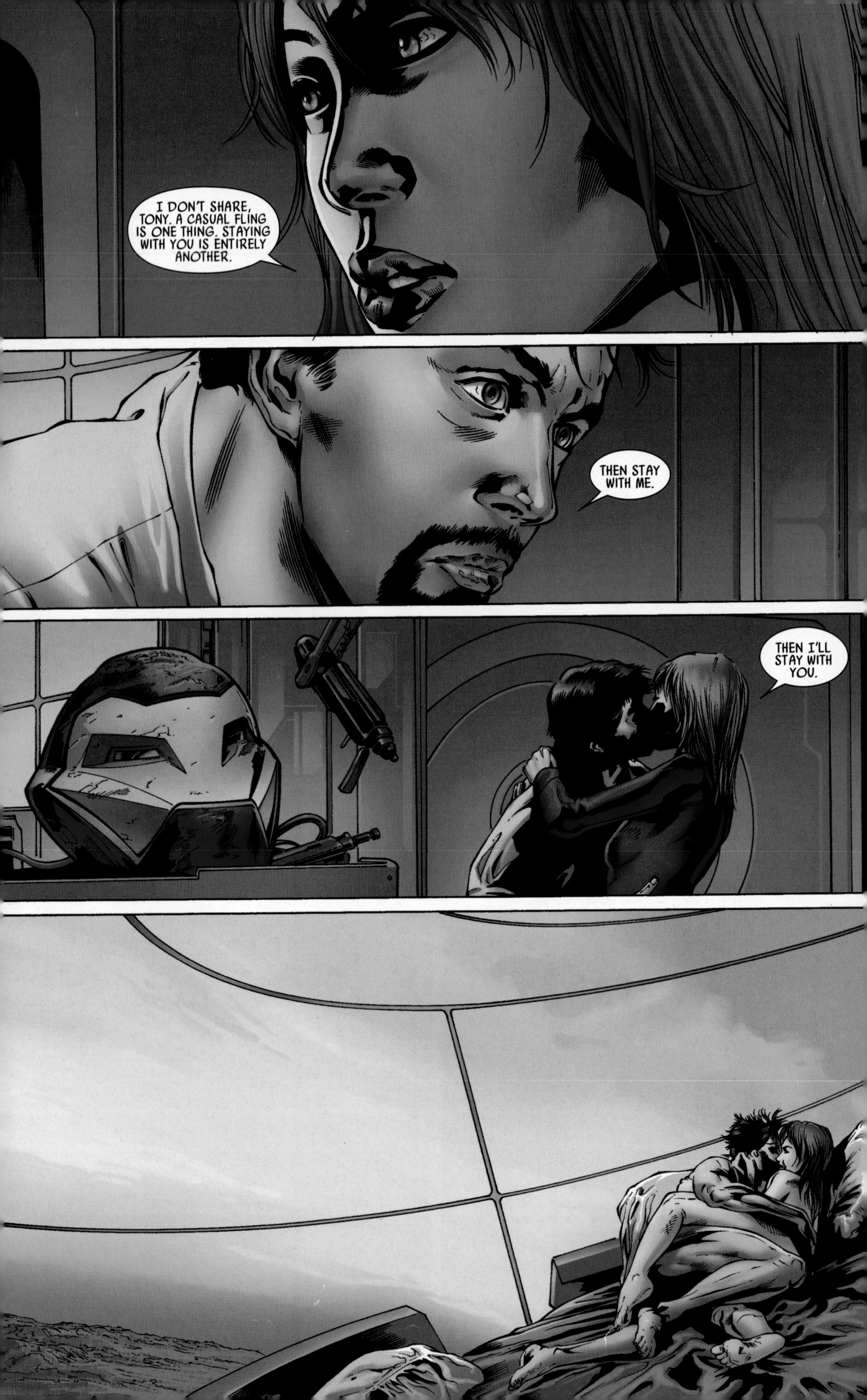
I DON'T SHARE, TONY. A CASUAL FLING IS ONE THING. STAYING WITH YOU IS ENTIRELY ANOTHER.
THEN STAY WITH ME.
THEN I'LL STAY WITH YOU.

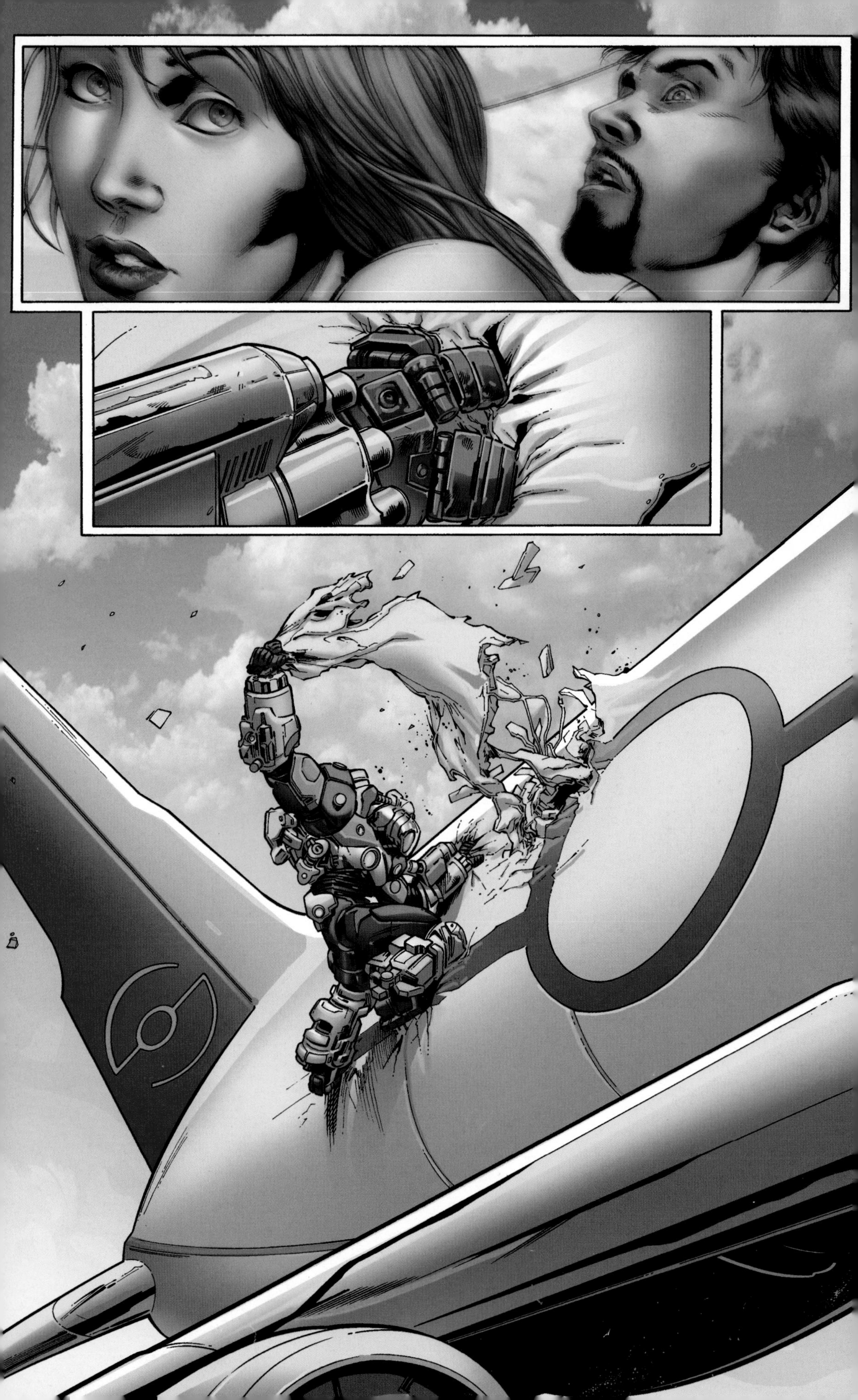

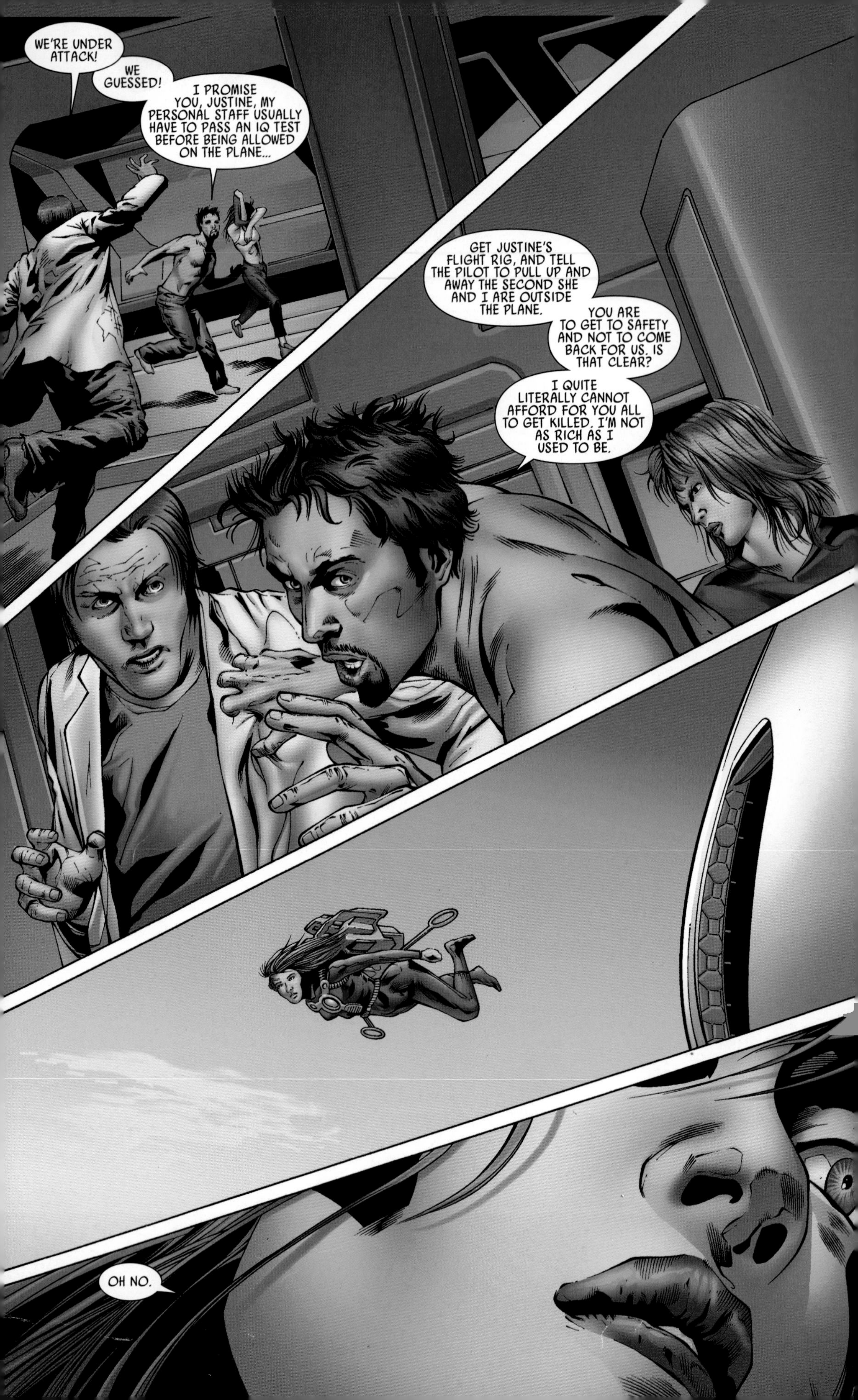
WE'RE UNDER ATTACK!
WE GUESSED!
I PROMISE YOU, JUSTINE, MY PERSONAL STAFF USUALLY HAVE TO PASS AN IQ TEST BEFORE BEING ALLOWED ON THE PLANE...
GET JUSTINE'S FLIGHT RIG, AND TELL THE PILOT TO PULL UP AND AWAY THE SECOND SHE AND I ARE OUTSIDE THE PLANE.
YOU ARE TO GET TO SAFETY AND NOT TO COME BACK FOR US. IS THAT CLEAR?
I QUITE LITERALLY CANNOT AFFORD FOR YOU ALL TO GET KILLED. I'M NOT AS RICH AS I USED TO BE.
OH NO.

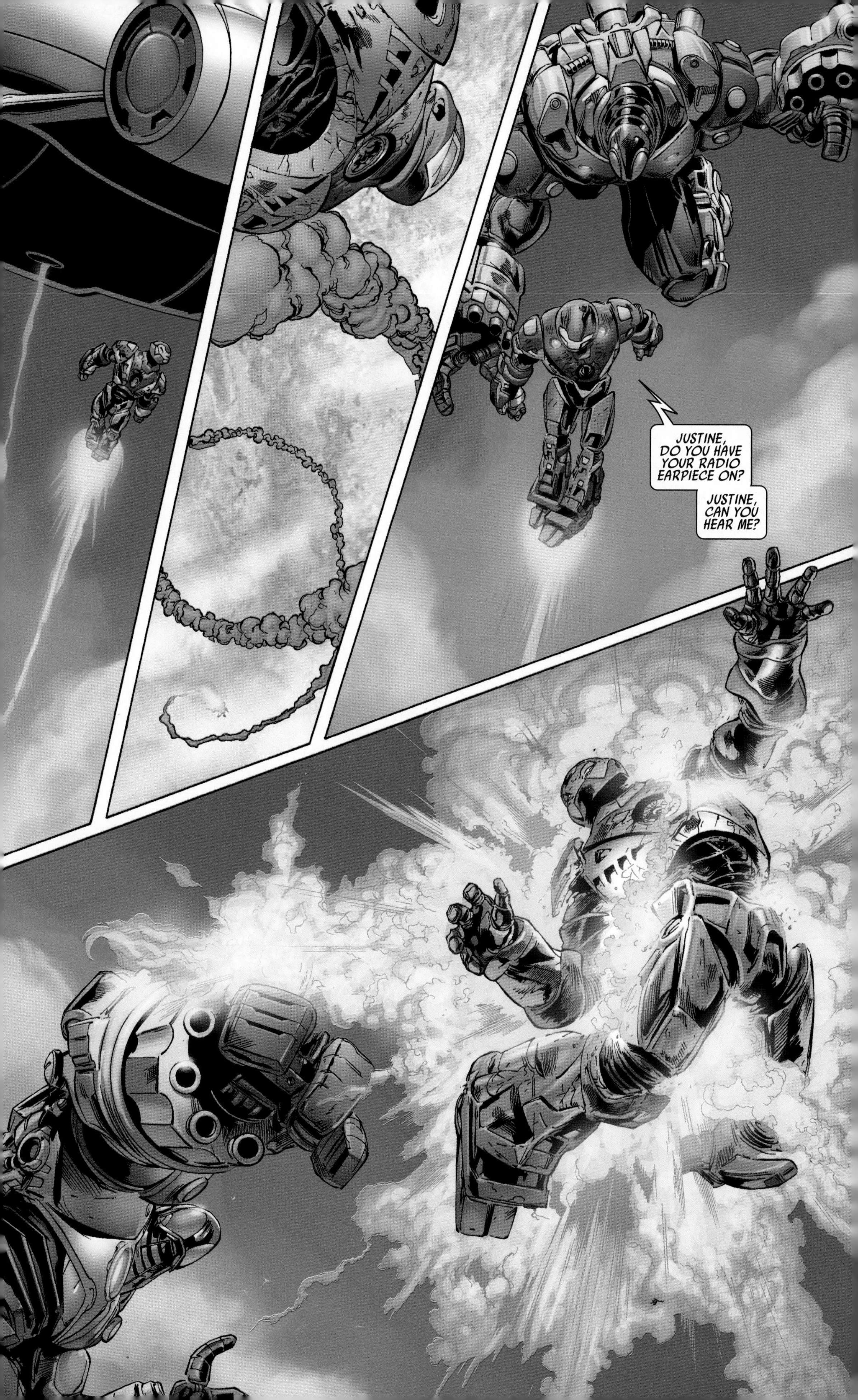
JUSTINE, DO YOU HAVE YOUR RADIO EARPIECE ON?
JUSTINE, CAN YOU HEAR ME?

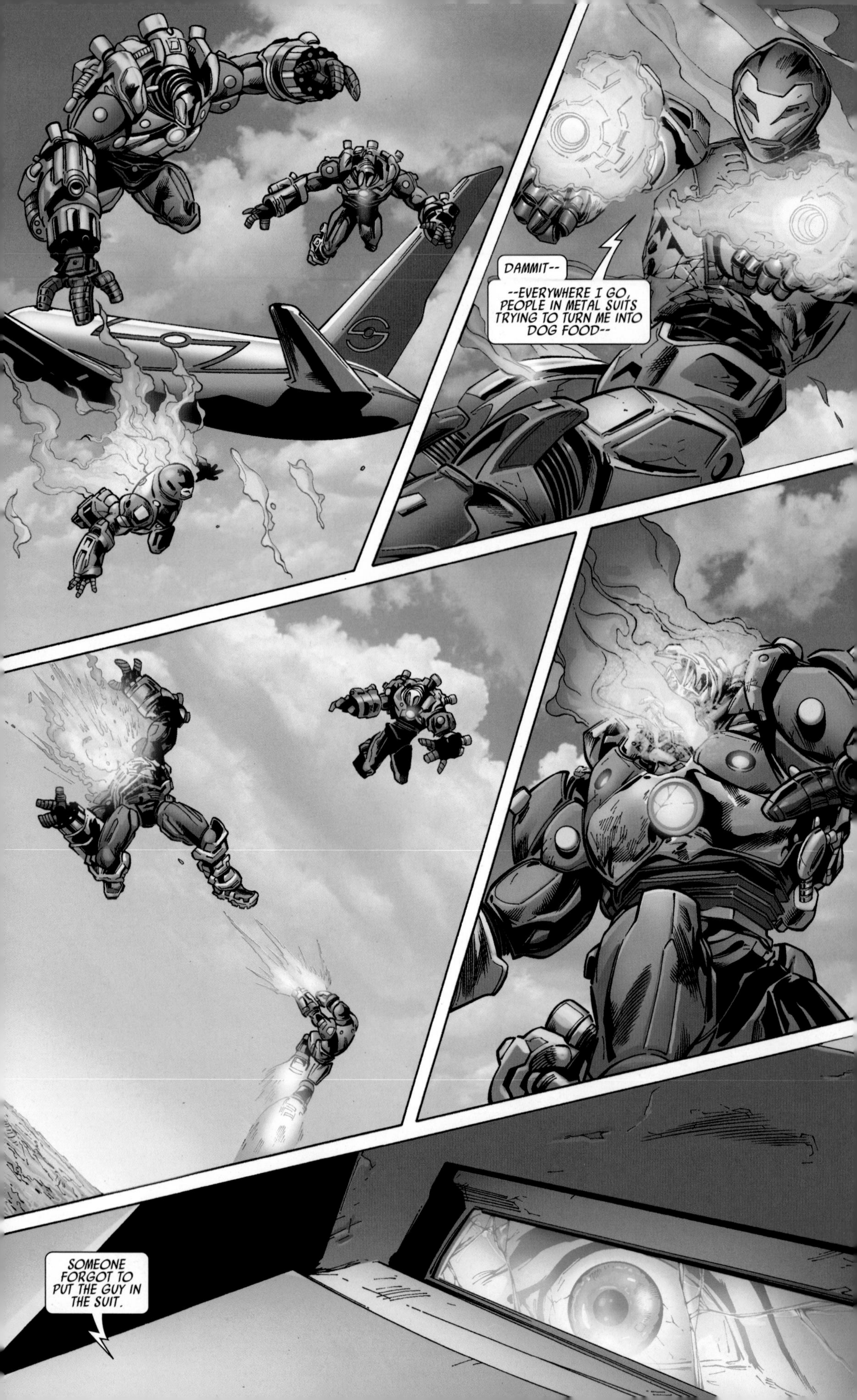
DAMMIT--
--EVERYWHERE I GO, PEOPLE IN METAL SUITS TRYING TO TURN ME INTO DOG FOOD--
SOMEONE FORGOT TO PUT THE GUY IN THE SUIT.

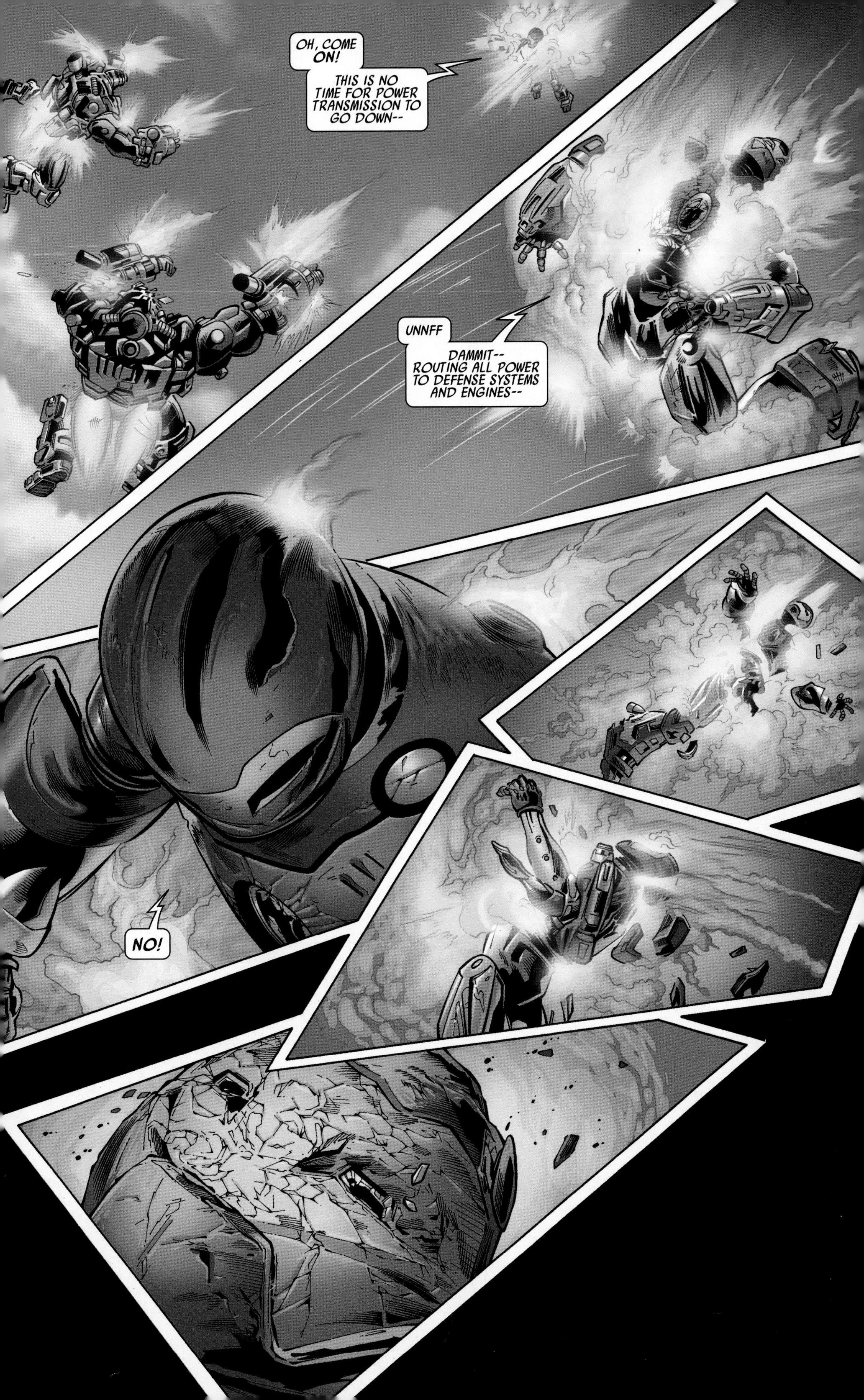
OH, COME ON!
THIS IS NO TIME FOR POWER TRANSMISSION TO GO DOWN--
UNNFF
DAMMIT-- ROUTING ALL POWER TO DEFENSE SYSTEMS AND ENGINES--
NO!

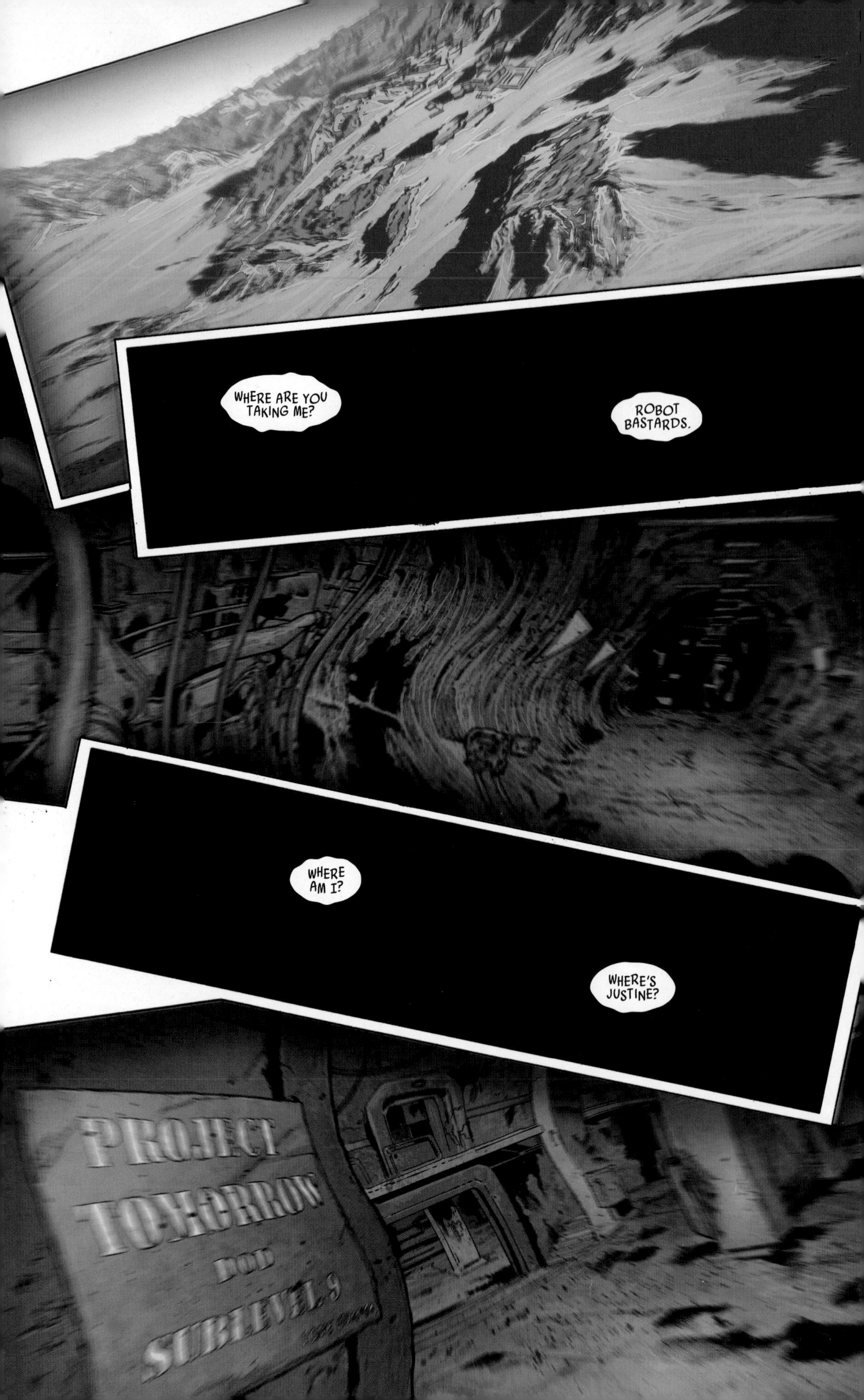
WHERE ARE YOU TAKING ME?
ROBOT BASTARDS.
WHERE AM I?
WHERE'S JUSTINE?
PROJECT TOMORROW
DOD
SUBLEVEL 9

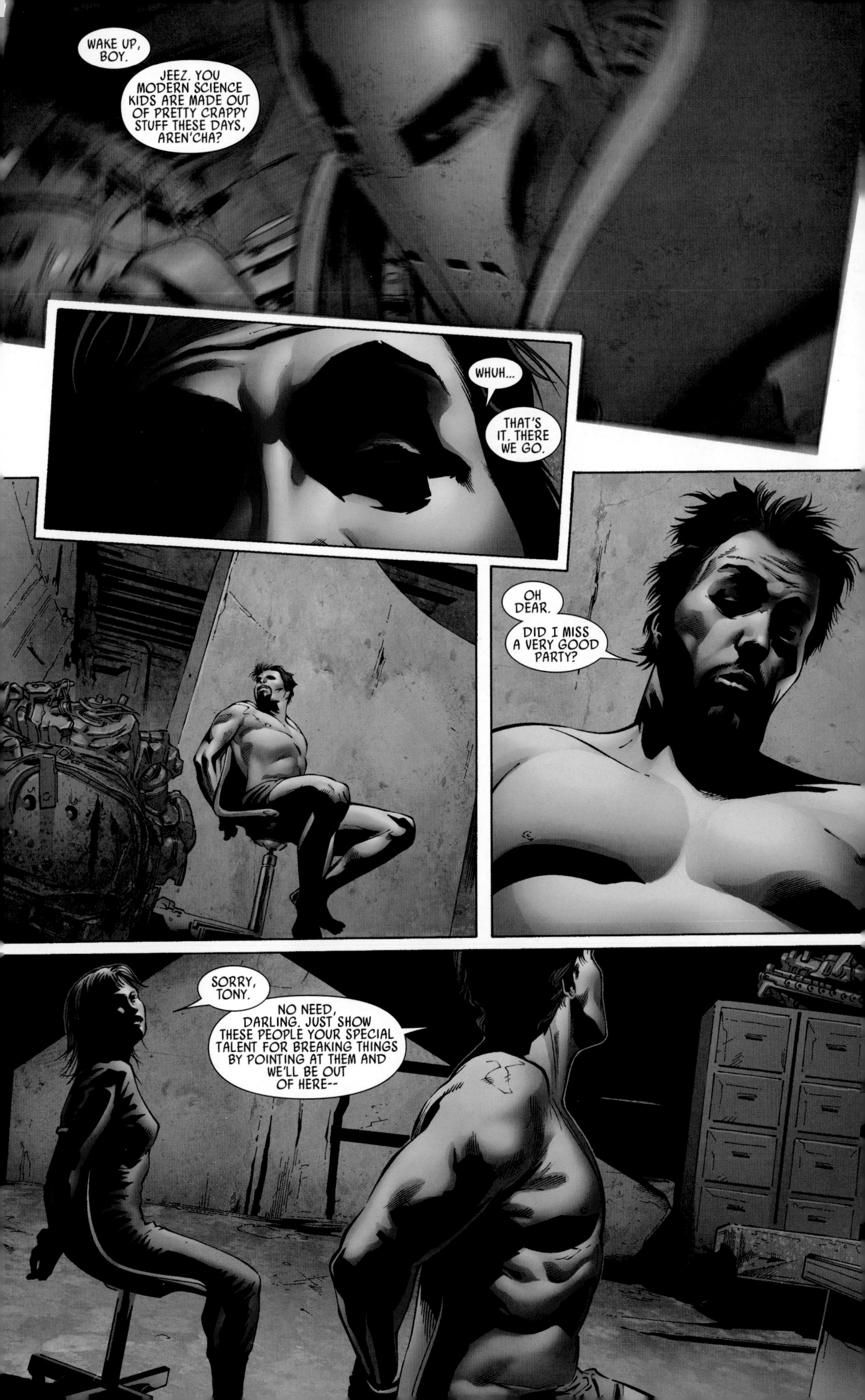
WAKE UP, BOY.
JEEZ. YOU MODERN SCIENCE KIDS ARE MADE OUT OF PRETTY CRAPPY STUFF THESE DAYS, AREN'CHA?
WHUH...
THAT'S IT. THERE WE GO.
OH DEAR.
DID I MISS A VERY GOOD PARTY?
SORRY, TONY.
NO NEED, DARLING. JUST SHOW THESE PEOPLE YOUR SPECIAL TALENT FOR BREAKING THINGS BY POINTING AT THEM AND WE'LL BE OUT OF HERE--

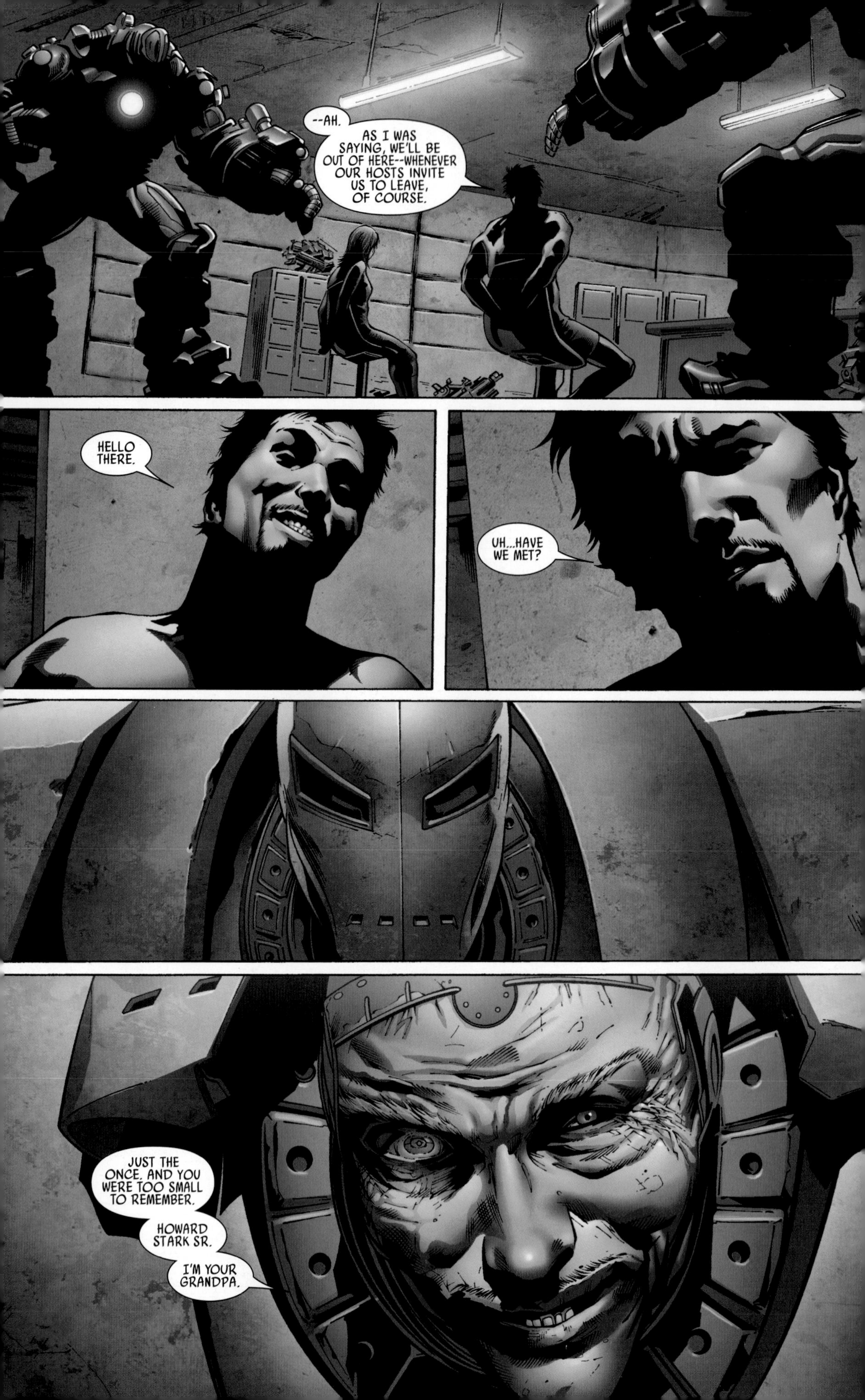
--AH.
AS I WAS SAYING, WE'LL BE OUT OF HERE--WHENEVER OUR HOSTS INVITE US TO LEAVE, OF COURSE.
HELLO THERE.
UH...HAVE WE MET?
JUST THE ONCE. AND YOU WERE TOO SMALL TO REMEMBER.
HOWARD STARK SR.
I'M YOUR GRANDPA.

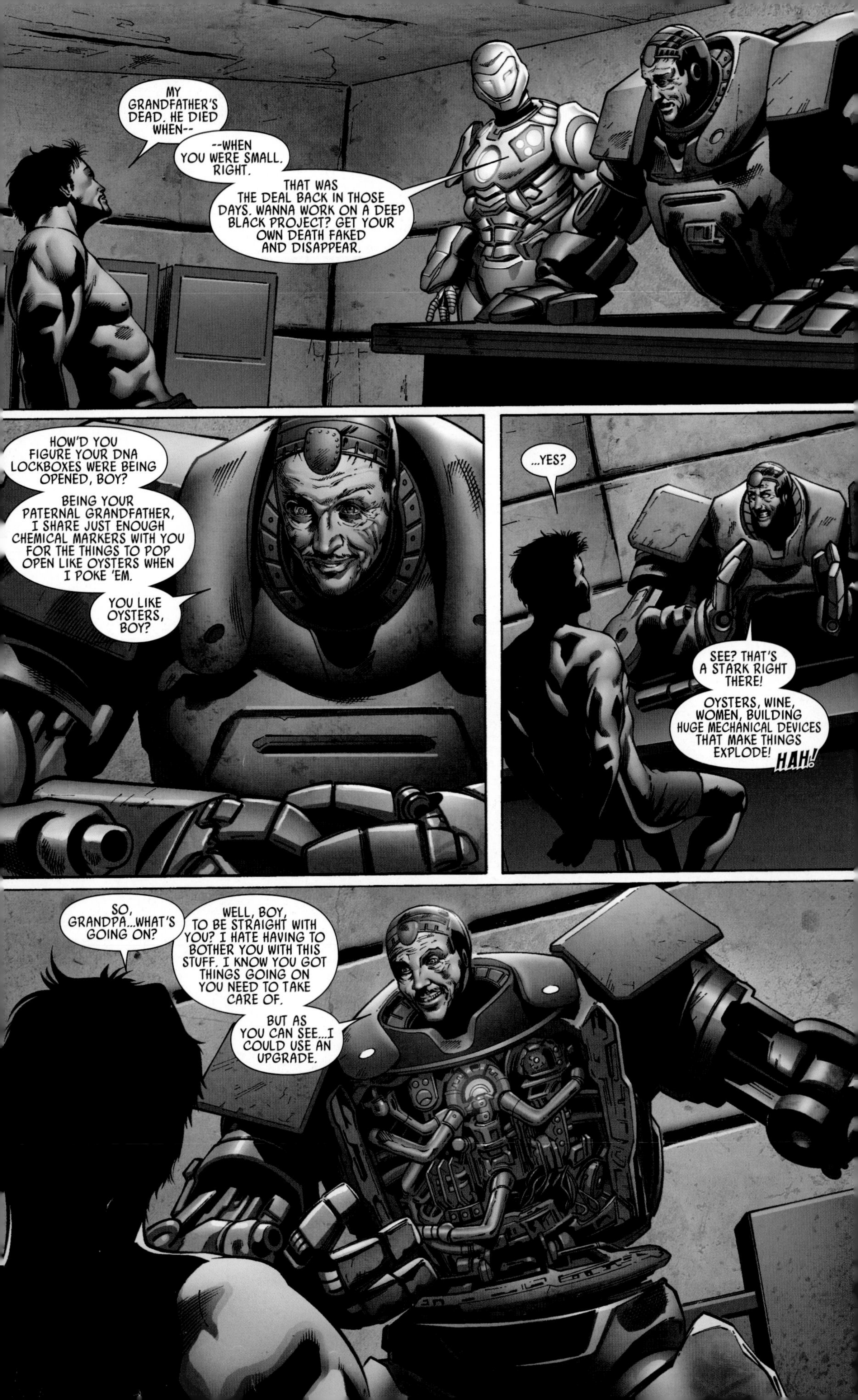
MY GRANDFATHER'S DEAD. HE DIED WHEN--
--WHEN YOU WERE SMALL. RIGHT.
THAT WAS THE DEAL BACK IN THOSE DAYS. WANNA WORK ON A DEEP BLACK PROJECT? GET YOUR OWN DEATH FAKED AND DISAPPEAR.
HOW'D YOU FIGURE YOUR DNA LOCKBOXES WERE BEING OPENED, BOY?
BEING YOUR PATERNAL GRANDFATHER, I SHARE JUST ENOUGH CHEMICAL MARKERS WITH YOU FOR THE THINGS TO POP OPEN LIKE OYSTERS WHEN I POKE 'EM.
YOU LIKE OYSTERS, BOY?
...YES?
SEE? THAT'S A STARK RIGHT THERE!
OYSTERS, WINE, WOMEN, BUILDING HUGE MECHANICAL DEVICES THAT MAKE THINGS EXPLODE!
HAH!
SO, GRANDPA...WHAT'S GOING ON?
WELL, BOY, TO BE STRAIGHT WITH YOU? I HATE HAVING TO BOTHER YOU WITH THIS STUFF. I KNOW YOU GOT THINGS GOING ON YOU NEED TO TAKE CARE OF.
BUT AS YOU CAN SEE...I COULD USE AN UPGRADE.

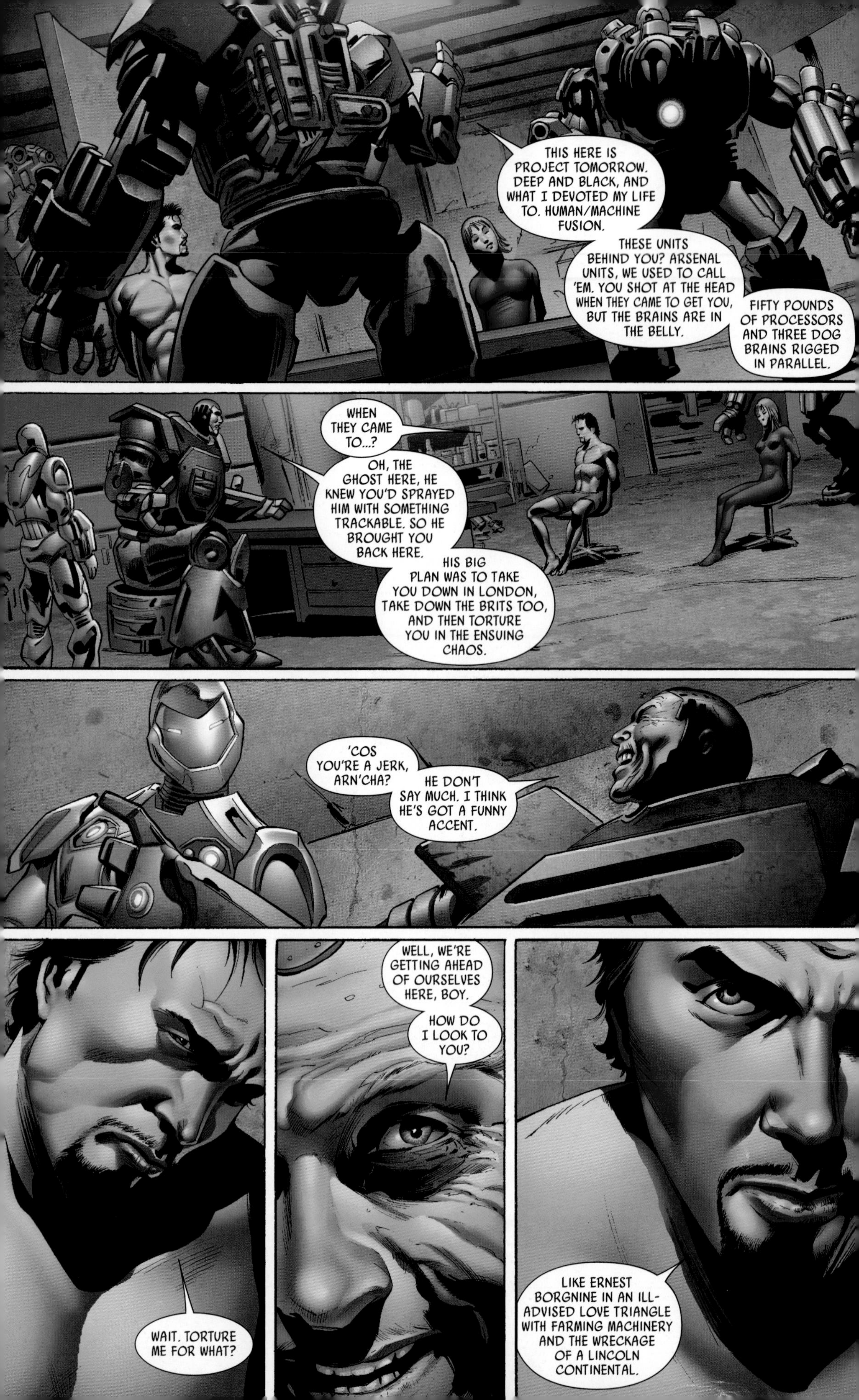
THIS HERE IS PROJECT TOMORROW. DEEP AND BLACK, AND WHAT I DEVOTED MY LIFE TO. HUMAN/MACHINE FUSION.
THESE UNITS BEHIND YOU? ARSENAL UNITS, WE USED TO CALL 'EM. YOU SHOT AT THE HEAD WHEN THEY CAME TO GET YOU, BUT THE BRAINS ARE IN THE BELLY.
FIFTY POUNDS OF PROCESSORS AND THREE DOG BRAINS RIGGED IN PARALLEL.
WHEN THEY CAME TO...?
OH, THE GHOST HERE, HE KNEW YOU'D SPRAYED HIM WITH SOMETHING TRACKABLE. SO HE BROUGHT YOU BACK HERE.
HIS BIG PLAN WAS TO TAKE YOU DOWN IN LONDON, TAKE DOWN THE BRITS TOO, AND THEN TORTURE YOU IN THE ENSUING CHAOS.
'COS YOU'RE A JERK, ARN'CHA?
HE DON'T SAY MUCH. I THINK HE'S GOT A FUNNY ACCENT.
WAIT. TORTURE ME FOR WHAT?
WELL, WE'RE GETTING AHEAD OF OURSELVES HERE, BOY.
HOW DO I LOOK TO YOU?
LIKE ERNEST BORGNINE IN AN ILL-ADVISED LOVE TRIANGLE WITH FARMING MACHINERY AND THE WRECKAGE OF A LINCOLN CONTINENTAL.

AND THERE'S YOU, DOING THE SAME WORK I'M DOING AND HAVING NO IDEA I WAS EVEN ALIVE.

IT'S IN THE GENES, BOY. THIS IS WHAT WE DO. WE WORK FOR TOMORROW.

AND YOU... YOU'RE AWFULLY GOOD AT IT.

HA!

A LITTLE BIT OLD SCHOOL, HUH?

LITTLE BIT.

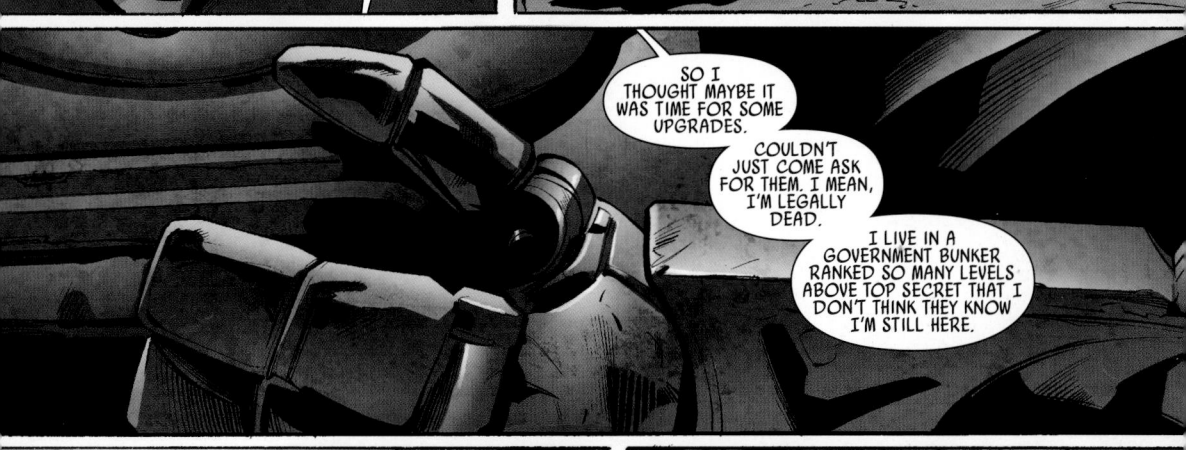

SO I THOUGHT MAYBE IT WAS TIME FOR SOME UPGRADES.

COULDN'T JUST COME ASK FOR THEM. I MEAN, I'M LEGALLY DEAD.

I LIVE IN A GOVERNMENT BUNKER RANKED SO MANY LEVELS ABOVE TOP SECRET THAT I DON'T THINK THEY KNOW I'M STILL HERE.

BUT ONE DAY--*ONE DAY*--THEY'RE GOING TO COME TO ME. THEY'RE GOING TO COME TO ME AND THEY'RE GONNA NEED THINGS, BOY.

AND I'M GOING TO BE THE BEST I CAN BE WHEN THAT DAY COMES.

SO YOU STOLE MY WORK.

WELL, NOT ME PERSONALLY. I COULDN'T DO IT IN PERSON, COULD I?

JUSTINE WAS A WELL-MOTIVATED YOUNG LADY.

I SUPPOSE THAT IF I'D MADE GOOD ON MY DEAL AND RELEASED THE NANOFLEET DATA TO HER, SHE MIGHT NOT HAVE GONE BACK IN AND GOTTEN HERSELF CAUGHT.

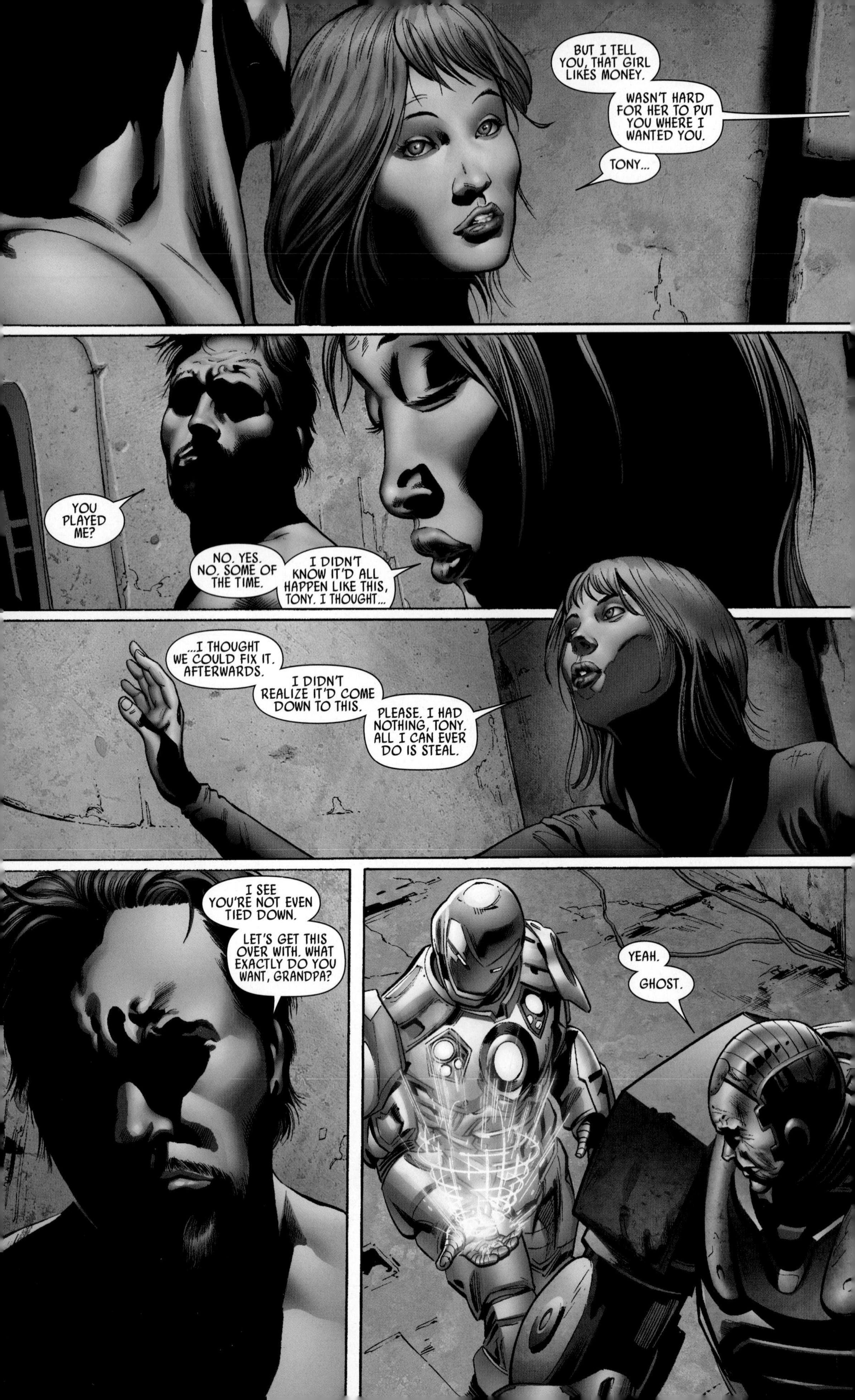
BUT I TELL YOU, THAT GIRL LIKES MONEY.
WASN'T HARD FOR HER TO PUT YOU WHERE I WANTED YOU.
TONY...
YOU PLAYED ME?
NO. YES. NO. SOME OF THE TIME.
I DIDN'T KNOW IT'D ALL HAPPEN LIKE THIS, TONY. I THOUGHT...
...I THOUGHT WE COULD FIX IT. AFTERWARDS.
I DIDN'T REALIZE IT'D COME DOWN TO THIS.
PLEASE. I HAD NOTHING, TONY. ALL I CAN EVER DO IS STEAL.
I SEE YOU'RE NOT EVEN TIED DOWN.
LET'S GET THIS OVER WITH. WHAT EXACTLY DO YOU WANT, GRANDPA?
YEAH.
GHOST.

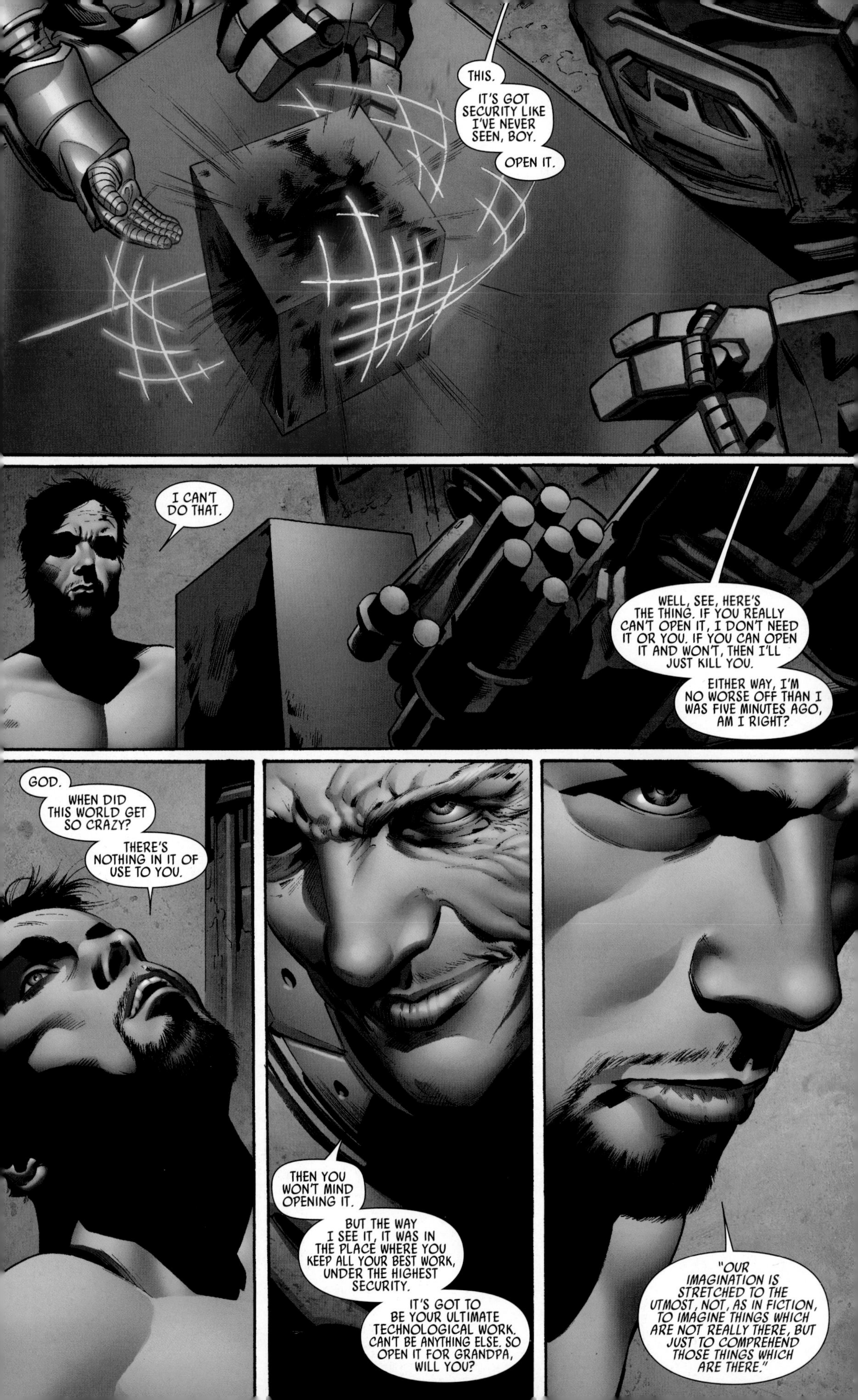
THIS.
IT'S GOT SECURITY LIKE I'VE NEVER SEEN, BOY.
OPEN IT.
I CAN'T DO THAT.
WELL, SEE, HERE'S THE THING. IF YOU REALLY CAN'T OPEN IT, I DON'T NEED IT OR YOU. IF YOU CAN OPEN IT AND WON'T, THEN I'LL JUST KILL YOU.
EITHER WAY, I'M NO WORSE OFF THAN I WAS FIVE MINUTES AGO, AM I RIGHT?
GOD.
WHEN DID THIS WORLD GET SO CRAZY?
THERE'S NOTHING IN IT OF USE TO YOU.
THEN YOU WON'T MIND OPENING IT.
BUT THE WAY I SEE IT, IT WAS IN THE PLACE WHERE YOU KEEP ALL YOUR BEST WORK, UNDER THE HIGHEST SECURITY.
IT'S GOT TO BE YOUR ULTIMATE TECHNOLOGICAL WORK. CAN'T BE ANYTHING ELSE. SO OPEN IT FOR GRANDPA, WILL YOU?
"OUR IMAGINATION IS STRETCHED TO THE UTMOST, NOT, AS IN FICTION, TO IMAGINE THINGS WHICH ARE NOT REALLY THERE, BUT JUST TO COMPREHEND THOSE THINGS WHICH ARE THERE."

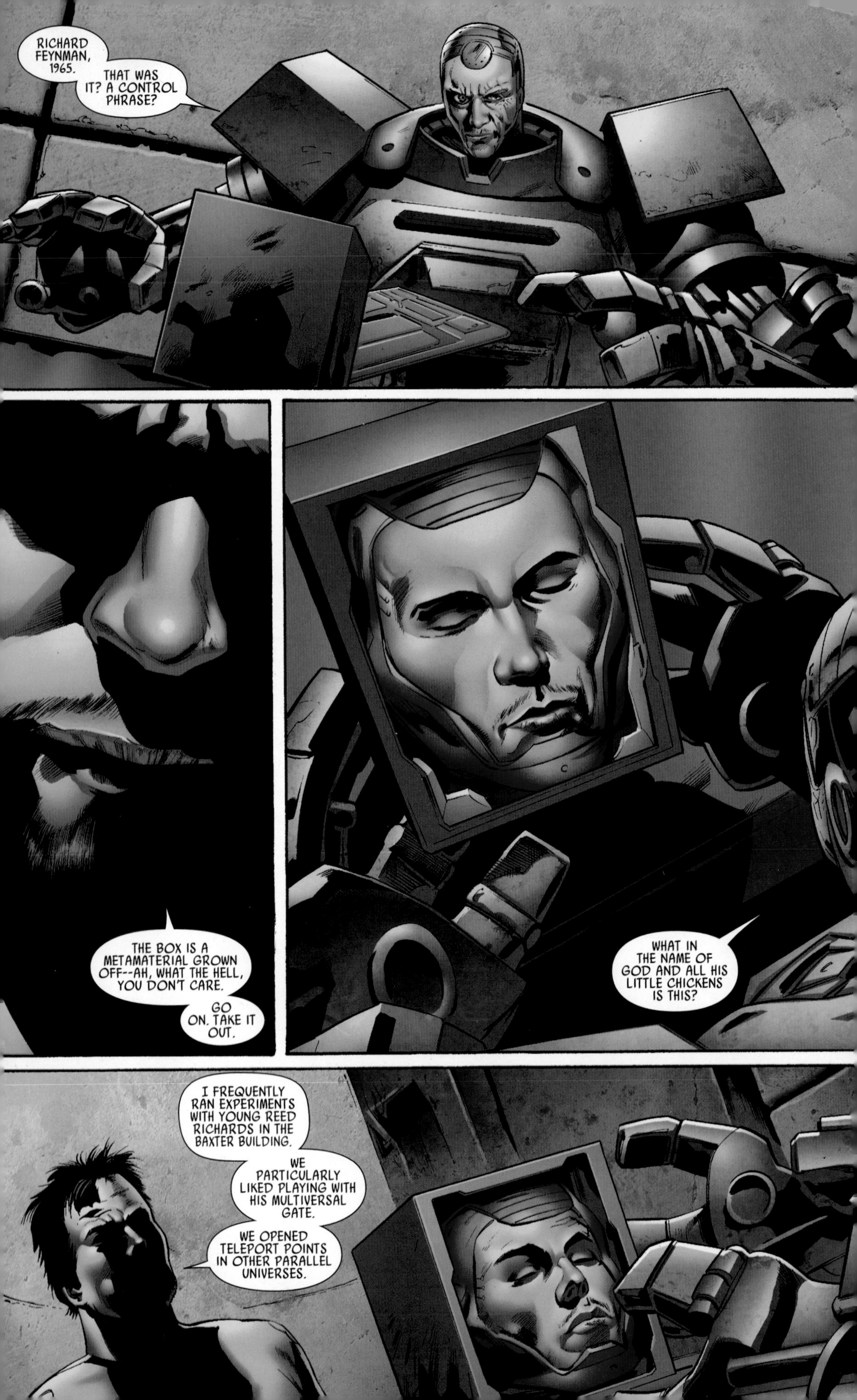
RICHARD FEYNMAN, 1965.
THAT WAS IT? A CONTROL PHRASE?
THE BOX IS A METAMATERIAL GROWN OFF--AH, WHAT THE HELL, YOU DON'T CARE.
GO ON. TAKE IT OUT.
WHAT IN THE NAME OF GOD AND ALL HIS LITTLE CHICKENS IS THIS?
I FREQUENTLY RAN EXPERIMENTS WITH YOUNG REED RICHARDS IN THE BAXTER BUILDING.
WE PARTICULARLY LIKED PLAYING WITH HIS MULTIVERSAL GATE.
WE OPENED TELEPORT POINTS IN OTHER PARALLEL UNIVERSES.

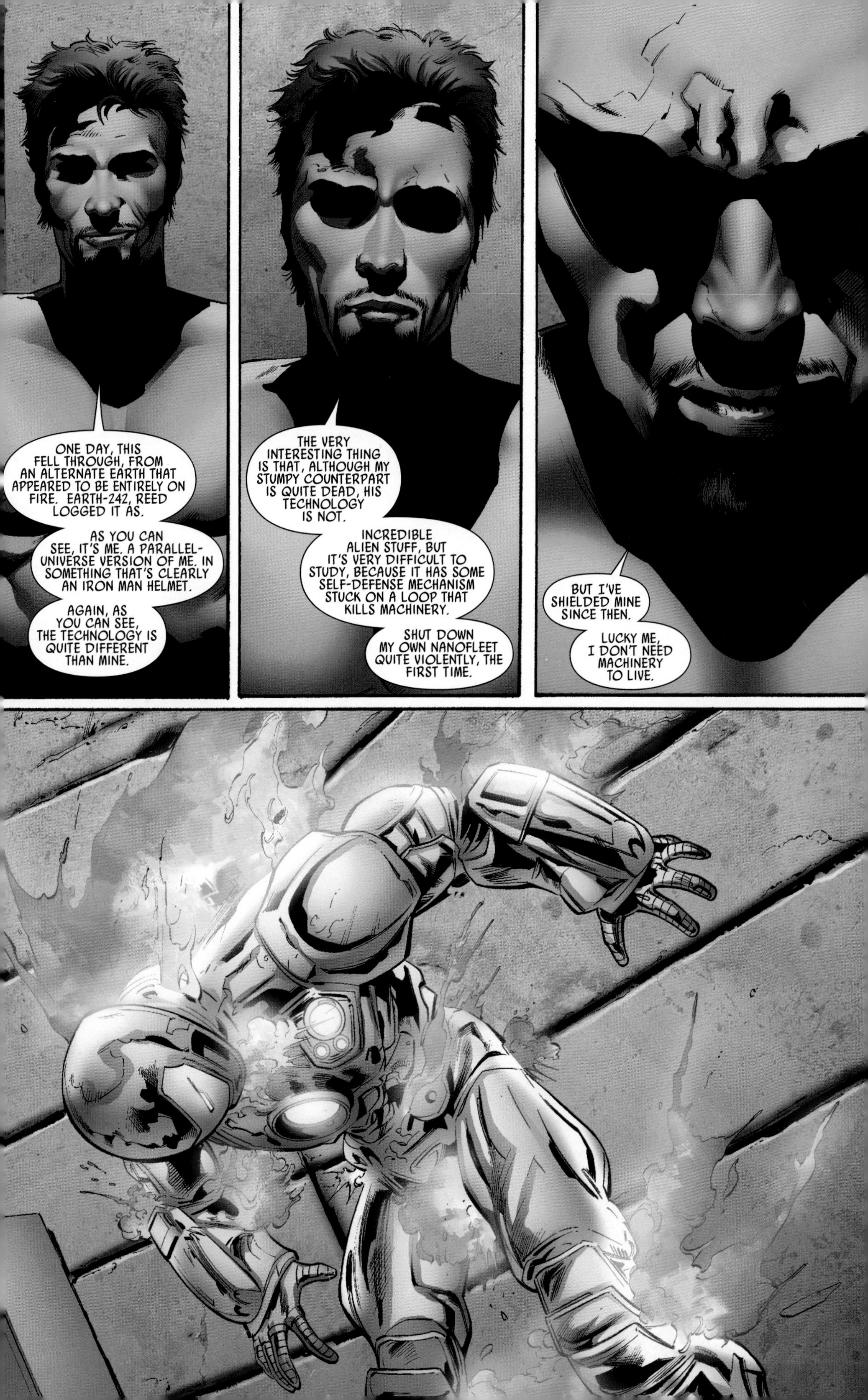
ONE DAY, THIS FELL THROUGH, FROM AN ALTERNATE EARTH THAT APPEARED TO BE ENTIRELY ON FIRE. EARTH-242, REED LOGGED IT AS.
AS YOU CAN SEE, IT'S ME. A PARALLEL-UNIVERSE VERSION OF ME. IN SOMETHING THAT'S CLEARLY AN IRON MAN HELMET.
AGAIN, AS YOU CAN SEE, THE TECHNOLOGY IS QUITE DIFFERENT THAN MINE.
THE VERY INTERESTING THING IS THAT, ALTHOUGH MY STUMPY COUNTERPART IS QUITE DEAD, HIS TECHNOLOGY IS NOT.
INCREDIBLE ALIEN STUFF, BUT IT'S VERY DIFFICULT TO STUDY, BECAUSE IT HAS SOME SELF-DEFENSE MECHANISM STUCK ON A LOOP THAT KILLS MACHINERY.
SHUT DOWN MY OWN NANOFLEET QUITE VIOLENTLY, THE FIRST TIME.
BUT I'VE SHIELDED MINE SINCE THEN.
LUCKY ME, I DON'T NEED MACHINERY TO LIVE.

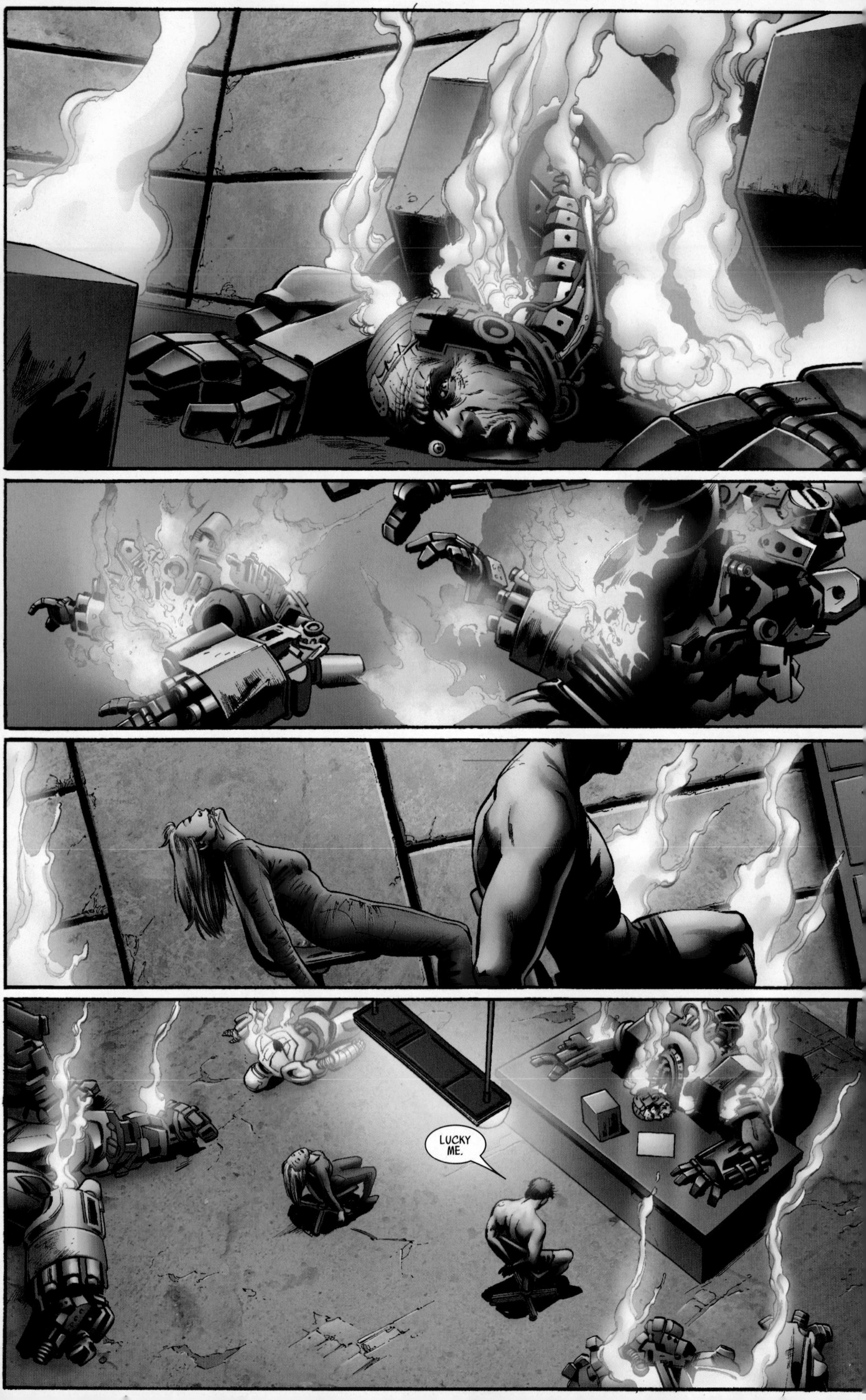
LUCKY ME.

BERLIN

HERE'S TO KILLING THINGS.

HERE'S TO STAMPING OUT EVIL. HEH. HERE'S TO LIARS AND CHEATS AND WHAT THEY DESERVE.

HERE'S TO THE LIFE OF A BACHELOR AND AN ORPHAN.

HERE'S TO SAVING THE WORLD.

FROM ME.

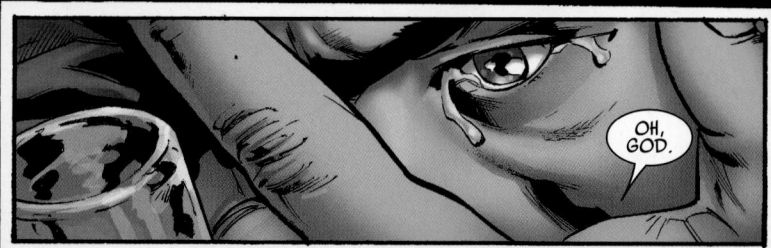

OH, GOD.

#1 VARIANT
BY STEVE KURTH

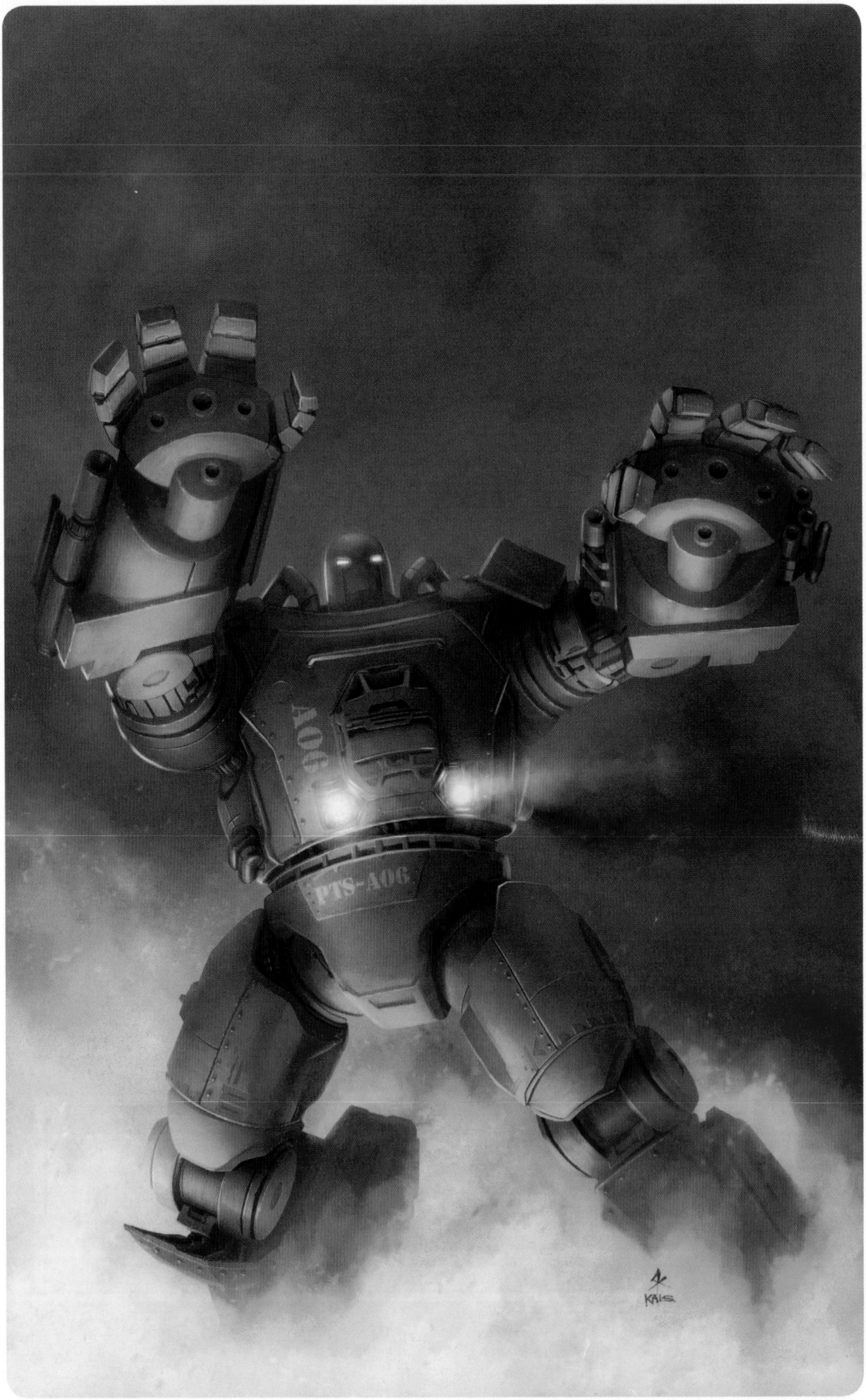
AO6
PTS-AO6

1 SKETCH VARIANT
BY STEVE KURTH

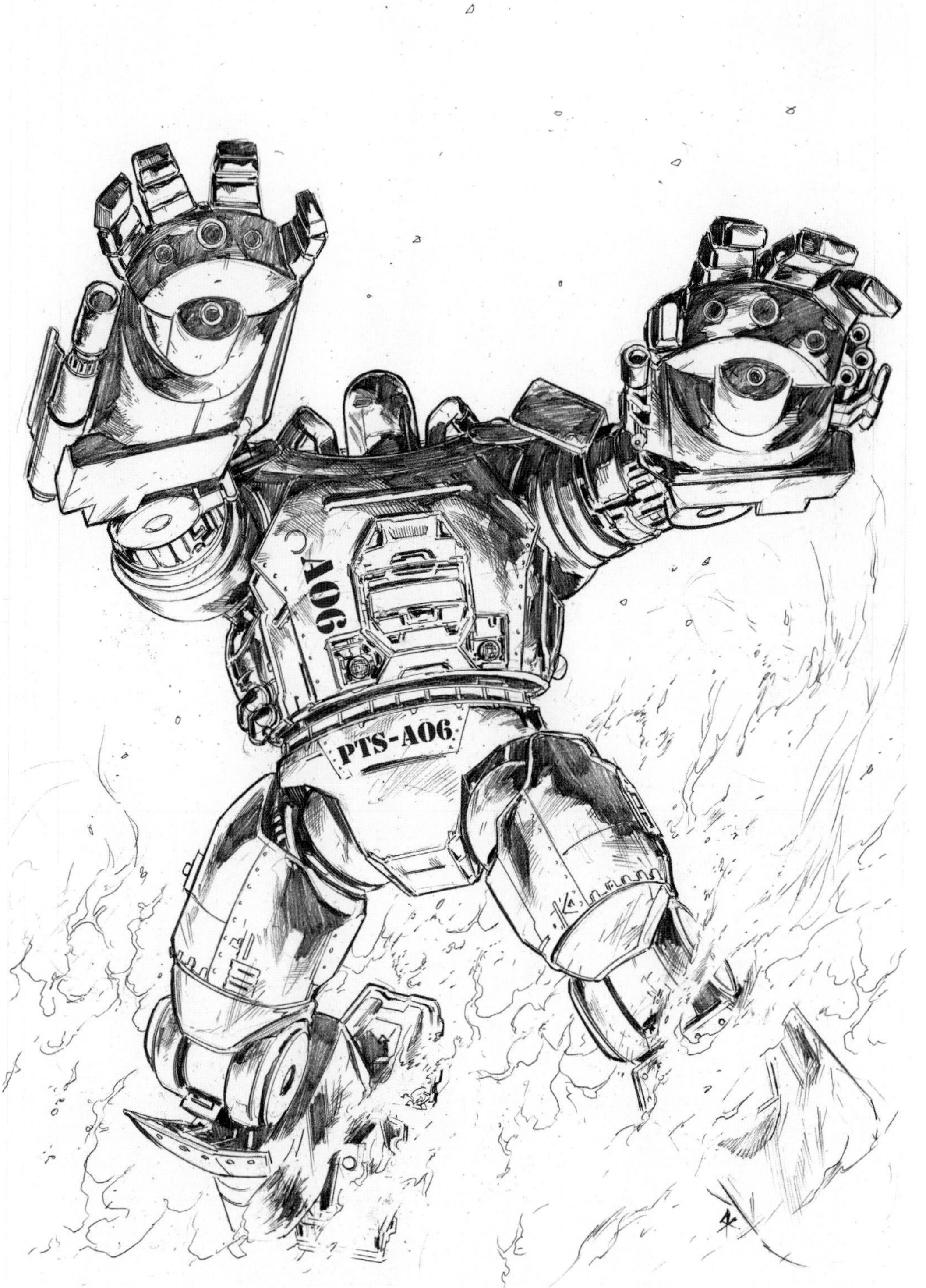

A06
PTS-A06

#1 VARIANT COVER PROCESS
BY STEVE KURTH

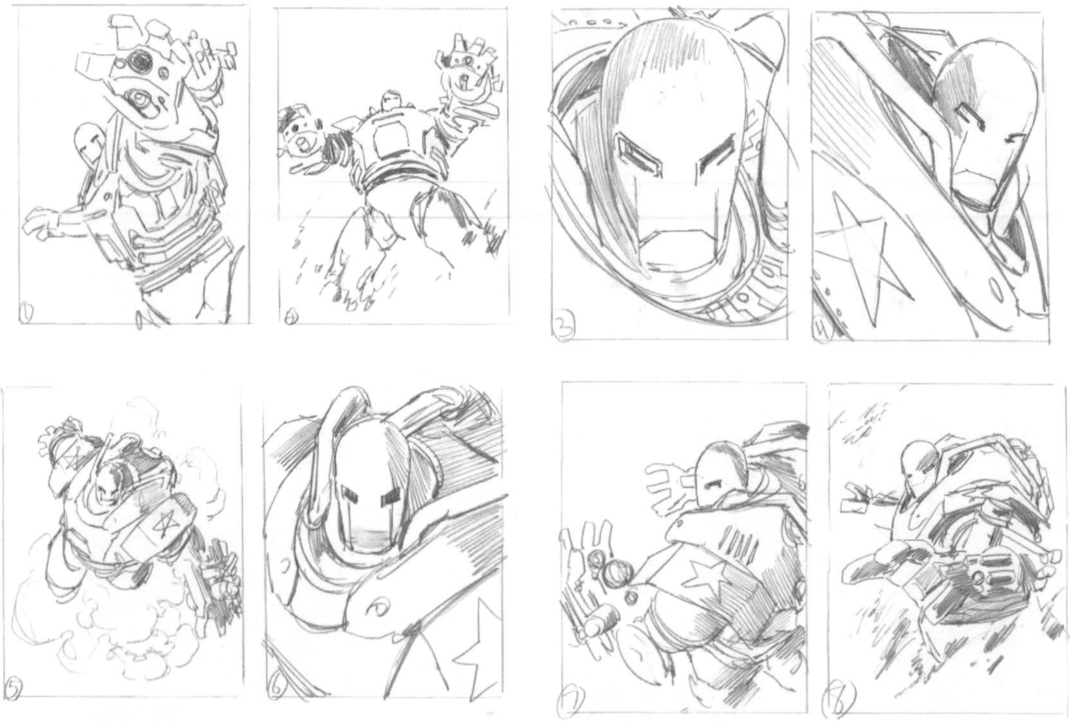

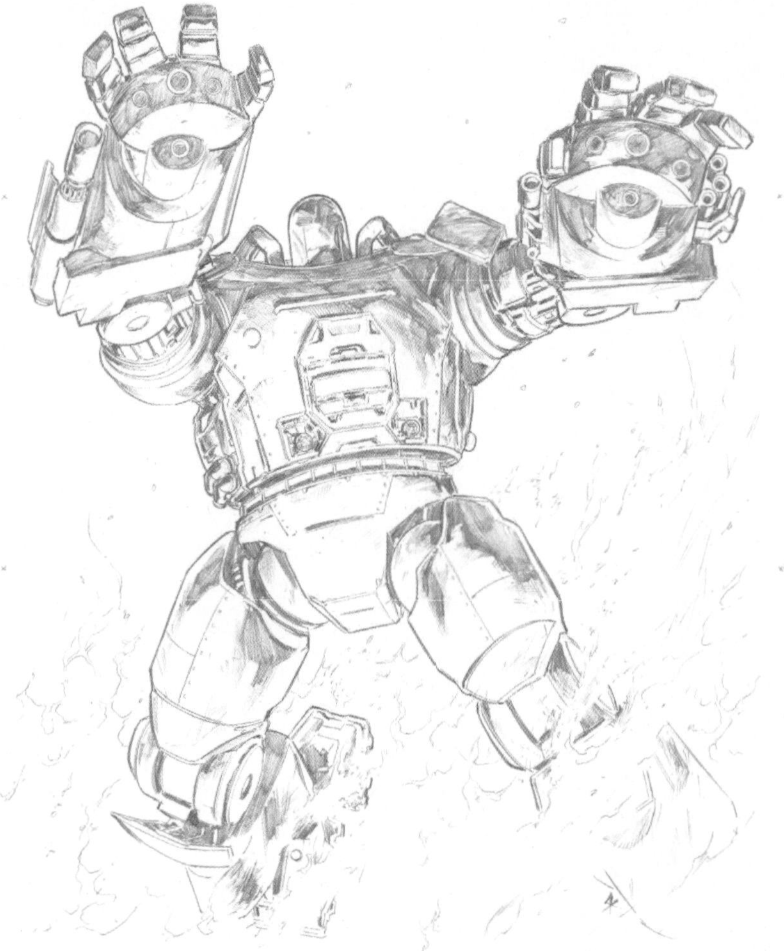

#1 COVER PROCESS
BY BRANDON PETERSON

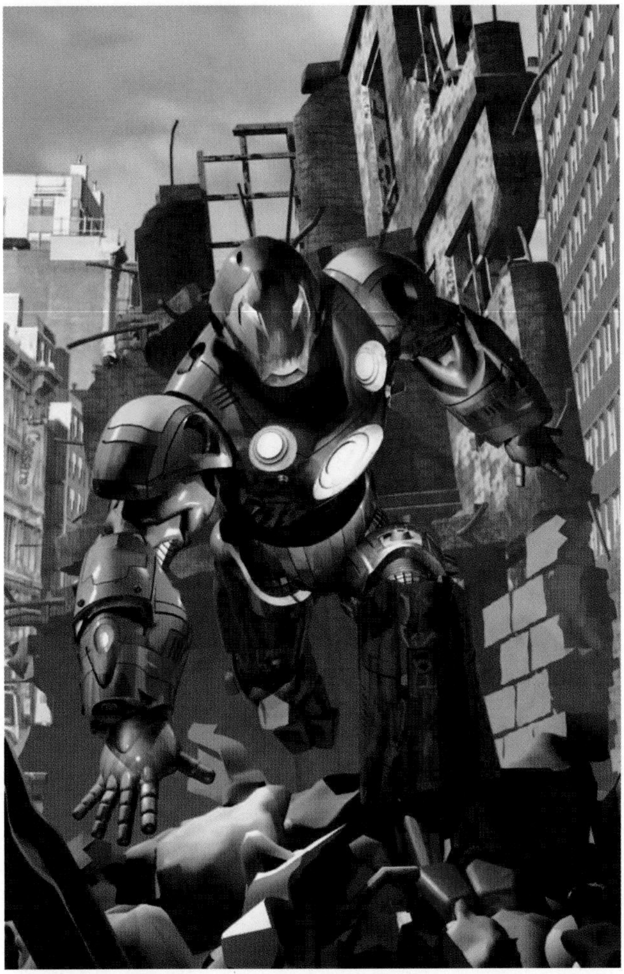

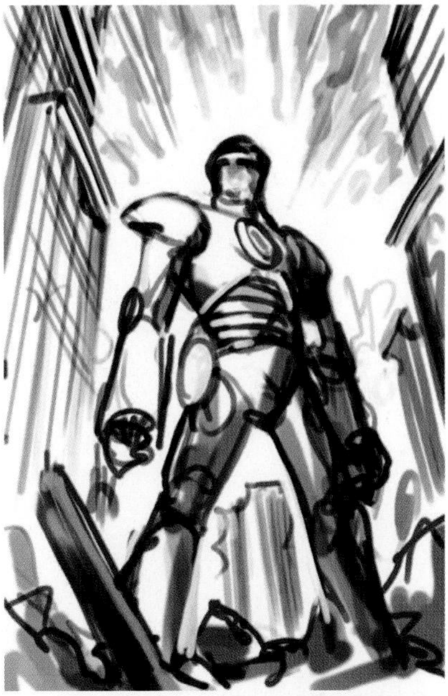

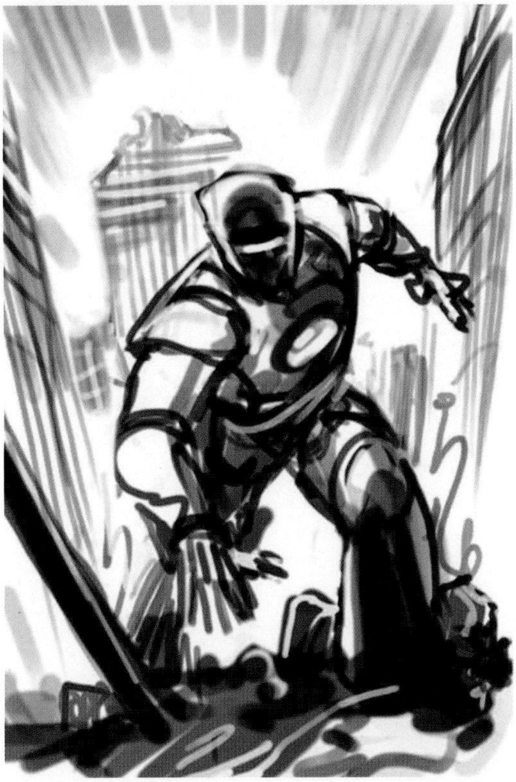

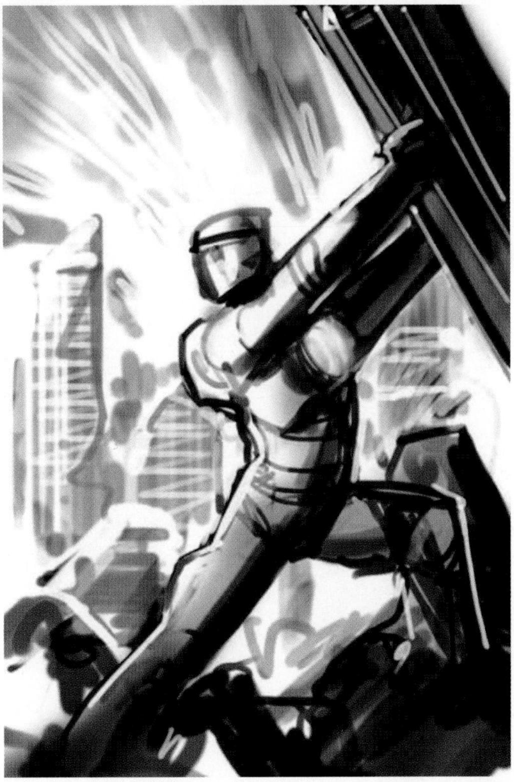

CHARACTER DESIGNS
BY STEVE KURTH

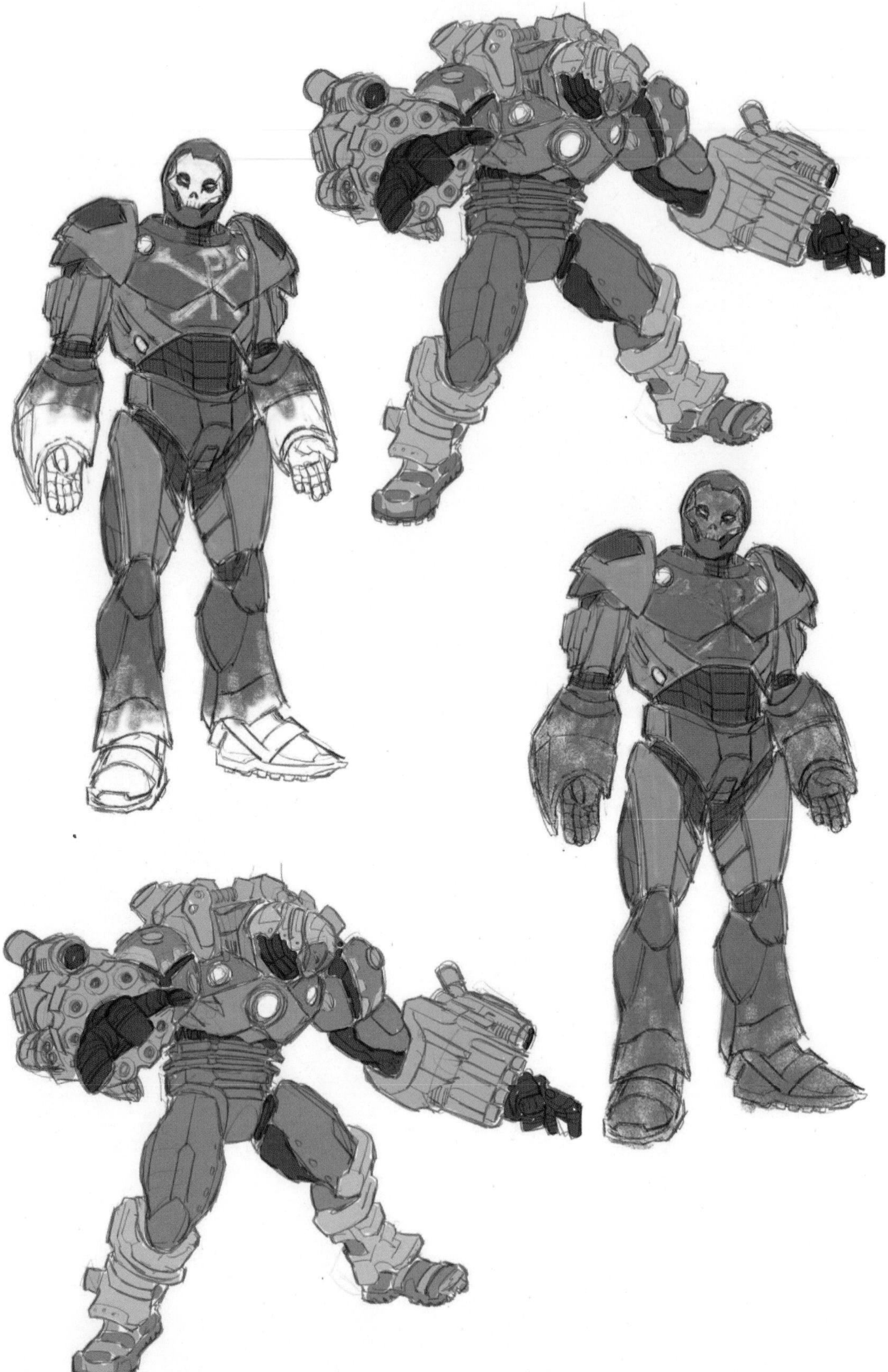

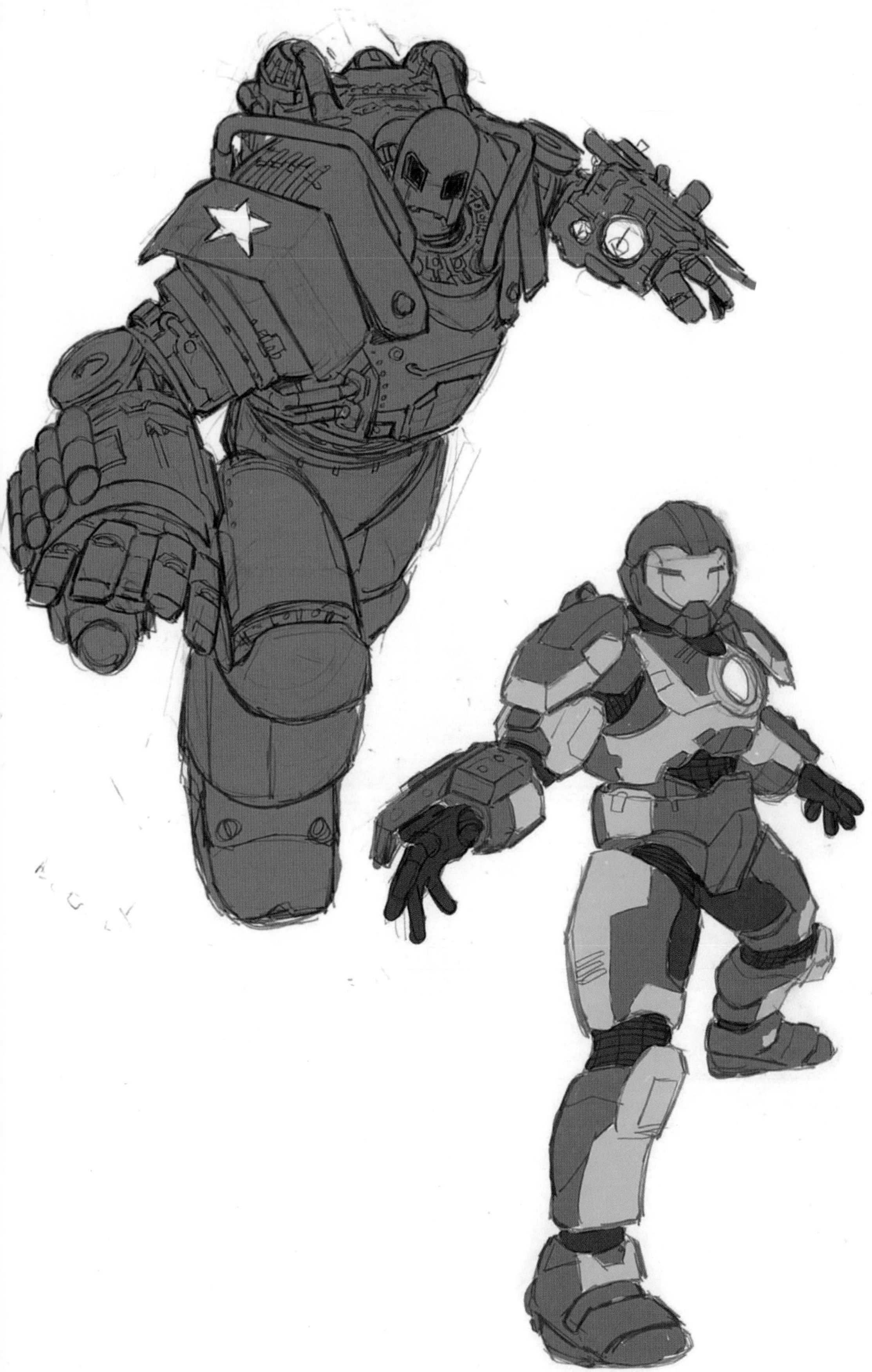

#2 PAGE 8 INKS

BY STEVE KURTH AND JEFF HUET

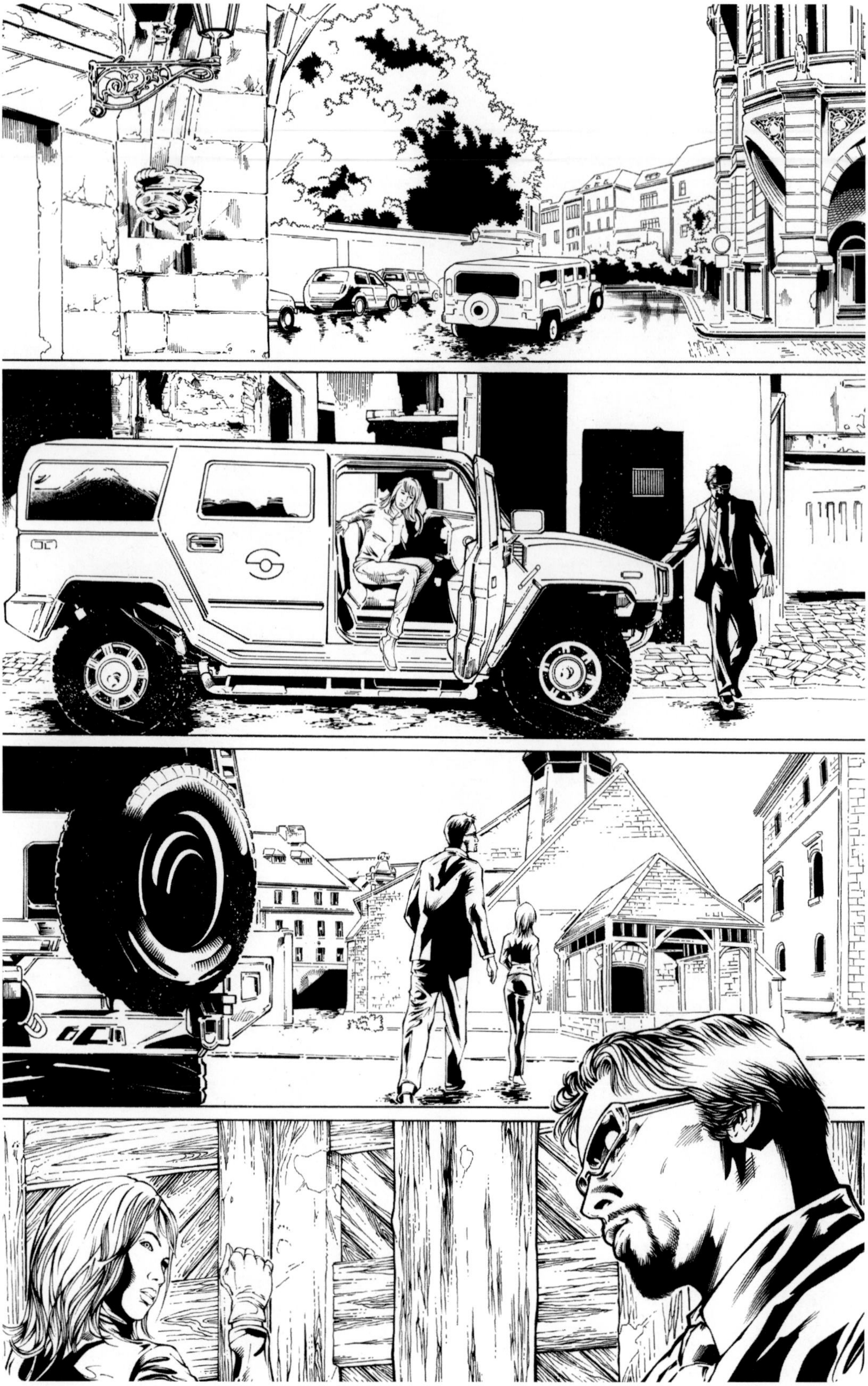

#2 PAGE 9 INKS
BY STEVE KURTH AND JEFF HUET

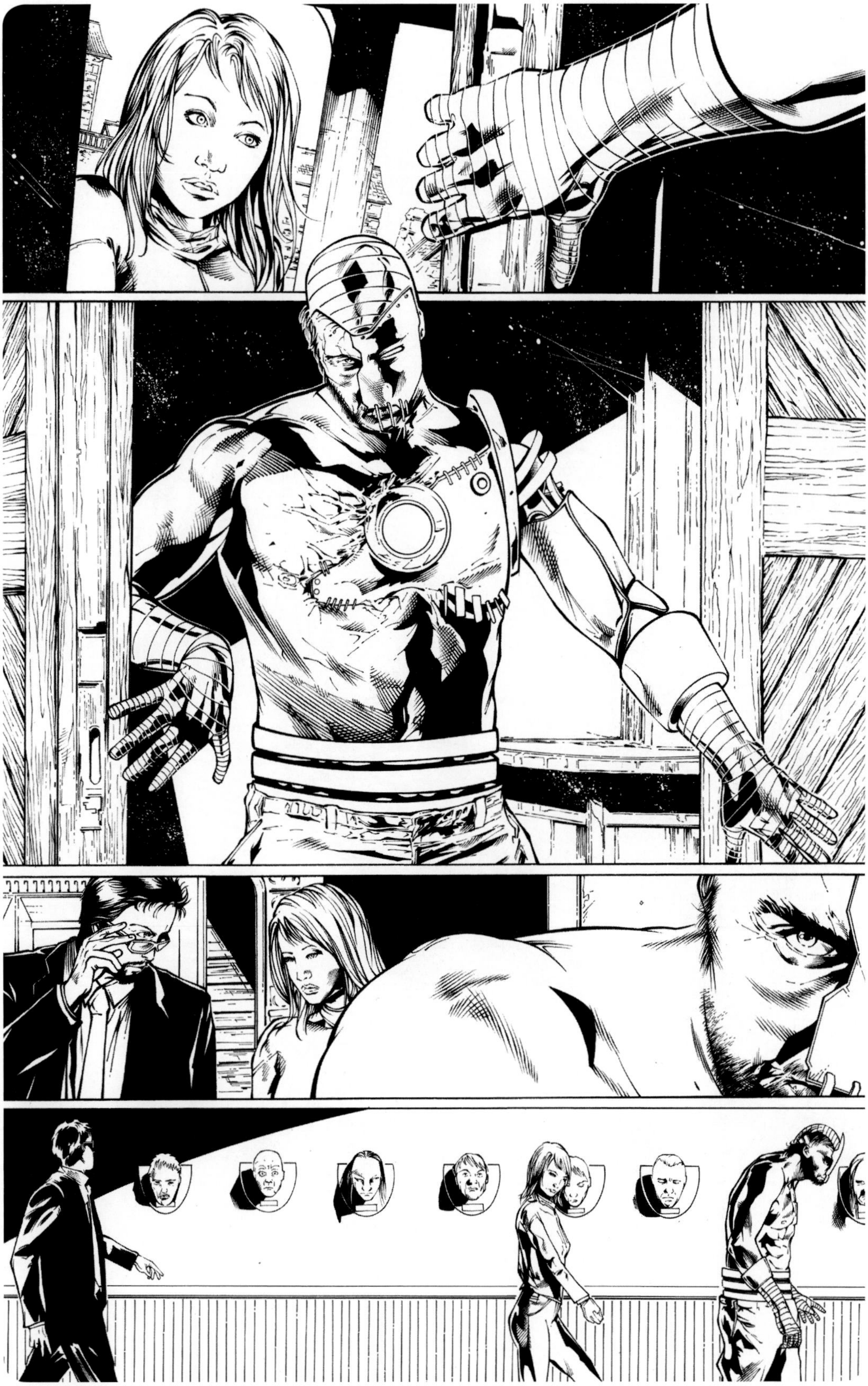

#2 PAGE 14 INKS
BY STEVE KURTH AND JEFF HUET

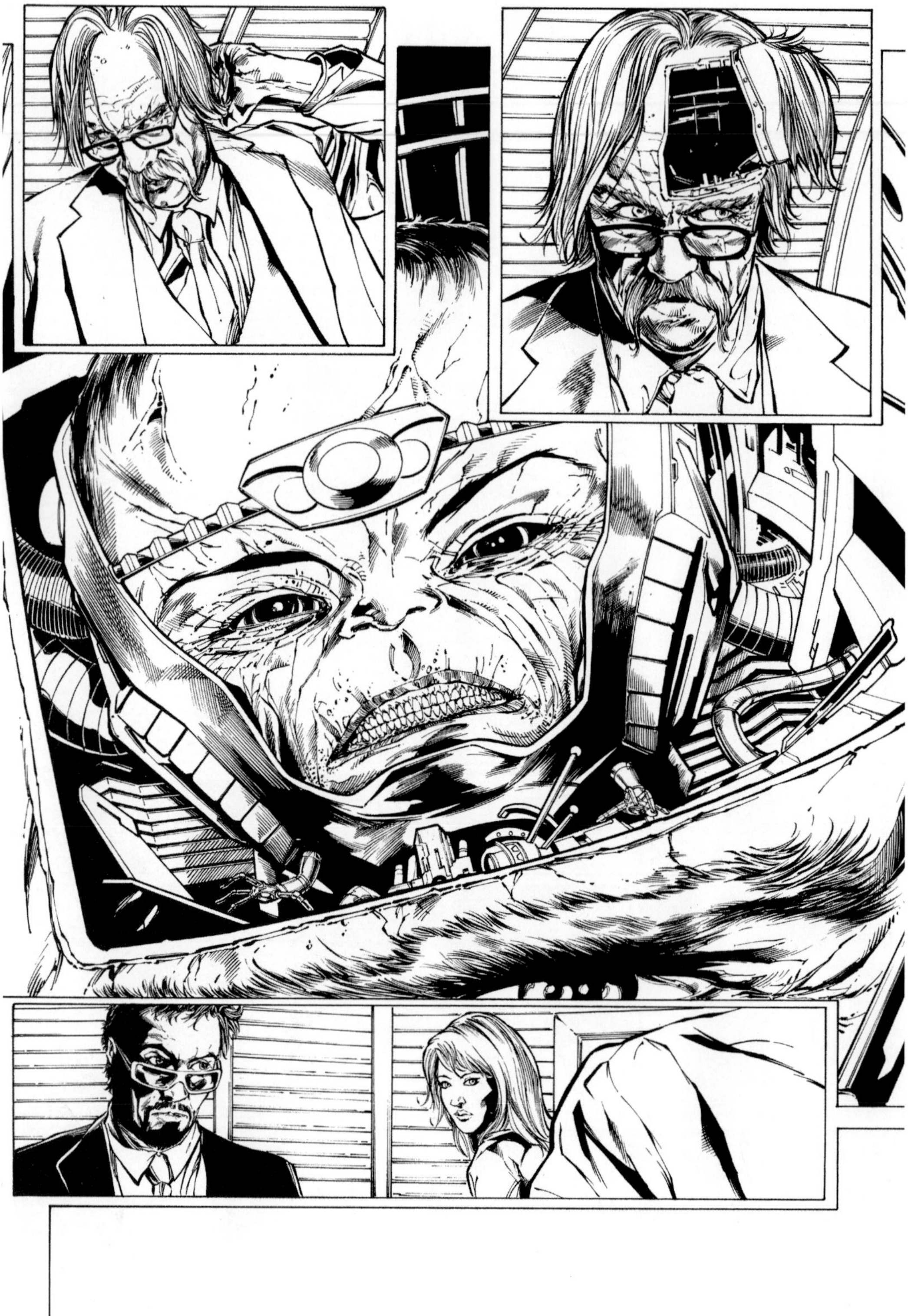

#2 PAGE 18 INKS
BY STEVE KURTH AND JEFF HUET

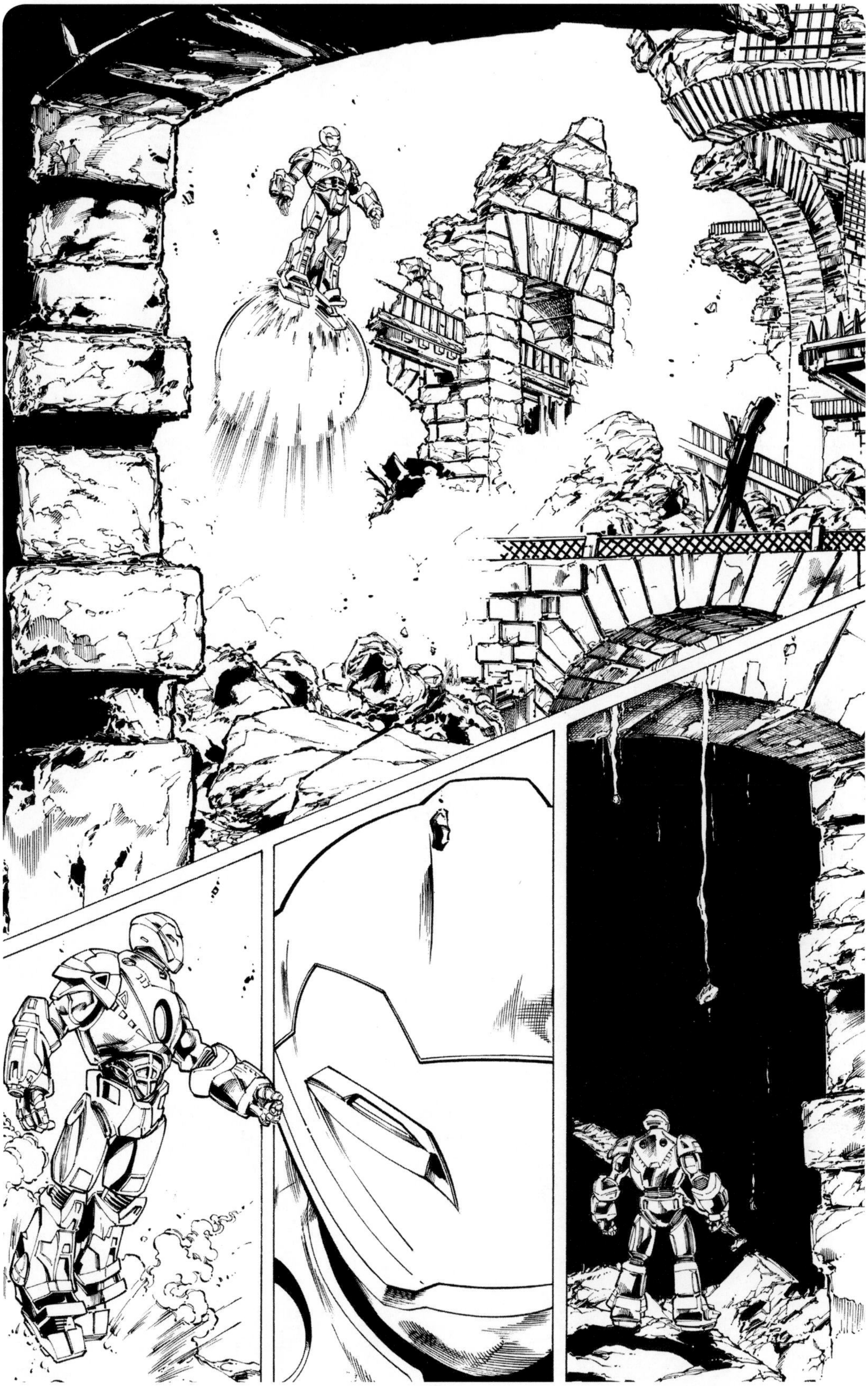

#2 PAGE 22 INKS
BY STEVE KURTH AND JEFF HUET

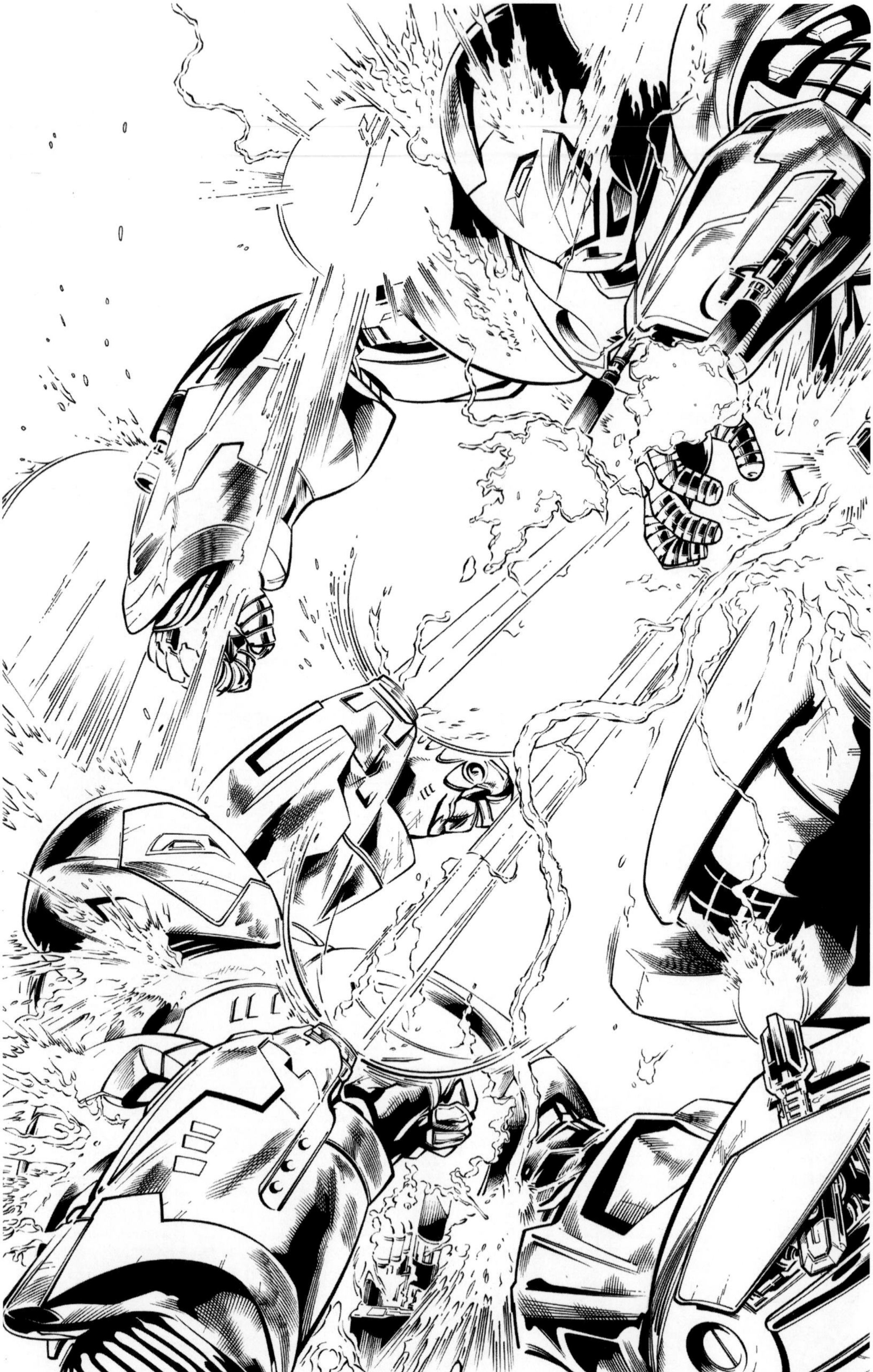

#3 PAGE 8 INKS
BY STEVE KURTH AND JEFF HUET

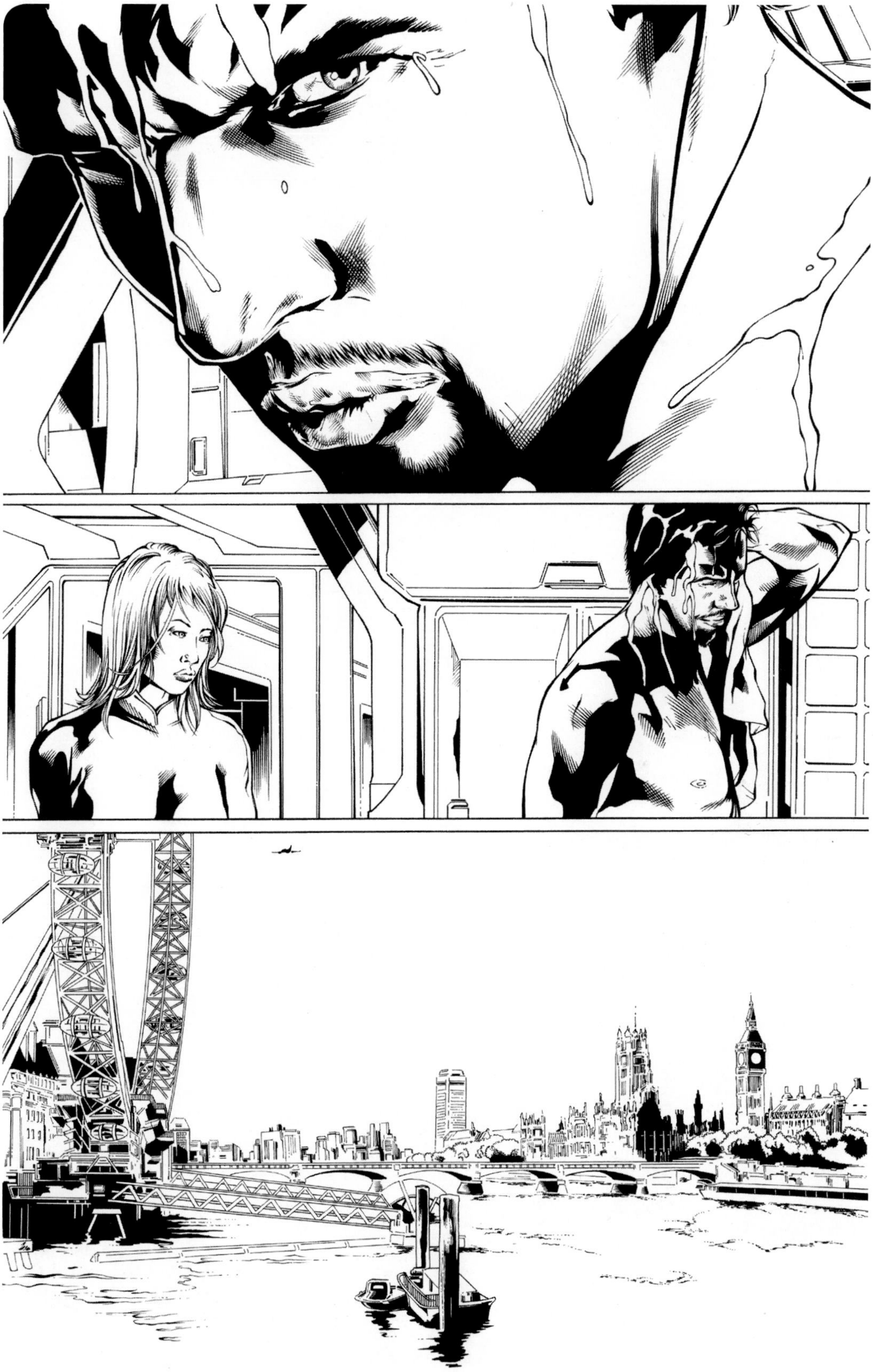

#3 PAGE 11 INKS

BY STEVE KURTH AND JEFF HUET

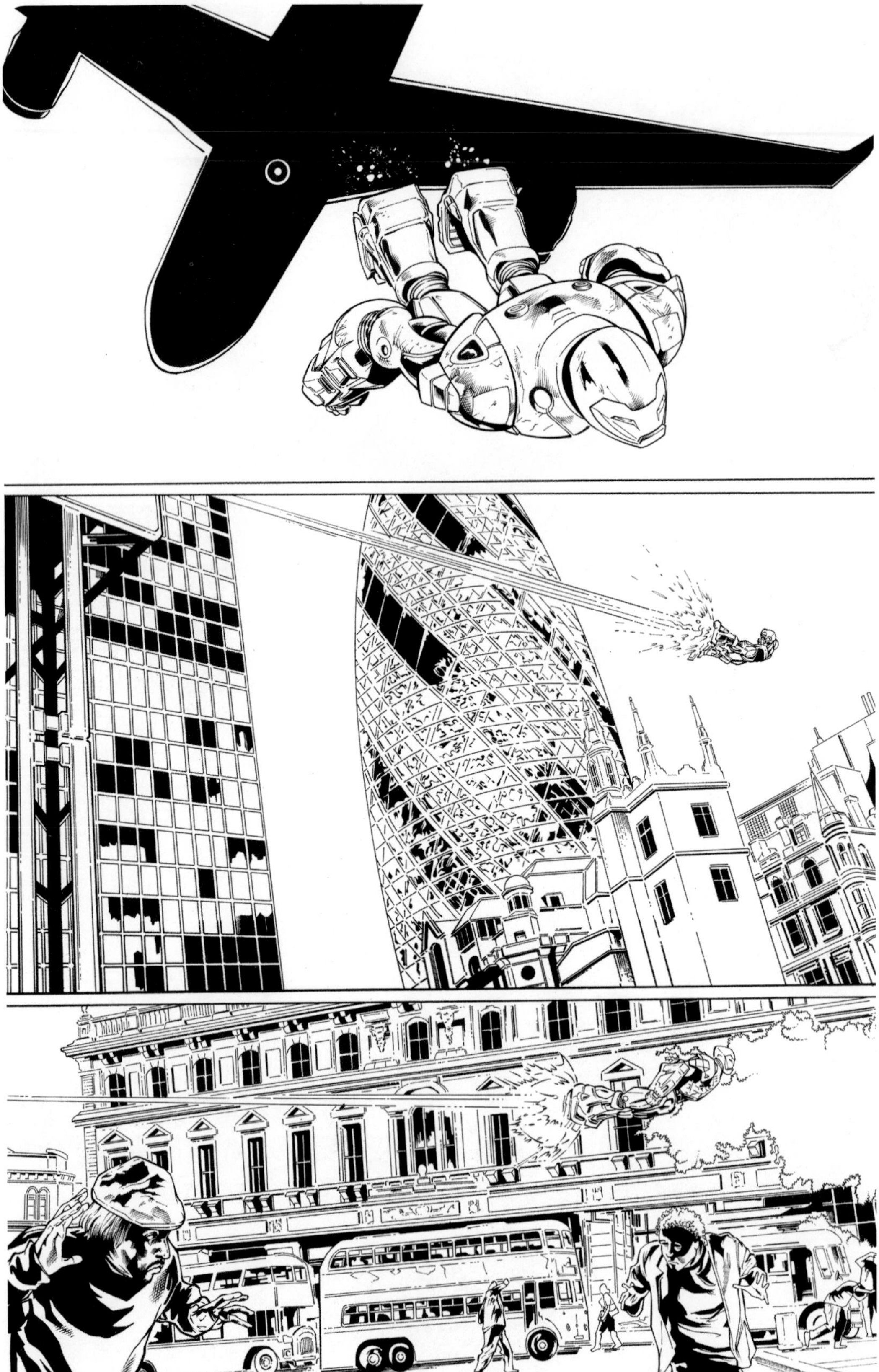

#4 PAGE 13 INKS
BY STEVE KURTH AND JEFF HUET

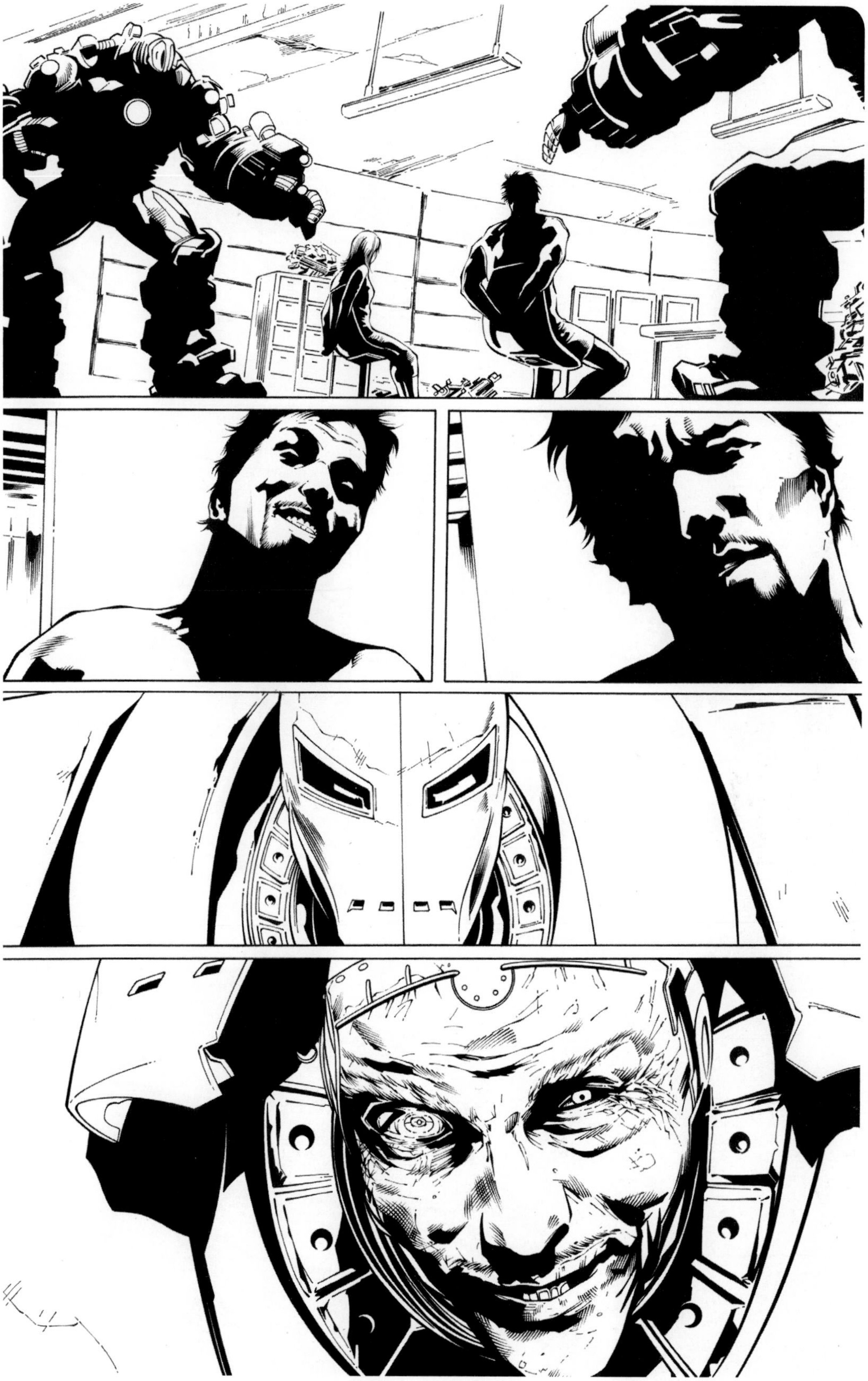

#4 PAGE 14 INKS
BY STEVE KURTH AND JEFF HUET

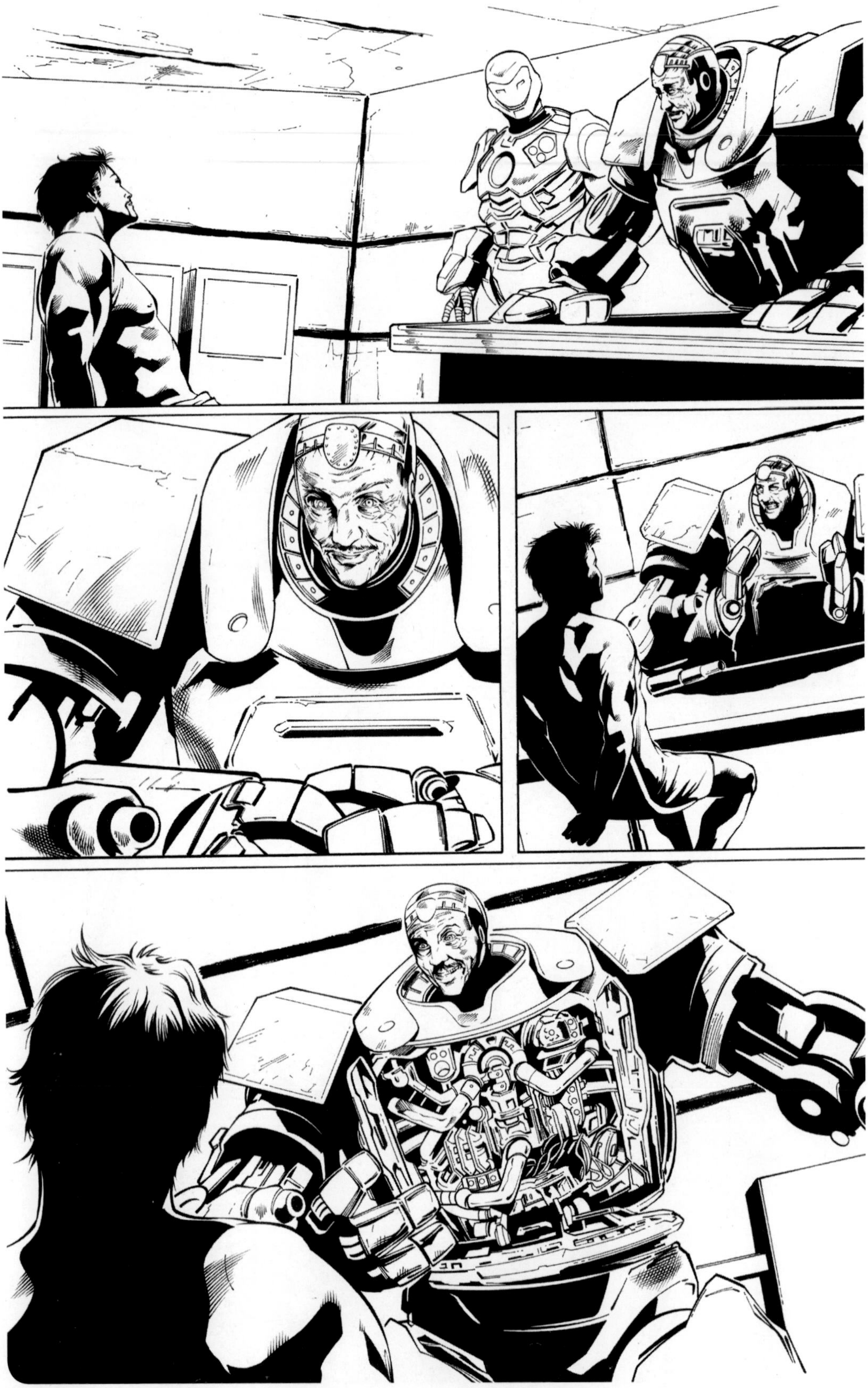